BULLIES AND VICTIMS IN SCHOOLS

A guide to understanding and management

VALERIE E. BESAG

OPEN UNIVERSITY PRESS
Milton Keynes · Philadelphia

Open University Press
Celtic Court
22 Ballmoor
Buckingham MK18 1XW

and
1900 Frost Road, Suite 101
Bristol, PA 19007, USA

First Published 1989. Reprinted 1991

British Library Cataloguing in Publication Data

Besag, Valerie
  Bullies and victims in schools: a guide to understanding
  and management
  1. Schools. Bullying
  I. Title
  371.5'8

  ISBN 0–335–09543–7
  ISBN 0–335–09542–9 (pbk)

Library of Congress Cataloging-in-Publication Data

Besag, Valerie.
  Bullies and victims in schools: a guide to understanding and
  management/by
  Valerie Besag.
    p.   cm.
  Bibliography: p.
  Includes index.
  ISBN 0–335–09543–7   ISBN 0–335–09542–9 (pbk.)
  1. School violence. 2. Abused children. 3. Deviant behavior.
  4. Personnel service in education. I. Title.
  LB3013.3.B47   1989
  371.5'8–dc20   89–3349
                                        CIP

Typeset by Scarborough Typesetting Services
Printed in Great Britain by St Edmundsbury Press Limited

To my father and my son, with thanks

Contents

Acknowledgements

I should like to acknowledge the help and encouragement I have received from a number of people. Professor Dan Olweus, Erling Roland and Professor Frank Coffield each gave unstintingly of their time and expertise to encourage me in the early stages of preparing this book. I should like to thank Professor Coffield in particular as on several occasions his words of encouragement and wisdom, combined with his boundless enthusiasm, have propelled me into new and rewarding territory.

Several friends supported me, each in their own way, throughout this project, from the first hesitant steps to the desperate last days as deadlines hurtled towards me. My gratitude goes to Liz Elliott, Dr Marion Farmer, Clare Howat and Margaret Murray, whose encouragement has been no less valued than their professional comment. My thanks extends to all my other colleagues for their support, psychologists and secretaries, especially Annette, in the Gateshead Psychological Service.

The most important contribution to this work has been made by those teachers in Gateshead, sadly too many to name, who listened to my suggestions, amended and developed them beyond my expectations, and with the highest degree of professional expertise and commitment, plus a great deal of Geordie humour, implemented them in their schools and generously shared their experiences with others.

I offer my grateful thanks to Pat Lee, Juliet Gladston and John Skelton of the Open University Press who turned a professional relationship into a friendship and patiently taught me the skill of writing a book.

I should like to acknowledge the following publishers for their permission to reproduce material: William Collins and Sons, Co. Ltd for the poem 'Pocket Money' from the book *So Far, So Good* by Mick Gowar; Faber for 'This Be The Verse' from *High Windows* by Philip Larkin; Allison and Busby Ltd for 'The Killing Ground' from *On The Beach At Cambridge* by Adrian Mitchell. My thanks also to Terence Ryan who wrote 'Lonely' during one of our discussions.

Introduction

Bullying in schools is one of the dark, hidden areas of social interaction, along with child physical and sexual abuse and adolescent violence in the home, which has thrived on a bed of secrecy and which has been neglected by professional investigation.

Parents and pupils alike have been concerned about the problem and, therefore, we need not be wary of escalating anxiety in bringing it out into the open for examination and discussion. Only professionals have underestimated the extent of the problem and the long-term trauma and damage caused both to the victims and bullies. We now understand that many victims hide and endure their stress over a period of years, and that the effects may be pervasive and long term.

One of the major difficulties in considering bullying is that it is not a phenomenon which is easily defined and measured. Definitions encompassing all possible facets of bullying become so cumbersome, that they are in danger of being counterproductive. It is, in my view, a problem to be considered within the context of normal social behaviour, where often both the bully and the victim have become enmeshed in a process of maladaptive social functioning which may suddenly escalate into crisis. Once put in terms of social interaction I have found that schools have been able to respond to the problem in a variety of productive ways.

The problem is covert, well hidden from the staff in school, buried in that curriculum organized by the pupils themselves. In addition to being hidden from sight, it may take the form of social ostracism, name calling, malicious gossip or a competitive academic approach, behaviours which are not easily identified as bullying behaviour by the victim. It is often an attitude rather than an act; it can be identified as bullying only by measuring the effect the acts have on a vulnerable child. Now, in legal terms, we recognize that mental cruelty can cause as much distress as physical damage, yet we may perhaps continue to be guilty of expecting pupils to cope alone with such psychological stress.

In searching for an explanation for bullying behaviour it is necessary to sift through a bewildering, often conflicting, array of research findings from biological, sociological, anthropological, psychological and other sources. Human behaviour necessarily rests on such a wide base of research; a myriad of causal factors, effects, repercussions and implications arise, not in an additive sense, but each interweaving and interacting with the other. The approach I have taken has been exploratory rather than explanatory, illustrative rather than exhaustive. The aim is to throw into focus various areas of work I consider relevant for future study.

So little research is available on this complex problem of bullying that, as yet, we can only identify high-risk factors rather than proffer, with confidence, firm conclusions. Empirical, large-scale research with a rigorous statistical design may not be the mode most suitable for the investigation of such a sensitive area. Small-scale, *in situ* pieces of research carried out in the individual school or classroom by practising teachers who know their pupils well, may be a more flexible and fruitful way forward. In my experience, proposals which arise from working with teachers on individual cases have, in the majority of instances, resulted in far-reaching and long-term changes in the organization of the school and professional practice.

In studying a behaviour which is often covert and secret, it may be pertinent to turn to such sources as literature to gain an understanding of the range and depth of feelings involved, and to gain a quality of insight often unattainable from those so reluctant to discuss their fear. For this reason, various sections of this book are prefaced by a literary extract.

Bullying is always with us. We encounter bullies in some form or other throughout our lives. There does seem to be some prevalent process by which there is a testing out of will and strength over others. It is not only as children that we encounter bullying, it happens in all strata of society and in all localities. As adults we have learnt to go where we feel safe, to confront only when we feel comfortable, to conform and to comply so as not to attract too much unwanted attention. Only those trapped by circumstances (as in the armed services and prisons), those trapped by emotional or financial bonds (such as cohabitees and marital partners), parents with violent children, those trapped by their frailty (such as the elderly), only adults so locked in a situation for any reason, experience the type of bullying some children encounter daily in school. Such research that has been carried out shows that only some of those children learn to cope and, of those, few will learn to cope quickly enough to avoid damage and distress. We cannot expect the victims to cope alone.

It is not their battle and, therefore, we need to offer training and support to those at risk.

If, as adults, we do fall foul of such an attack, we can turn to others for aid – the police, the legal system, or the trade unions. Are we then leaving the most vulnerable sector of our society unprotected? We need to ensure that the school circumstances in which our children spend the greater part of their lives are those we would wish for ourselves.

The problem is multidimensional and I have found that schools are able to respond best by using a multifactorial response. Prevention is far better than crisis management and a team response by all teachers taking the responsibility for all children at all times, in a variety of ways, is perhaps one of the most effective preventative measures possible. The specific intervention programme implemented on discovering a case of bullying must be two-fold: the bullying must stop and firm action must be taken to ensure the safety of pupils at risk; and, in parallel, the social behaviour of the bully and the victim must be analysed and amended. Simply to stop the bullying is to leave the work half done, and to put pupils at further risk. The bullies may need to revise their code of conduct, and the victims will need support to help them gain confidence and guidance so that they might solve their problems themselves and, therefore, reach a stage of comfortable maturity rather than being overprotected.

There does appear to be a need for a change in attitudes at all levels. The majority of pupils in our schools, I believe, have a clear sense of justice and they themselves are often secondary victims, as a large number of schoolchildren are known to worry about bullying behaviour they witness or hear discussed. We need to help the 'silent majority' of our young people to see that they are taking responsible action in reporting incidents and not 'telling tales'. We must, however, ensure that they do not put themselves at risk in doing so. As a society we need to address ourselves to the question of what type of young person we want to emerge from the school experience, what constellation of characteristics we should encourage in our young people; and we need to ensure, perhaps by an explicit approach to other bodies forcibly, that we have time during the school day to develop those facets of social life we feel to be important. Long-term studies are beginning to indicate that children with social problems in school – victims and bullies – are at high risk of taking those problems with them into adult life and even passing them on to their own children. Academic success is important, but unless our pupils are socially secure and well adjusted, we may not see the fruition of their labours or our own.

PART ONE

How to understand bullying

1
Researching bullying

Overview

There has been surprisingly little research, or informed opinion, published on the subject of bullying. The sparse research available is confounded by the terminology used. The majority of current studies have been carried out in the Scandinavian countries, where the definition of bullying differs from that widely accepted in Britain and the USA. The Scandinavians, other than Olweus (1987) and Roland (1988), consider bullying to necessarily involve more than one attacker harassing one or more others (Lagerspetz *et al.*, 1982). The word 'mobbing' is used to describe this form of bullying. Pikas (1975b) describes necessary criteria for defining a behaviour as mobbing. It has to be a negative activity exerted by two or more individuals against one or a well-defined group. Those who act negatively have to interact with each other, in some way reinforcing each other's behaviour. The bullying, Pikas suggests, is a goal in itself, often executed with no other intent than to persecute the victim.

In Britain we accept that bullying can be an attack carried out solely by one individual against another, one individual against a group, one group against another group or a group against one individual. Olweus (1987), who has worked extensively in the field, offers this definition: 'A person is bullied when he or she is exposed, regularly and over time, to negative actions on the part of one or more persons.' Roland (in prep.) defines it as 'The long term and systematic use of violence, mental or physical, against an individual who is unable to defend himself in an actual situation.' Bjorkquist *et al.* (1982) note that bullying is 'a special case of aggression which is social in nature'.

Most definitions agree that three factors are implicit in any bullying activity: it must occur over a prolonged period of time rather than being a single aggressive act; it must involve an imbalance of power, the powerful attacking the powerless; and it can be verbal, physical or psychological in nature. When children themselves are asked to define bullying they too offer these three parameters (Arora and Thompson, 1987). In addition, in one study, they added that the attacks seemed to take place for no good reason, because little appeared to be gained other than the bully's personal satisfaction.

My own definition would propose that there are four facets to the problem:

1. It may be verbal, physical or psychological in nature.
2. It may be in the form of a socially acceptable behaviour, as in a highly competitive approach to academic, sporting or social success, which, by intent, makes others feel inferior or causes distress.
3. It is necessarily a repetitive attack which causes distress not only at the time of each attack, but also by the threat of future attacks.
4. It is characterized by the dominance of the powerful over the powerless in whatever context.

In summary, bullying is a behaviour which can be defined as the repeated attack – physical, psychological, social or verbal – by those in a position of power, which is formally or situationally defined, on those who are powerless to resist, with the intention of causing distress for their own gain or gratification.

Definitions which aim to encompass all the aspects of this highly complex behaviour are necessarily clumsy and unwieldy. Too rigid a definition could be counterproductive, as some of the most traumatic and terrifying instances of bullying have been seemingly innocuous acts, such as giving the victim 'the wink' or 'the look'. It is in the interpretation of the behaviour by victim and bully that the power lies.

There appears to be little evidence of serious concern other than in the Scandinavian countries and Japan. We can only surmise as to the reasons for this surprising lack of research and knowledge about bullying worldwide. Bullying in schools is, on the whole, a covert activity occurring without adult witness; teachers only hear about it second-hand, if they are aware of it at all, and parents are often the last to know. The bully, victim and any observers remain silent, because there is still a stigma in our society against telling tales. It would appear that the problem has been underestimated by adults. This may be because it is difficult for us as secure adults to comprehend the extent of the trauma encountered by the victim, even when the attacks have been continuing for some time. Research now indicates that bullying can continue undetected by adults for a number of years because the effects, distressing and pervasive though they are, may be missed or misinterpreted by unwary adults (Cole, 1977). The act of bullying may cause anxiety and stress out of all proportion to the actual event.

One reason for the paucity of research could be that uninformed professionals are insensitive to the problem and so carry out no research. As long as there is little research, however, professionals will remain ill-informed. This circularity leaves many children at risk.

A further reason for our apparent lack of concern could be that primarily it is only the victim who suffers. The teacher and the rest of the group may remain unaffected. Even if the victim makes a tentative complaint or shows slight signs of distress, these could be missed in the bustle of a busy classroom. As our knowledge grows, we can look to research which shows that it is not only the victim who suffers, but also that those who passively witness the attacks or threats can also become anxious and distressed (Elliott, 1986 and Davies, 1986).

In many cultures there is a traditional expectation that children will learn to look after themselves – that they will learn to cope with hurdles and hazards – and, in so doing, be better prepared for life. Those who do not do so are thought to have failed to meet some undefined social criteria of success. Bullies, by definition, pick out those children who are vulnerable and who are unable to defend themselves no matter how hard they try. It may, in retrospect, have been a character-building experience for some more physically robust children, but for others the erosion of self-confidence and self-esteem is such that even in adulthood their social interactions remain affected (Cowen *et al.*, 1973).

There may be a reluctance on the part of the school or local authority administrators to admit to the problem of bullying. An admission could be read as incompetence and reflect badly on the school.

In my own experience, I have found that any initial reluctance to help most often stems from the fear of adults that they might make things worse for the victim should they intervene. It is not easy to know what to do, for there are few obvious solutions or easy answers. There are no published studies of long-term, detailed and evaluated intervention. Teachers often fear that their involvement would simply drive the problem underground. Suggestions of surveys, action-research or discussion groups frequently meet this wary response. Preventative programmes have been rejected in case they should escalate and encourage what is believed to be an almost non-existent problem. Yet I have not myself known of any situation where such work has escalated any bullying. Indeed, the reverse has been the case, in that once out in the open and discussed freely, the secrecy, which

I believe supports the situation, is lost and the tension eased. The exposure of the problem in itself can go a long way in curtailing the bully's activities. It is a problem which flourishes best on a bed of secrecy, hidden from those who could help.

The most obvious reason for the lack of information we have about bullying is that children themselves will not discuss the difficulties they encounter with bullies. Do they justly lack confidence in our expertise to sort out this particular problem? In our past state of knowledge and experience perhaps our track record has not been impressive. In addition, the victims may feel so ashamed and degraded by the attacks and insults that they are quite unable to admit to this social failure. I have found that some victims are more easily able to draw a picture about a humiliating incident, such as being spat on, than to speak about it. They feel so ashamed that they are unpopular that they begin to feel themselves social pariahs. Parents, too, can feel ashamed that their child is not a social success and is unable to call on class support. This could contribute to parents' reluctance to approach the school for help or to return if an initial strategy has not worked. Parental pressure on professionals to address themselves to this problem has been lacking and may have contributed to the lack of available expertise.

It is not only from the attacker(s) that the child may fear reprisals. If the bully and victim are of the same age, the victim's parents may expect him/her to fend off attack, to protect possessions and clothing. The vast range of physical strength and confidence found in any one age group is often underestimated by parents who, understandably, become angry at the loss or destruction of property.

A child may not admit to difficulties encountered at school for fear of worrying his/her parents, especially if the family is experiencing some trauma. Sadly, it is possible that those very problems, such as marital disharmony, may have been contributory to the child's lack of confidence and self-esteem which, in turn, may have resulted in his/her current vulnerability.

Finally, even older children do not always understand the subtleties of bullying situations. Socially isolated children may endure loneliness and ostracism without being able to verbalize the confused emotions they experience. Teachers may see it only within the normal spectrum of disruption or aggression in the bustle of the school day, particularly as separate incidents may be reported to separate teachers, if they are reported at all.

With so few studies available, the contamination of cross-cultural effects, the differences in terminology, the array of research designs employed and, above all (the fact we cannot lose sight of) that we only know what the frightened young people are willing to tell us, it would be foolhardy, at present, to extrapolate anything from the research so far other than a few tentative hypotheses.

The main body of research originates in the Scandinavian countries. Peter Paul Heinemann, a Swedish physician, first drew attention to the problem after observing bullying in the playground on his routine visits to schools (Heinemann, 1973). His work aroused public interest and prepared the ground for the academic research of Olweus. The work of Olweus requires special note, as no other body of work is comparable in size or complexity. Olweus alone, having been working in this field for over 20 years, has access to important longitudinal data. The impact of the early work of Olweus led the Norwegian Ministry of Education to initiate a nationwide campaign against bullying in schools (Norwegian National Campaign, 1983). This preventative programme of booklets, videos and workshops for both teachers and parents is currently being evaluated by Roland and, at the time of writing, the findings are shortly to be published and will provide data on 140 000 students. I understand that the findings suggest that those schools which were initially most receptive to the programme (especially secondary schools) have had the greatest successes.

Olweus continues his large-scale, long-term research in both Norway and Sweden. Those boys studied at 13 and 15 years of age and identified by Olweus as bullies, have been found now, at approximately the age of 24, to be more likely to be involved in criminal and antisocial activities (Olweus, personal communication and 1987). Olweus is currently looking at the levels of testosterone and adrenalin, and the neuropsychological features of a sub-group of boys taken over a period of 7 years. As yet, a huge body of work awaits collation and publication.

There are, however, major differences between Scandinavia and Britain which do not allow for the careless comparison or adoption of data between studies. In the Scandinavian studies, little variation was found between the number of incidents reported in rural and urban schools. Olweus disputes what he terms the myth of the idyllic rural school, whereas a higher incidence of bullying was found in urban compared with rural schools in Britain (Stephenson and Smith, 1988). It may be relevant that there are less large conurbations in Scandinavia. Fewer differences between schools were reported in Scandinavia, but their largest schools have a role of 800 pupils, compared with Britain where it is possible for there to be up to 2000. The vast majority of pupils in Scandinavia continue on to further education and post-school prospects are better because unemployment figures are, at present, as low as 4 per cent (Council for

Cultural Cooperation, 1988). It may be, therefore, that there is a more homogeneous feel to Scandinavian schools. Olweus (1987) considers, however, that it is such factors as parenting skills which are crucial, rather than socioeconomic variables.

Japan is the only country outside Scandinavia to have taken an interest in bullying at a national level. The degree of concern is such that a national survey is currently being carried out throughout Japan. White (1987) quotes the National Police Agency as defining *Ijime* (bullying) as:

> attacks on a particular individual, physical and/or through the force of words, involving threats or pushing, shoving or punching, being shunned by their classmates, psychological pressure continually repeated, resulting in suffering to the victim.

The police have organized a telephone help line for the use of both parents and children. The public and media concern is not mere sensationalism; the education of children is a high national priority in Japan. Education is seen first as a way for the individual to gain social status, recognition of achievement and personal growth; and, secondly, the key to national cohesion and continuity, and the way forward towards international development. Any weakness noted in the system causes an immediate alert (White, 1987).

This national concern with education is thought to have contributed to the intense pressure put on even very young children to succeed and conform in school. By secondary age, White reports 90 per cent of students are receiving private tuition after school. On leaving school, less that 1 per cent of students are illiterate, yet 1000 characters must be mastered for a minimum level of literacy. There is an implicit understanding that no child has a finite potential to learn and that there is no ceiling on ability. The international press has frequently implied that the stress imposed by this system is to blame for the number of suicides among young people in Japan, but a recent survey disputed this and found the figures to be less than those from the USA (*Wall Street Journal*, 1985).

There is a heritage in Japan of group-consciousness – to be a good group member is not only necessary but is considered to be a skill in itself. This is manifest in the harsh treatment given to outsiders, such as children returning from abroad who, in the past, have suffered such stress and rejection, that there is now a national programme to help with reintegration (White, 1987). Interestingly, the emphasis is to change the victim, to help them to become a good group member. There would appear to be little evidence of bullies having to face their responsibility for the situation.

Children in modern Japan are often caught between two ideologies – the recent economic growth gnawing away at the rural, cultural traditions (Yamazaki *et al.*, 1986). Even in the home, change is evident – as fathers are spending more time at work, it is the mother who becomes the main disciplinarian. More than half of those surveyed by White (1987) found the task extremely stressful.

Even though it would be rash to transpose facts and figures from one cultural setting to another without due caution, it must be with interest that we await the findings of this national survey.

Critique

Most of the research published so far on bullying has been based on pupil reports and replies to a wide variety of questionnaires. This means that we only know what we have been told. The reliability of the data rests on the assumption that the responses given reflect the true situation. As bullying is a behaviour characterized by anxiety, fear and threat, and perhaps a boastful demonstration of power by the dominant, reservations which are voiced about such research designs are even more relevant when this style of research is used to investigate bullying. Olweus and Roland have tried to ensure the anonymity of replies to all their questionnaires but, even so, it could be that some degree of apprehension on the part of vulnerable children, and bravado on the part of the more confident, causes contamination of the data. Both Olweus and Roland, however, have used parent and teacher interviews and peer ratings to confirm their findings, and a surprisingly good correlation has been found between results, so that pupil responses do appear to constitute reliable data. Teacher responses alone have been found to be an unreliable means of identifying victims and bullies by Lowenstein (1978) who found that teachers tended to confuse bullying with aggression and disruption, putting the behaviours on the same continuum.

A major difficulty is that there is no one accepted definition of bullying, bullies or victims. Even within Scandinavia, Pikas (1975b) holds the view that it is a group mobbing, whereas Olweus allows the concept of the lone bully. The categorization of bullies has only recently included the anxious bully (Stephenson and Smith, 1988) and the neurotic bully (Mitchel and O'Moore, 1988). A category that I have identified, the false victim, has not been studied. Lowenstein (1978), although one of the more rigorous researchers, does not distinguish between the provocative and the passive victim, so making it impossible to relate his data to the work of Olweus. Lowenstein describes the victims as being more aggressive than the controls, presumably because the provocative, passive and colluding victim groups have not been distinguished. One of the more obvious flaws in attempting to compare data is the variation in defining what constitutes bullying behaviour, e.g. how long the attacks need to continue for it to be classified as bullying. In addition, some of the parent surveys have asked only whether the child has ever been bullied and, therefore, cannot be compared to studies giving rates of current incidence. Both Olweus and Roland have a firm criterion for the length of time the attacks must have continued to be rated as serious: at least once a week for a month or more. Lowenstein uses stricter criteria: the attacks must have continued for at least 6 months and they have to be confirmed by two or more children and two or more teachers. Other studies offer no criteria other than the opinion of children or parents that the bullying takes place. Bullying is a subtle behaviour, taking many forms and involving highly complex interactions. It is, at least, a two-way interaction, possibly depending as much on the response of the victim as on the initial intent of the bully. It may be that a questionnaire or written response could miss the vital components of the problem. Checklists may, at best, only indicate rates of incidence, and not further our knowledge in a more meaningful way.

One of the more controversial issues to arise from research is the question of whether or not a child can be both bully and victim. The traditional bully is a lonely child, socially or academically inadequate, a child bullied by others, but who attacks weaker victims to compensate. Olweus (1978) states that the personality and home background of bullies and victims are so diverse that only a few children could encompass both roles. Those studies which have looked at the comparative ages of bullies and victims show that bullies tend to be 1–2 years older than their victims (Olweus, 1987). In such a situation, they may feel confident enough to bully; however, among their peers, or at home, they may themselves be the victims of others. As yet, no research has explored this possibility.

A few studies that set out to investigate quite different problems such as sexual abuse, truancy, aggression or disruption, found that bullying was a related problem (West and Farrington, 1973; Reid, 1983a). Understandably, these studies can offer little detailed data on any aspect of bullying. The results of a further group of studies, specifically undertaken to look at the problem of bullying in schools, have as yet only been published in precis form (Mitchel and O'Moore, 1988; Byrne, 1987).

The most exhaustive and complex work undertaken so far is that of Olweus and the follow-up survey by Roland, which is similar in concept: all other investigations are far smaller or still in the embryonic stage.

A summary of the research findings is presented in Tables 1–5 at the end of this chapter.

Summary of research findings

Frequency

One conclusion which may be drawn from the sparse and diverse research is that at least 10 per cent of children in our schools are probably, at any one time, involved in bullying to a marked degree, whether as bully or victim. Olweus (1978, 1985a) found that in Scandinavia 5 per cent could be considered seriously involved and 15 per cent occasionally so. Ten per cent were classified as victims, 8 per cent as bullies. These figures are supported by studies using similar definitions of bullying, bullies and victims (Mitchel and O'Moore, 1988; Byrne, 1987; Lowenstein, 1978). Some studies put the figure higher if parents were surveyed. Newson and Newson (1984) found that 26 per cent of parents had come across the problem. A further informal study by *Mother* magazine in 1987 reported that 25 per cent of primary pupils interviewed had encountered the problem and 75 per cent of the parents of the children had found it to be the worst problem their children had been required to face. A MORI report (1987) found that one in four parents interviewed said that their children had been seriously intimidated by others. Elliott (1986), who interviewed 4000 children about abuse, found that 38 per cent had been bullied by other children badly enough to describe the experience as terrifying. Of the sample, 8 per cent of the boys and 2 per cent of the girls had found the experience to have had a chronic and severe effect on their everyday lives. Of the parents of the children surveyed, 30 per cent were anxious about bullying, but only 4 per cent had any idea as to how to help their child. Could this be why Olweus found that only half the victims of primary age and 35 per cent of older students had reported the problem to their parents? In the same survey, Elliott found that of those children who approached their teacher for help only 60 per cent of primary children and 40 per cent of older children considered that adults were either willing or able to alleviate their distress. Very few bullies of any age had been approached by teachers or parents about their behaviour. A study by Riley (1988) of bullying in a comprehensive school, found that of 30 cases of bullying – with 24 pupils witnessing the bullying – only 5 were reported to staff and only 2 were observed by staff. There was a massive degree of non-referral.

Stephenson and Smith (1988), studying primary age children, indicated that a wide discrepancy occurred between schools. They found that the number of children involved in bullying in each school group varied from nil to 50 per cent; on average, 23 per cent were involved as bullies or victims. Riley (1988) also found that one of the four feeder schools he studied had the reputation of being 'violent'; however, this finding may have been influenced by the high percentage of pupils from ethnic minorities in the school, because the study found that these children were most at risk of being bullied. Arora and Thompson (1987) studied children in a secondary school and also found the frequency to vary widely from class to class. In this latter study, 50 per cent of 14-year-old boys stated that they had been kicked the previous week in school, 30 per cent had had a possession damaged and 19 per cent had had money taken from them. Using a different approach, Reid (1983), in his work on truancy, discovered that approximately 19 per cent of truants had started to skip school because of bullying and continued to miss school for this reason.

There is some evidence, not yet published in detail, which would seem to indicate that the incidence of bullying is even higher in specialist settings, among those pupils with emotional, behavioural or learning difficulties. Mitchel and O'Moore (1988) found that 16 per cent of children in primary remedial groups bullied others, compared with 6 per cent in non-remedial groups. Byrne (1987) came to a similar conclusion in his study of a secondary school – 9 per cent in remedial groups compared with 5 per cent in ordinary classes. Stephenson and Smith (1988) found the incidence of bullying to be higher among children in specialist settings for emotional and behavioural problems. Sixty-five per cent of these children had been involved in bullying prior to admission. Other studies (e.g. Olweus, 1978) suggest that both victims and bullies are most often children of average ability, but it would seem that the stress engendered by the bullying could result in many victims, especially those with long-term problems, underachieving.

It must be stressed that much of this work has been based on pupil reports; we only know what they have told us. The studies were, however, all anonymous and the figures do seem to be replicated from other sources such as teacher, parent and peer reports, and from studies which did not originally set out to look at the problem of bullying, as in the truancy and abuse surveys.

Even these figures perhaps mask the true extent of the damage, because they do not take into account the effect of bullying on those merely observing it. It is clear that many children become highly anxious after witnessing a bullying incident. Students about to transfer from primary to secondary school rated it as their main concern about their new school (Davies, 1986). The figures quoted do not take into account such phenomena as the ripple effect of malicious gossip or the effect one bully alone can have if backed by the group in socially isolating a child. In legislation, non-physical attacks, such as slander and libel, are recognized as potent, and mental cruelty is considered alongside physical cruelty as valid ground for divorce, yet in such issues as bullying it could be that we continue to underestimate the damage non-physical bullying may have upon the target child.

A distressing factor emerging from the research is that the bullying is often sustained over a long period of time, being handed on from class to class or even year to year. Cole (1977) found that two-thirds of teachers facing the problem had inherited it from the previous year. Sadly, the majority felt that they themselves had not been able to implement realistic change and would, therefore, pass the problem on yet again at the end of the year. Other studies have reported similar findings. Riley (1988) found that over 50 per cent of bullies had been identified by the feeder schools previous to entering the secondary school. The Scandinavian studies found similar stability: Lagerspetz *et al.* (1982) reported a 93 per cent stability of incidence over 1 year. The attacks do not appear to be constant, rather they ebb and flow over time, but it is clear that specific children are targeted for attack and that their misery is prolonged. A general conclusion which could be drawn from the research is that teachers may recognize the problem but severely underestimate both the extent and the direct and indirect effect it can have on both the victim and the group.

Categories of victim and bully

Several subgroupings may be identified from the two categories of victim and bully (see Tables 1–5 for references).

Passive victims

These are children who are ineffectual, for whatever reason, in the face of attack (Olweus, 1978). They avoid aggression and confrontation and lack the confidence or skill to elicit support from their peers. These children are described as being fearful, physically weaker than their peers, cautious, withdrawn, and often find it difficult to make friends. When attacked they display helpless, futile anger. Olweus (1978) considers that a significant number have coordination difficulties and a low level of self-esteem.

Provocative victims

A small group of children intentionally provoke the antagonism of others. They tease and taunt yet are quick to complain if others retaliate. About one-seventh of the victim group was found to fall into this category (Olweus, 1978). In extreme cases, such a child may be in need of specialist help. Unlike the passive victim, these children would probably be at risk even if there were no bully to act as catalyst.

Colluding victims

These children take on the role of victim to gain acceptance and popularity (Olweus, 1978). They may play the part of class clown or join in disruptive behaviour to be safely included in the group. It is common for children to mask their true academic ability to avoid becoming outcast from their group, as they could then find themselves in a vulnerable position.

False victims

I would suggest that a category exists which could be defined as false victims. No specific research has highlighted this group, but all teachers know of children who complain unnecessarily about others in the group. It is usually attention-seeking behaviour, but even so there may be a reason for this, e.g. it could be a cry for help.

Bully-victims

A group of children are victims in one situation yet bully in another. Olweus (1985a) found that 6 per cent of those who were seriously bullied, and 18 per cent of those who were bullied occasionally, in turn bullied others. It is suggested by Olweus that the characteristics of the bully and victim differ so widely that this group will necessarily be small. Children subjected to harsh discipline at home, to the extent that they are bullied by their parents, are more likely than others to be aggressive to those younger and more vulnerable. In this way they would seem to have the dual role of both victim and bully. These children were found to be physically strong and able to assert themselves. Stephenson and Smith (1988) found them to be less popular with their peers than the main group of bullies.

Bullies

The research is in general agreement about the characteristics of the bullies (Olweus, 1978). They are considered to be physically stronger, and to have more energy and confidence than any other group. Several studies noted that they appear to enjoy conflict and aggression, seeking out situations where their aggression can be witnessed by their peers (Wachtel, 1973; Bowers, 1973). These bullies are not as unpopular as one would expect, although Olweus found them to be isolated, apart from two or three satellites, and that they lost their popularity in their teens.

Anxious bullies

This group has been identified by Stephenson and Smith (1988). They are the least confident children and are less popular than other bullies. These children appear to have other difficulties, such as problems at home or educational failure. This group made up 18 per cent of the category identified as bullies. This would appear to be the type of child labelled as the bully who is a coward at heart, the 'oaf' of literature who torments the school swot. Mitchel and O'Moore (1988) defined a small group of bullies as 'neurotic' and Olweus and Roland (1983) identified a group they named as 'hangers on', which had similar character-istics to the anxious bullies.

Gender differences

There is general agreement with the finding of Olweus (1978) that boys are more violent and destructive in their bullying than girls. Boys bully in a direct way, using physical aggression or threat. Girls favour the more indirect modes of malicious gossip and social ostracism. Boys bully both boys and girls, but mainly other boys, whereas girls bully, almost exclusively, other girls (Olweus, 1987). Roland suggests from his results that boys bully both boys and girls and find victims from other classes, whereas girls bully mainly girls and choose victims from their own class. This would seem feasible since Roland found that the girls in his study were using alienation from the group as their bullying technique, and this would be more effective among girls in the same class (Roland, in prep.).

The finding that boys bully more than girls, in the ratio of three to one, is a finding common to several pieces of research, but as the behaviour of the girls is more covert, it could be that the incidence among girls is higher than we at present assume. Parents and teachers, however, report that there is an equal amount of bullying between girls as there is between boys. This

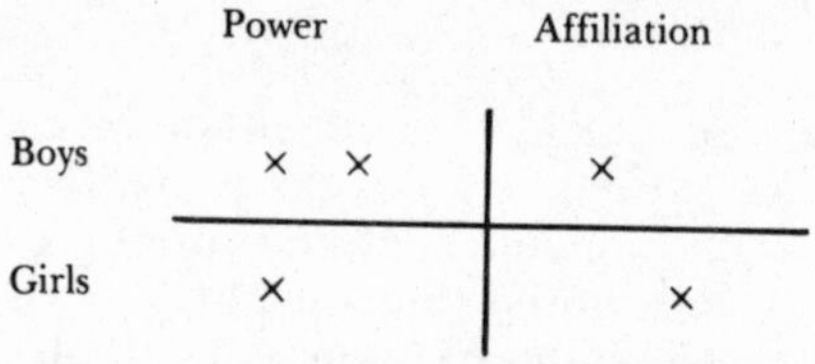

Figure 1 Rationale for bullying Roland (personal communication) suggests that boys bully to display their power, girls for reassurance.

could be because the girls complain to adults about being excluded without realizing that it is a form of bullying, whereas adults do label the behaviour in this way.

Roland (in prep.) has looked closely at the behaviour of girls who bully and suggests that they are seeking out an affiliation with others by alienating the victim to prove that they are 'in' the group and, by definition, that the target girl is 'out'. It is suggested that girls bully for reassurance, whereas boys bully to display their power (Wachtel, 1973). Affiliation and power are considered by Omark *et al.* (1975) to be the basic factors which regulate our social behaviour (see Fig. 1).

Age factors

Olweus (1987) has compared data from primary and secondary schools. Comparisons between other studies are difficult to obtain due to differences in the definition of terms such as bully, victim and bullying, and differences in the choice of methodology. Olweus found the incidence of bullying to be twice as high in primary as in secondary schools. The time of greatest risk for victims was found to be on entry to school, at each stage. Bullies were found to be active in the last year of both primary and secondary school, presumably when they are the oldest present and so in a position to dominate and several studies confirm a peak at about 13 years. This hypothesis is supported by the finding that the bullies were least active on entry to the secondary school, i.e. when they are the youngest students. Bullies of any age were found to be older than their victims and this has been substantiated by several other studies. Over the school years bullying among girls decreases, whereas it increases among boys, although there was found to be a general decrease in physical bullying among the older pupils.

Family factors

Family factors will be considered more fully in a later chapter, but it is of relevance to note that all studies which investigated the family background found it to be an influential factor common to both bullies and victims (Lowenstein 1978; Stephenson and Smith 1987a, b). The negative attitude of a mother to her son was found to be most significant (Olweus, 1987; Roland, in prep.). This negative attitude, characterized by indifference and a lack of involvement, is termed 'silent violence' by Olweus.

Behavioural problems

Some studies have made reference to bullying in relation to other behavioural problems. Mitchel and O'Moore (1988) noted that of the 19 bullies they studied, 15 were rated as antisocial and 3 as neurotic on the Rutter Behaviour Questionnaire. Several studies on aggression and disruption in schools mention bullying as one of a constellation of behaviours exhibited by these pupils but, sadly, little information specific to bullying has been collated (Foy, 1977; Mills, 1976; Lawrence *et al.*, 1984; Wilson and Irvine, 1978). One recent study indicated that a high proportion of bullies were disruptive in class but the study was small and within one school (Riley, 1988). Wider research is needed to confirm the hypothesis.

Racial bullying

There is little research available on the bullying of ethnic minority children, although small-scale studies indicate that these pupils are especially at risk (Riley, 1988). Seven out of ten children nominated as bullies were found to have strong racist attitudes. This bullying would appear to start at an early age (Akhtar and Stronach, 1986). Riley observed that there were two separate communities at playtimes in the school he studied, and sociometric work not only showed that a high proportion of these children were victims of attack but that there was very little positive contact between the children from ethnic minorities and the other pupils in the school. The victims did not talk of racism but they did speak of being bullied (further discussion of racial bullying is to be found in Chapter 3).

One clear finding from all the research presented is that at least 10 per cent of children of all ages in our schools are involved in a bullying situation. In looking at the incidence of bullying, we need to consider whether or not it is of paramount importance to identify large numbers of children at risk before we initiate preventative work in our schools. Does our intervention depend on a head count alone? Without doubt, for some children and their parents, their one case alone is sufficient to warrant our help.

Table 6 presents a summary of authors, samples, methodologies and results.

Table 1 Thumbnail sketches: The characteristics of children in the major categories of bullies and victims

Victim	Bully
1. Anxious, insecure, cautious, sensitive, quiet, submissive	1. Aggressive to parents, teachers, peers, siblings, impulsive
2. Reacts to attack by crying, yelling, withdrawal, helpless anger, ineffective retaliation, temper outbursts	2. Positive attitude to aggression and aggressive means, little anxiety; not a tough surface hiding a deeper anxiety (maybe in the case of anxious bullies)
3. Negative view of self and the situation	3. No guilt, shame or embarrassment, little empathy with the victims
4. Feels a failure, stupid, ashamed, unattractive, lonely and abandoned, no single close friend or supporter in the school, not provocative, bewildered and confused, unable to understand why bullied and how to find ways to become accepted	4. Strong, tough, powerful, well coordinated, dominant, confident; peers perhaps confuse this with leadership skills
5. Poor communicator, unable to talk way out of trouble	5. Good communicator, quick-witted, fast verbal responses, able to talk way out of trouble
6. Secondary nervous habits, e.g. stammering, biting nails or rocking	6. A sense of fun, more popular than victim, popularity decreases with age
7. Physically weaker, poor coordination, frequently younger than the attacker, small stature	7. Bullying may be only one component of a general pattern of antisocial and rule-breaking behaviour, a predictor of later antisocial and criminal behaviour in adulthood
	8. Girls: an exaggerated loudness, shouting, rudeness to staff, domineering to staff and peers
Summary. An anxious personality pattern combined with physical weakness (Olweus, 1987). Their behaviour and attitude signal to others that they feel insecure and worthless and will not retaliate if attacked	*Summary. Constellation of antisocial and disruptive problems, spirit of violence, i.e.* aggression considered to be an acceptable form of behaviour

Table 2 Personality factors

Victim	Ref.	Bully	Ref.
1. Enjoys home life, close relationships with family	Lagerspetz et al. (1982)	1. Little time spent at home, fewer positive family interactions	Lagerspetz et al. (1982), Lowenstein (1978)
2. Shy, withdrawn, anxious, passive non-gregarious, showing little interest in others, poor communication skills	Olweus (1978) Lowenstein (1978)	2. Confident, good communication skills, quick-witted, slick replies, can talk their way out of trouble	Olweus (1978), Hamblin (1978a), Lagerspetz (1982)
3. Socially insensitive, obsessive behaviour, ineffectual social skills, poor ability or wish to conform, submissive	Lowenstein (1978)	3. Conforms to own social ideal of dominant and powerful male, 'macho' image accepted by peer group	Lowenstein (1978)
4. Anxiety problems; eating, sleeping difficulties, ineffectual, temper outbursts, depression	Robins (1966a)	4. No anxieties; a rare exception is the anxious bully	Olweus (1978), Stephenson and Smith (1988)
5. Feelings of inferiority, below average self-esteem, rate themselves low in intellectual ability and attractiveness, but this could be due to modesty; self-report: detached, critical, aloof	Lowenstein (1978), Lagerspetz et al. (1982), Olweus (1978), Mykletun (1979), Byrne (1987)	5. Self-image of power, see themselves as tough, successful and capable, no focused dissatisfaction, not compensatory bullying; rate themselves more intelligent than their school work shows, remain confident, out-going, easy-going	Olweus (1978), Bjorkquist et al. (1982), Lowenstein (1978), Byrne (1987)
6. Feel unable to cope alone or to elicit support from peer group, feel helpless and ineffective	Lowenstein (1976)	6. Good coping skills, independent, effectively assertive	Olweus (1978)
7. Come to accept they deserve the bullying	Bjorkquist et al. (1982)	7. Come to believe the victim deserves the punishment	
8. Described as 'threat-sensitive'	Byrne (1987)	8. Described as 'socially bold'	Byrne (1987)

Table 3 School factors

Victim	Ref.	Bully	Ref.
1. Positive attitude to school work	Lagerspetz et al. (1982)	1. Less positive attitude to school work, staff and authority figures	Lagerspetz et al. (1982)
2. Below average popularity, may be rejected by peers, social isolate	Olweus (1978), Lagerspetz et al. (1982)	2. Below average popularity, more popular than the victim, possibly a leader due to dominance being confused with leadership, popularity declines with age; not so unpopular as to be rejected; not a cause for retaliatory bullying; 43% popular in ordinary classes – none found to be popular in remedial classes	Olweus (1978), Lowenstein (1978), Mitchel and O'Moore (1988)
3. Negative view of peer relationships, unable to muster support or form friendships	Lagerspetz et al. (1982), Olweus (1978)	3. Negative attitude to peer relationships outside own supporters, but able to elicit more peer support than the victim	Lagerspetz et al. (1982), Olweus (1978)
4. Peers have no clear picture, no stereotype	Olweus (1978)	4. Peers have a clear picture, a stereotype	Olweus (1978)
5. Average intellectual ability	Olweus (1978)	5. Average intellectual ability, possibly low attainments, underachieving	Olweus (1978), Lowenstein (1978)

6. Negative attitude to aggression, never provoked, fear when provoked, helpless anger, possible temper outbursts due to provocation and frustration	Olweus (1978), Lowenstein (1978)	6. Positive attitude to aggression, clear social ideal of 'macho' man, tough/powerful, poor control over aggressive impulses, no guilt, no embarrassment	Olweus (1978), Bjorkquist et al. (1982), Lagerspetz et al. (1982)
Possible cluster of anxiety and emotional problems		Enjoys the discomfort and the distress of weaker students; seeks out aggressive situations, no motive other than for power and kudos has been identified by peers	Ekman (1977) (quoted in Olweus, 1979), Wachtel (1973), Bowers (1973), Arora and Thompson (1987), Bjorkquist et al. (1982)
		Feels tough, powerful, able to meet own expectation of social ideal, lack of sensitivity to others, think of themselves as impulsive and having low control over impulses	Olweus (1987a), Bjorkquist et al. (1982), Lagerspetz et al. (1982), Lowenstein (1978)
		Possible cluster of antisocial, disruptive problems	Mitchel and O'Moore (1988)

Table 4 Family factors

Victim	Ref.	Bully	Ref.
1. Over-protected and dependent on the family	Olweus (1978), Lagerspetz et al. (1982)	1. Low level of home supervision and monitoring, such as times for returning home	Patterson (1984)
2. Close relationship within the family	Lagerspetz et al. (1982)	2. Low empathy and negative emotions between parents and child defined by Olweus as 'silent violence'; too little love and care considered the most detrimental factor	Olweus (1978)
3. Feels unable to meet parental expectations – feels unassertive and unable to defend him/herself		3. Inconsistent control and discipline, i.e. over-lax or over-punitive, physical means of control	Olweus (1978)
		4. Use of aggression condoned, social image of 'tough and powerful' encouraged	
		5. Parents likely to have been bullies themselves	Lowenstein (1978)
		6. Marital conflict, chaotic home background	Lowenstein (1978), Stephenson and Smith (1987)
		7. Family factors considered to be most important	Olweus (1987)
Three times as many bullies and victims were found to be experiencing family problems of some kind, as were the controls			Stephenson and Smith (1987a and b)
77% of bullies and victims were experiencing family problems			Mitchel and O'Moore (1988)

Table 5 Physical factors

Victim	Ref.	Bully	Ref.
1. Weak physical strength, unable to retaliate	Olweus (1978)	1. Physically strong, robust, confident to attack	Olweus (1978)
2. 8/19 victims weak, 6/93 of the well-adjusted weak	Lagerspetz et al. (1982)	2. 10/27 bullies very strong, 7/93 of the well-adjusted very strong	Lagerspetz et al. (1982)
3. 17/20 victims with coordination problems, no aptitude for sport, low motivation and poor at playground activities; could be an influential factor on social behaviour from an early age	Olweus (1978)	3. Well coordinated, good at sport, games and playground activities, could influence social skills, popularity and confidence from an early age	Olweus (1978), Jersild (1966)
4. Low energy level	Olweus (1978)	4. Energetic, active	Olweus (1978)
5. Low level of pain tolerance, fearful, lacking in confidence	Olweus (1978)	5. High pain threshold, robust, 'dare devil'	Lagerspetz et al. (1982), Olweus (1978), Jersild (1966)
6. Younger, smaller than the bullies	Elliott (1986)	6. Older, stronger than the victims	Elliott (1986), Olweus (1987)
7. Possible physical deviations, e.g. glasses, obesity, tall, small	Olweus (1978) Lagerspetz et al. (1982), Byrne (1987)	7. Average appearance	Lagerspetz et al. (1982), Lowenstein (1978)
No physical deviations Some physical deviations	Lowenstein (1978)		
8. Below average attractiveness	Lowenstein (1978)	8. Average attractiveness	Lagerspetz et al. (1982), Lowenstein (1978)

Table 6 A summary of methodologies and results

Author	Sample	Methodology	Results	Other information
Lowenstein (1978a) (1978b)	10 000 boys and girls	Teacher, parent and pupil interviews and assessments; Maudsley Personality Inventory	5 to 7-year-olds (2%) 7 to 11-year-olds (1%) 11 to 16 years, boys (5%), 11 to 16 years, girls (1.5%)	Family factors significant, strict criteria used, e.g. bullying had lasted at least 6 months
Bjorkquist et al. (1982)	430 boys and girls aged 14–16 years	Semantic differential survey, peer ratings, ego picture study	5% victims 5% bullies 10% involved	Three times as many boys as girls
Lagerspetz et al. (1982) Reid (1983)	434 boys and girls aged 12–16 years 128 boys and girls	Q-sort technique, teacher interviews, peer ratings Survey on truancy	13.7% boys 5.4% girls involved First study (15%), Second study (19%) involved	Bullies had positive attitude to aggression These truants reported they were not attending due to bullying
Newson and Newson (1984)		Study on parenting, parent interviews	26% parents aware child had been bullied, 4% seriously	Few mothers admitted to own child bullying, majority were worried about the problem of bullying
Wall Street Journal (1985)			58% involved	USA
Elliott (1986)	4000	Children and parents surveyed	38% victims at some time	Bullying found to be the priority concern, identified older children bully younger children, identified sibling bullying
Cole (1977)	Primary age boys and girls	Sociometric studies, teacher ratings		Two-thirds of teachers had encountered it; long-term problem as teachers felt unable to resolve the situation

Reference	Sample	Method	Incidence	Findings
Roland (in prep.) (preliminary results, 1988a, b)	Janus Project; evaluation of the Norwegian Campaign	Parent and teacher interviews, questionnaire of own design given to pupils, sociometric studies	5% victims 3.5% bullies } severe	Family factors significant, no difference between rural and urban areas. Situation had improved in secondary schools but worsened in primary schools
Roland (in prep.) Arora and Thompson (1987)	Study of families Secondary age boys and girls	As above Action research design: questionnaire formed from pupil information	Mother–son relationship important 24% involved	Wide variation in incidence between age groups and classes, three times as many boys as girls involved.
Byrne (1987)	600 secondary school, boys only 720 primary boys and girls	Teacher survey using Cattell High School Questionnaire	5% incidence	13% of remedial group were classed as victims, 9% as bullies
Mitchel and O'Moore (1988)		Teachers and children surveyed. Rutter Behaviour Questionnaire and teachers' free description	5% incidence, 16% bullies in remedial group	15/19 bullies classed as antisocial; 3/19 classed as neurotic, high proportion in remedial group
Stephenson and Smith (1987)	1078 boys and girls aged 10–11 years	Teacher and pupil interviews, questionnaire of own design	23% bullies and victims 7% victims 10% bullies } severe	18% of bullies were anxious bullies; 7% of victims and bullies had family problems; wide range of incidence (0–50%) between schools, more in social priority areas
White (1987)	Japan		40% involved	Emphasis on changing the attitude and behaviour of the victim
Olweus (1978)	Solna Study, 900 boys aged 13 and 15 years	Self-reports, Q-sort, teacher and mother interviews, specific definition of bullying given	10% victims, 7% bullies, 5% severe bullying problems, 10% less severe	Detailed information in the book *Aggression in Schools: Bullies and Whipping Boys*, 1978 (Summary publication)

continued

Table 6—continued

Author	Sample	Methodology	Results	Other information
Olweus (1985)	Sample survey of 85% of all Norwegian primary and junior high schools	Teachers and pupils – given extensive inventory of own design	5% incidence/severe, 11% primary age victims, 5% secondary age victims	
Olweus (1985)	Long term study of primary and junior high school pupils	Parent and teacher interviews, pupil self-reports, peer ratings, teacher inventories	7–8% bullies, 9% victims	50% bullied by older pupils, 3 times as many boys as girls involved, 18% of bullies were anxious bullies, 6% of serious bullies were also victims
Olweus (1987)	Summary of all the above studies plus a parallel study in Sweden and an indepth study in Norway		9% victims, 7% bullies 3% victims } severe 2% bullies 5% seriously involved	Family factors and parenting influential. Long term social difficulties prognosed for those involved in bullying

2
The bullies

When I was a laddie
I lived with ma granny
And many a hiding ma granny gied me.
    Now I'm a man
And I live with ma granny
And do to ma granny what she did to me.
                    (Traditional rhyme)

Most definitions of bullying encapsulate the idea of there being an uneven distribution of power, i.e. a lack of physical strength or assertiveness on the part of the victim. It is a situation where the powerful clash with the powerless. Is there then some intrinsic need for humans to exercise and display their power over others, an inevitable instinct for the powerful to assert their dominance over the weak? It is commonly assumed that it is natural for all animals to fight and ethological examples are quoted freely.

In general terms, all animals do display aggression and clearly certain animals establish their dominance firmly over the more submissive of the species (Edelman and Omark, 1973). This is done through play fights, elaborate ritual and display; disputes are settled before serious injury, and gratuitous violence is rare (Krebs, 1984). Similarly, in almost any primary school playground, play fights are common between young boys as a means of informally establishing a hierarchy of dominance. Even among older boys, in corridors or at bus stops, one sees this playful, casual behaviour, but careful observation clearly shows who is the more dominant of the dyad. Most primate groups, including young children, do establish this hierarchy of dominance (Edelman and Omark, 1973). It occurs as a matter of course throughout casual interactions, an eminent position in the group being allocated, in the case of children, to the tough, smart, kind and popular.

However, according to some theorists, the element of cruelty involved is exclusive to humans:

> It is a sad fact that, with the exception of certain rodents no animal habitually attacks or destroys members of its own species to the same extent as humans. (Storr, 1975)

> We are the cruellest, most ruthless species ever to walk the earth and hence action has to be taken to protect us from ourselves. (Jamieson, 1984)

There appears to be little evidence of intra-species aggression among other animals which does not serve a definite function (Lorenz, 1966). For example, domestic animals will use violence if space or food is limited. Also, newly dominant male lions may kill off the offspring of previously dominant males. However, this is rational behaviour, because the females come into oestrus faster, there will be no future competition between the established cubs and those the new male will produce, and only his genes will be left in the pride (Krebs, 1984).

In contrast, there seems little rationale to the verbal, physical and psychological taunting of bullying children in terms of species preservation. Witnesses are rarely able to offer any ready explanation for the bullying. Sadly, over time, a cognitive change seems to occur in both bullies and their victims; the victims begin to believe that they deserve the attacks, the bullies that their actions are warranted (Bjorkquist *et al.*, 1982).

The rationale which appears to emerge is the need of the bullies to demonstrate or confirm their power over others (Bowers, 1973; Wachtel, 1973). It would seem that the human race has always had a preoccupation with seeking power – wars and invasions embody the principles of bullying behaviour:

> Man has always been fascinated by power. He has reason to be for, as scholars we are fond of reminding him he belongs to a violent species. Look at his history: a long succession of wars with interludes of peace in localized times and places. His myths and his religion are saturated with concern for power. (McClelland, 1975)

Highly aggressive children appear not only to seek out conflict situations, but to choose those where they may best be observed by their peers (Wachtel, 1973). McClelland (1975) proposes that there are two faces to power: a socialized power where there is a need for positive influence in the group, and a personalized power – an 'I win, therefore you lose' situation. Both are evident in bullying behaviour but the latter, especially, seems relevant in this context. There is perhaps a balance between the power of the bully and the feelings of fear and vulnerability of the victim; a symbiotic relationship where the signs of helplessness of the victim give the bully licence to use power-oriented techniques to dominate (Rubin, 1980).

The need to feel dominant over others, as is shown in bullying among children, may remain through the adult years but be expressed in a different manner. Attempts to measure a 'power motive' in adults suggest that it expresses itself in a variety of ways throughout the stages of maturity, often in an indirect or vicarious manner in the areas of work or leisure (McClelland, 1975). Younger males may seek power-arousing cues in magazines where women are portrayed as submissive or compliant, or they may favour guns or powerful cars. In later maturity power may be courted by possessions, e.g. collections of paintings or antiques or by committee work. Women, it is suggested, display their need for dominance through an obsession with their body image, clothing or home decor. Bullying among children, however, often involves a less subtle bid for power and dominance and frequently incorporates some form of direct aggression.

Aggression

Bullying is not a new phenomenon, it is simply one form of aggression which is social in its nature (Bjorkquist *et al.*, 1982). Indiscipline and aggression have always been a permanent feature of schools: Gallup (1984) found disruption a major problem in American classrooms; Dunning *et al.* (1988) write of the 'wild and riotous folk antecedents of modern football hooliganism', which can be traced back to the fourteenth century; the violent mutinies of schoolboys in the seventeenth century are documented by Ariès (1960); and Ogilvie (1953) notes that more than one public school has been razed to the ground by its pupils. A perusal I made of school logbooks dating back to the last century showed that violent attacks on pupils and teachers were not uncommon at that time. Aggression in schools is not a contemporary problem but there are perhaps contemporary factors, such as media coverage, which could lead us to believe that this is so. Olweus (1979) defines aggression as:

> any act or behaviour that involves, might involve, and/or to some extent can be considered as aiming at, the infliction of injury or discomfort; also manifestations of inner reactions such as feelings and thoughts that can be considered to have such an aim are regarded as aggressive responses.

The concept of aggression covers a myriad of events from toddler temper tantrums to grievous bodily harm. The target for the aggression may not be obvious; some forms of aggressive behaviour can be misinterpreted or overlooked. A deliberately slow speed of working, the repeated ignoring of explicit instructions, some forms of school refusal or even elective mutism could, perhaps, be a covert form of bullying. Any behaviour causing deliberate and repeated annoyance, with the intent of distressing another powerless to stop it, for whatever reason, could perhaps be considered within the context of bullying.

Aggression is not a preserve of a pathological minority of children; all children are aggressive in some manner at some time, none are aggressive all of the time. In seeking explanations for maladaptive behaviour we need to consider the whole context in which the behaviour occurs, and also the conditions when the behaviour of the child is appropriate. From the dissonance between the two situations and the personnel involved we may elicit clues as to why maladaptive responses are employed.

There are various models of aggression, and those noted here appear to be directly pertinent to bullying:

1. *Organized vs collective aggression* (Nielsen and Stigendal, 1973). A group of children, having planned to lie in wait for another, on the way home from school, is an example of organized aggression. This premeditated attack may be more dangerous and damaging, reflecting a negative feeling common to the group, than a case of *ad hoc*, collective bullying where one or two make an initial attack and a mob forms in a casual fashion due to a transient interest and the promise of excitement.

2. *Direct vs ritualized aggression.* Aggression can be in the form of a direct attack on another with deliberate intent to harm. There is, however, a ritualized aggression – a symbolic form – as can be seen in the elaborate displays of weaponry and aggressive dress style used by some young people to emphasize their power and potency. A latent ritualized aggression may be triggered and become active by provocation or, for example, by over-policing at a rally (Marsh *et al.*, 1978). Applied to bullying, the dramatic threats which are initially 'peacock displays' of power may, if mishandled, erupt into direct attack.

3. *Direct vs indirect aggression.* Bullying behaviour is divided by Olweus (1978) into direct aggression (e.g. physical or verbal attack) and indirect aggression (e.g. covert malicious gossip, cruel jokes, sarcasm, social ostracism). Girls, he suggests, are more likely to be subjected to the latter, whereas boys are prone to both types of attack, as can be seen from several of the case studies presented later.

4. *Instrumental aggression.* Bullying can be used as a means to an end (e.g. extortion) and it can be instrumental if used as a means of expressing anger or disappointment. Aggression is, of course, the instrument used in bullying to express dominance over others in a variety of ways.

The aggressive personality

A vast amount has been written about aggression but we still have no conclusive evidence to explain why one particular child should behave in an aggressive manner more frequently than others:

> Little currently is known about genetic origins of aggressive behaviour or about the physiology of why some people find it more enjoyable to behave in this way. (Dunning *et al.*, 1988)

The debate continues as to whether children are born with a personality predisposing them to behave in an idiosyncratic manner or whether they are born free from any prenatal influence, in a state of *tabula rasa*, so that all behaviour is the result of experience. If the latter is true, there is perhaps more optimism for change. New behaviours may be learned, maladaptive ones unlearned.

Personality is a concept familiar to all, yet difficult to define: 'Personality is a hypothetical construct designed to bring order and consistency to the explanation of individual behaviour' (Monte, 1977). Most definitions imply that in addition to any predisposition, people assimilate experiences throughout their lives and act accordingly: 'Temperament represents the interaction between a biologically anchored predisposition and environmental demands' (Thomas and Chess, 1976). The comparative studies of monozygote (identical) and dyzygote (non-identical) twins, have found no conclusive evidence as yet, but encouragement is given to the idea that some degree of innate predisposition is contributory to what we know as personality (Mittler, 1971).

Longitudinal studies of temperament have been carried out to look for stability over time, presuming that this would support the hypothesis of genetic predisposition (Chess and Thomas, 1984). Robins (1966a) followed a cohort of children over 30 years and found some stability of temperament; Cowen *et al.* (1973) also found stability and, interestingly, noted that opinions of classmates given by peers were as good a predictor of adult behaviour as professional opinions and psychometric measurements. Classmates spend a great deal of their time together and share a wide range of experiences and, therefore, it is reasonable to assume that they know more about each other than anyone else. Irritable and non-conforming children (Block, 1971) did not alter despite experiencing radical environmental change, and Kagan and Moss (1962) discovered that socially anxious children grew up to become non-competitive, insecure adults. The results of Thomas *et al.*'s (1963) vast cohort indicate that some early infant indices reliably predict adult social problems. Most relevant to bullying is the work of Olweus (personal communication and 1987), who has shown that a high proportion of boys bullying others at 8 years old are likely to display troublesome behaviour at 16, and to pursue an antisocial or criminal career by age 24. In summary, there would appear to be some degree of stability evident, for whatever reason, in the personality of some, if not all, children.

A different interpretation of these studies has, however, been made by Clarke and Clarke (1984), who offer a lively debate. They suggest that a simple measure of stability of response to environmental stimuli is not necessarily proof of a predisposition of temperament, but could simply indicate a learned pattern of behaviour showing a high resistance to change. In addition, there may be considerable stability in the environmental factors involved. Wolff (1986) states that as no findings are ever totally conclusive, we can never predict the outcome for any one particular child. Without doubt, a high number of subjects in the studies did show stability, but it is important to recognize that in every study a considerable number did not. MacFarlane (1964), wrote retrospectively of the 30 year long Berkley Guidance Study:

> Many of our most mature and competent adults had severely troubled and confusing childhoods and adolescences. Many of our highly successful children and adolescents have failed to achieve their predicted potential.

Robins (1966a) wrote that 90 per cent of the sociopathic adults in her cohort had displayed antisocial behaviour as children. It is not as easy, however, to predict from the incidence of disturbance in children, which of them will grow up to have problems in adulthood. While agreeing that there is a degree of constancy of temperament, Clarke and Clarke (1984) stress most strongly the potential for change, i.e. the plasticity of human behaviour. They suggest that four categories of factors – biological, sociological, environmental and chance – tend to militate against the idea of constancy in human development.

Whether or not there is some degree of predisposition in

personality, there do appear to be some factors which counter adverse circumstances and provide highly positive effects in the most serious of cases: a special talent or interest, a commitment to a career, a rewarding relationship outside the family, perhaps with a particular teacher. Any or a combination of these factors can have a profound effect on the eventual development of the child faced with extremely difficult circumstances (Quinton and Rutter, 1985b). Factors which offer the young person self-esteem, confidence and independence seem factors critical to success. If the aggressive tendencies of some children can be identified in the very early years it would seem expedient to look at our work with preschool children as it could be that at this young age they are more responsive to adult intervention. Clarke and Clarke (1984) suggest that we need not rush to intervene without deliberation, because the flexibility and resilience of the human organism do not decrease with age and, therefore, there is always opportunity for change.

Only in the middle of the last century did there begin to be any systematic consideration given to causal factors within the environment for child behaviour. Previously, the child was deemed good or bad from birth; prevalent explanations being sought in hereditary or religious fatalism. Simple rewards and punishments were the only inducements or deterrents used in attempting change. There are now many explanations offered to account for the behaviour of children.

Some explanations for aggressive behaviour

A wide range of explanations has been offered for aggressive behaviour: decor, food additives, diet, medical conditions and, of course, previous experiences of all forms. Those mentioned here are those relating to the responses of a child which may be considered in a programme for change to be initiated by a school. These explanations are not discrete but interrelated, so that more than one could be at the root of any aggressive act perpetrated by any one child.

A child using bullying tactics may not have attained the same stage of moral development as the others in his/her group (Kohlberg, 1981), and attitudes can vary greatly within any one age band. Some children may have genuine difficulty in under-standing the view of others and, being unable to empathize with the distress of their peers, regard their own teasing and taunting of them as just 'messing about'.

Many bullies appear to experience little guilt or sympathy for their victims. Unlike the group above, some children have a cold and calculating approach to their misbehaviour and their intent to cause pain to others. Such children in ordinary schools may be receiving specialist help.

It is common for some pupils, in my own experience, to reflect on and justify their actions solely from an egocentric stance; to hold a skewed perception of a confrontation so that their own contribution to a crisis goes unacknowledged. The inevitable punitive reactions of others are seen as erroneous, over-harsh or vindictive. In many cases, this does seem to be due to a genuine ignorance of their own part in the escalation of the crisis.

A poor self-image, little confidence and feelings of hopelessness can result in some children failing to understand the effect of their behaviour on others. Pupils considering their own efforts to be irrelevant to their future success or failure are unlikely to make a determined effort to change (Kaplan, 1980).

Knowing how to behave does not necessarily result in a successful execution of the behaviour. A volatile, impulsive response to a real or imagined threat or provocation could stem from low self-value (Meichenbaum, 1977). There is a poor prognosis for the success of a simple social skills programme for such children (Spence, 1983). These candidates do not possess the prerequisite self-control and, therefore, an intermediary programme of relaxation may be necessary to slow such children down to a level where they can premeditate and predetermine their behaviour (Spivack and Shure, 1974).

There is a developmental pattern to aggressive behaviour, in the light of which, incidents need to be viewed. In the first years aggression with intent to hurt is rare: the pushing and snatching of toddlers is mainly for gain (Manning and Sluckin, 1984). Once the child has the cognitive ability to distinguish self from others, focused fear arises. At this stage they are able to understand that not only can they be harmed but that they themselves can harm others. Along with the first attempts to hurt and harm others, guilt, remorse and conscience emerge. With increasing sociability there is a correlated increase in aggression. More interactions result in more conflicts. A hierarchy of dominance is established and even young children become aware of when to challenge and when to comply. A better command of language allows squabbles to be settled without resort to physical violence and a developing intellect allows for both coping with and avoiding conflict (Patterson and Guillon, 1976). In adolescence, conflicts have a more abstract, less tangible source, involving status, obligations, rights, beliefs and trust. At this age a wider range of options is available and, whereas younger children can only choose between the hierarchy of dominance or playing alone, adolescents have the intellectual and physical ability to draw upon this wider array of choices (Patterson and Guillon, 1976).

The bullying child may select to offend, for whatever reason, from a large repertoire of behaviours (Clarke, 1985). There may be a well-established habit of acting in an aggressive manner. Past experiences may have coloured the perceptions and attitudes of the child. The excitement of the conflict could have incited others to join in, so reinforcing the fun of an attack.

It could be that the child has a restricted array of behaviours to choose from due to impoverished experience (Jamieson, 1984). Aggression being the simplest and most accessible of behaviours is the one most readily chosen. The individual, of whatever age, interacts in a complex manner with all aspects of the environment and from these transactions a repertoire of behaviour is formed.

Regardless of the scope of behaviours at their disposal some children have a faulty decision technique (Tversky and Kahnmann, 1974): a misreading or misinterpretation of the situation could be at fault; the problem-solving skills could be weak or the information-processing skills impaired; or there could be an inability to predict with accuracy the consequences of any behaviour (D'Zurilla and Goldfried, 1971). Rarely is there wanton purposeless aggression. Interestingly, we are now beginning to understand that there are rules and a structure to disruptive behaviour in schools.

During puberty hormonal changes correspond to parallel emotional development, leading to a stage where there can be a severe lack of confidence and an increase in confusing moods and phases of regression. The difficulties of coming to terms with a new body structure may be underestimated. Regressions in behavioural and emotional stability could prove confounding both for the young person and others alike. Most, however, gradually emerge throughout the teenage years as independent individuals, seeking out their abilities, limitations and boundaries. There is not necessarily more aggressive behaviour among older pupils in schools but, because of their greater size and strength, it can be more effective and dangerous.

Maturation implies independence. Young people are often given little autonomy and responsibility compared to that they take upon themselves in after-school hours when their lives may closely mirror those of adults. This can encourage a sense of frustration and boredom. In addition, as children grow towards adulthood, the immediate influence of parents may decrease, to be replaced by stronger ties with their peer group. Young people often look towards their contemporaries for guidance and confirmation regarding codes of behaviour as well as to other role models, e.g. those promoted by commerce and the media.

The role of society

Is there a section of our society more prone to use aggression and aggressive means than the culture of our schools accepts as the norm? If so, why should this be? Dunning *et al.* (1988) write on football hooligans:

> If our observations are correct there is a specific aggressive masculine style which, in Britain at least, nowadays tends to be characteristic mainly of males from particular sections of the lower working class.

Dunning *et al.* stress that this is a particular deviant sub-group, an under-class, and that no generalization can be made about, what is referred to in general terms as, the working class. Certain characteristics are noted, such as maintaining strong ties with an unusually wide range of kin, most of whom live in the immediate locality. Therefore, the most salient emotional links are with others like themselves, within a community made up from an aggregate of structurally similar groups. The result is a strong cohesive community with narrow social horizons and a hostile attitude to outsiders.

Several studies have shown parenting practices to be highly influential in controlling or encouraging aggressive behaviour. Low levels of supervision and monitoring of a child's where-abouts can result in the early socialization of the child occurring on the neighbourhood streets or further afield, where the young child only has equally young or slightly older role models (Dunning *et al.*, 1988). In addition, the adults in the community may have a positive attitude towards aggression, the young males being encouraged to 'stand up for themselves' – physical prowess, for example, being more highly prized than the academic competence promoted by some schools. Elias (1978) suggests that power has gradually been transferred over the centuries to the police and the legal system, and that this collective monopoly protects the individual from sudden attack. Parents, therefore, should be able to demand that their offspring suppress aggressive impulses because, in a situation of law and order, those impulses are redundant. The result is that we now experience guilt if we transgress and behave in a violent manner. Some parents, however, do not train their children to suppress their aggressive impulses, perhaps because they live in communities where law and order are not as much in evidence. In some of the more impoverished communities, the most vulnerable families are scapegoated and bullied by the more robust, and this is evident in the case studies of Michael and Andrew presented in Chapter 10.

Dunning *et al.* (1988) propose that there are two different response patterns to the aggression of children; the response of families with a non-positive attitude to aggression being different from the response of families with a positive attitude to aggression.

Responses made to aggression by families with a non-positive attitude to aggression include:

● restraint on any overt expression of aggression;
● it may be pushed behind the scenes or channelled into other activities;
● a high level of guilt and remorse may be inculcated by others;
● it may be deflected legitimately by playing sport or enlisting in the army;
● intellectual and academic qualities are prized (over, or as well as, physical strength);

Responses made to aggression by families with a positive attitude to aggression include:

● little restraint on any overt expression of aggression;
● a public display of strength may be sought;
● permission might be given by adults;
● there is little guilt or remorse;
● legitimate modes are considered too tame;
● street credibility is essential for community kudos.

From my own experience I would suggest that even within an aggressive culture there are rules and regulations. Anyone overstepping the mark earns a derogatory label such as 'nutter' and group disapproval. Rather than making a simplistic judgement of such behaviour, it is necessary to view it in the context in which it occurs. These young people may be severely restricted in their options – they may not be faced with free-floating moral choices which can be taken outside of their limited experience. It is no mean achievement for such pupils to straddle the two cultures of home and school.

For a further explanation of aggressive attitudes in some young people, we must look to the heritage of industry to explain an admiration of physical strength and prowess. Muscle power was needed to gain and maintain most employment in the not too distant past, whereas weakness led to the inevitable loss of job and livelihood and crippling medical bills. It was essential to be strong for the survival of self and dependents. In most industrial areas, there is much less manual work now, but those cultural values remain and continue to be transmitted without any awareness of their original purpose, so all that remains is an overemphasis on masculine strength (Taylor, 1979). Kudos is gained by a display of physical power over those who are weaker.

Is there perhaps some imbalance in the structure of our society which encourages aggressive behaviour? Fitzgerald (1980) states that 'No society can at one and the same time hold out a common goal to all its members and block off access to the achievement of that goal and not expect problems.' The ethnographic studies of Coffield *et al.* (1981, 1986) are extremely enlightening, for they give a vivid picture of how it feels to be pushed to the margins of our affluent society. It must be stressed, however, that there is no suggestion that bullying is a prerogative of the poor and disadvantaged. Some of the more distressing and damaging cases I have come across have been among pupils with advantaged, in some cases privileged, backgrounds. Donnie (see Chapter 10) came from a privileged family background where dominance over others was condoned, even encouraged. Bullying is not the product of status deprivation or financial disadvantage alone – that would be a myopic stance to adopt. None of the studies quoted have inferred that such factors are anything but contributory to the problem of violence in our society.

Gender differences

If a difference was discernible in the behaviour and relationships between boys and girls from a very early age, this might offer support to the theory of some degree of prenatal influence. Whether this is the case or not, any differences found in the social behaviour of boys and girls would offer valuable insights into the more covert behaviour of bullying.

The previous discussion emphasized the part society perhaps plays in eliciting aggressive behaviour from young boys and youths. There does seem to be a difference in the bullying behaviour of girls and boys – girls resort to physical aggression less often than boys, instead preferring social exclusion or malicious rumour (Roland, 1988). Many girls, both perpetrator and victim, do not consider this to be bullying even when it causes considerable distress. The less frequent physical attacks by girls do attract disproportionate attention compared to boys, as does any violent crime, presumably as it contravenes current social expectations.

The popular viewpoint that there may be a combination of both inherited and learned influences which result in the differing behaviour of boys and girls, is supported by Hinde (1988):

> The answer to the question of the ontogeny of gender differences lies partly at the biological level in the prenatal influences of maternal and infant hormones and partly at the social level in the effects of cultural and socialization influences.

It is the view of Hinde that the biological influences are far outweighed by the sociocultural structure – the norms, values and institutions of society. Human behaviour is almost infinitely malleable and there is no evidence to show other than that males and females are equally able to be influenced by cultural pressures.

In an attempt to discern how much of the behaviour of young children is socially induced, observers in one study were asked to identify toddlers as boys or girls by their behaviour alone, for all were wearing snowsuits (Condry and Ross, 1985). This proved impossible, but when told the gender of each child, stereotyped labels for play and behaviour were assigned to the children by the observers. In a different study, newborns were shown to observers from behind a screen. Those named as boys were immediately described by the observers as robust and strong, those named as girls were described as gentle and having fine features (Rubin *et al*, 1974).

Such stereotyping must start at birth, for it is not socially acceptable to refer to a baby as 'it'; therefore, once named, society colludes with the labelling. There is more pressure on a boy to be tough than on a girl not to be a tomboy, and fathers have been found to be more boisterous and robust in playing with their baby sons than they are with their daughters (Maccoby and Jacklin, 1980b). The higher incidence of verbal and physical aggression in boys has been noted as early as the second year and is thought to be one of the most established gender differences (Maccoby and Jacklin, 1980b), and it is common to most cultures worldwide (Whiting and Whiting, 1975). Maccoby and Jacklin (1980b) suggest that boys may perhaps be more biologically prepared to learn dominance, competitiveness and aggression, whereas girls may be more receptive to training in inhibition. This hypothesis is, however, challenged by Tieger (1980).

Relationship differences between boys and girls

By looking for gender differences in friendship patterns it may be possible to gain insights into the differing methods of bullying used by boys and girls. The traditional hypothesis is that the friendships and relationships of boys differ from those of girls in fundamental and observable ways. Boys are considered to be primarily interested in objects and their manipulation, and their friendships are considered to be spread wider than those of girls. Girls show a preference for the more intense twosome, or even a group of three or four, but if there are more than two at any one time one girl, almost certainly, will be on the periphery (Douvan and Adelson, 1966). Casual playground observations show that boys play team games more than girls and often commandeer the largest play area for their game, pushing small groups of girls and the less robust boys to the periphery. Even across cultures, boys of primary age play more often in gangs than girls (Omark *et al.*, 1975); it would be interesting to know whether this is so in cultures where there is no heritage of team sport.

It may be that boys need the support of the group in their quest for adventures and escapades, or for support in a collaborative bid to usurp adult authority. Rubin (1980) refers to the reminiscences of B. F. Skinner, who enjoyed the traditional games of gangs of young lads everywhere, i.e. ringing the doorbells of neighbours and then running off, or pulling string taut across paths to trip up pedestrians. Such pranks were, according to Skinner, devised and executed in an atmosphere of conspiracy and close companionship. I suspect girls make less of an overt group bid to defy authority. Boys are thought to emphasize the hierarchy of dominance within their group more than girls who perhaps stress intimacy and other affective aspects in relationships. Perhaps from a young age boys learn the skills of getting along in a large group but are less proficient than girls in developing and sustaining intimate relationships. The smaller, more exclusive groupings of girls may elicit more commitment than boys. By definition, girls' friendship patterns are more intimate by simple virtue of fact that they are smaller (Maccoby and Jacklin, 1975).

Girls appear to make fewer new friends, show a preference for sharing with their friends and maintain a stronger boundary between those they regard as close friends and others, than do boys. The looser friendships are more trouble-free; the closer the relationship the more conflict occurs (Shapiro, 1967). It is interesting to watch children at playtime in schools; the girls seem to seek out their particular friend, whereas the boys rush around looking for anyone with a football!

Research on bullying suggests that boys seek power and dominance, whereas girls need a sense of affirmation and affiliation, a feeling of belonging and a shared intimacy expressed in exchanging confidences and gossip (Roland, in prep.).

Comparisons have been made between the friendship of two young girls and a love affair (Lever, 1976): teenage girls may hold hands, keep in constant contact by telephone, copy details of each other's dress, hairstyle and musical taste, write notes to each other in class and openly show mutual affection. This need for intimacy is manifest in bullying: bullies either exclude the targeted girl from the intimate group or, by use of malicious gossip, they try to prove that whereas they are acceptable, the discredited victim is not. This type of ploy can be executed with the skill of an army general on manoeuvres.

This hypothesis – that boys enjoy a more extensive frame to their friendships, whereas girls prefer fewer but more intimate relationships – does not go unchallenged (Bigelow and La Gaipa, 1980). It would seem, however, that research specific to bullying does support the hypothesis to some degree. Roland (in prep.) proposes that girls who bully may have had a poor relationship with their mothers: 'A long standing situation of low primary affiliation will create a motive system within the child which will increase the need for secondary affiliation in class.'

Boys who use physical aggression are considered by many to be modelling the behaviour of significant others, or perhaps simply using this method of interaction because they have not been taught that it is socially unacceptable.

It is not suggested by any theorist that either boys or girls use one or other technique exclusively, only that there do seem to be gender differences regarding the preferred method of bullying, which may reflect a possible difference in friendship behaviour.

3
The victims

Pocket Money

'I can't explain what happens to my cash.'
I can, but can't – not to my Mum and Dad.
'Give us ten pee or get another bash' –

That's where it goes. And though their questions crash
Like blows, and though they're getting mad,
I can't explain what happens to my cash;

How can I tell the truth? I just rehash
Old lies. The others have and I'm the had:
'Give us ten pee or get another bash.'

'For dinner Dad? . . . just sausages and mash.'
'That shouldn't make you broke by Wednesday, lad.'
I can't explain. What happens to my cash –

My friends all help themselves. I get the ash
Of fags I buy and give, get none. 'Too bad.
Give us ten pee or get another bash.

For being You.' And still I feel the thrash
Of stronger, firmer hands than mine. The sad
Disgust of living like a piece of trash.

I can't explain what happens to my cash.
'Give us ten pee or get another bash.'

Mick Gowar (1986)

Even though the research on bullying is sparse, certain characteristics are now emerging which indicate the predisposition of some
children to the risk of being bullied. This does not, however,
explain why any child at all should be at risk, nor why, throughout
history, vulnerable individuals, communities and nations have
been bullied by the more powerful. It is sometimes difficult for
adults to appreciate the distressing effect name-calling and

scapegoating can have on a young victim. We may be guilty of being dismissive for, as adults, we may fail to understand the terror of the unknown which may be confronting a child bullied in this way. We have the advantage of an understanding, a factual knowledge and accumulated experience; a child may be left confused and terrified by verbal threats and provocation.

Scapegoating and labelling

The historical perspective on the phenomenon of scapegoating suggests that in biblical Judea a goat would be invested with all the sins of the community and then driven out. This is probably the origin of the word 'scapegoat'. The Greeks in Asia Minor in the sixth century are thought to have practised choosing an ugly or deformed person to take on the evils afflicting the community. This unfortunate would be fed, beaten and then burnt to death (Frazer, 1923).

Name-calling also has roots in anthropology. The power of labelling may be seen in the historical and prehistorical tradition of word magic: 'The name of a thing or a group of things is its soul; to know their names is to have power over their souls' (Malinowski, 1923). Other writers have noted the intrinsic power of names. Frazer (1923) wrote: 'A name can only be given by one who has power invested in him, and that knowing the name gives one power over an object or person.' Later writers such as Goffman (1968) suggest that 'A man without a name has no existence.'

The power of name-calling was no doubt intensified by nicknames being associated with Old Nick, the devil. Name-calling in bullying often draws upon non-human names such as wimp, louse, pig, plus colourful local variations. This is an effective way of dehumanizing the victim, thus assuaging any guilt and giving permission for the process to continue once it is outside the human context. It may be a contributory factor in the escalation of some incidents of bullying to a dangerous level.

Names and labels are necessary. They are the most economical way of knowing and defining, naming being the demarcation process set down by society. Without labels we would be swamped by a myriad of anomalous characteristics to remember. We ourselves are named to define our inclusion in or exclusion from families, localities and nationalities, among other things. Maladaptive labelling, however, as in the name-calling in bullying, is used to exclude a child from the group. One sociological perspective would suggest that it is perhaps necessary for society to scapegoat some members in order to better define the boundaries of 'normality': the sane from the mentally ill, the criminal from the law abiding, the able from the handicapped. In his influential book *The Myth of Mental Illness*, Szasz (1961) proposes that we use labels in an insidious way to enable us to cope better with issues of great difficulty:

> Our adversaries are not demons, witches, fate or mental illness. We have no enemy whom we can fight, exorcise or dispel by 'cure'. What we do have are problems in living . . . mental illness is a myth whose function it is to disguise, thus render more palatable the bitter pill and moral conflicts in human relations.

A psychoanalytical explanation of scapegoating and labelling is that it is a projective process of transferring the unacceptable aspects of our own personality, which are normally repressed, on to another who is more vulnerable and who displays more overtly those very same characteristics (Klein, 1946). The word stigma originates from the tattoo worn by those Greeks who were either devoted followers of the gods or, conversely, by those who were slaves and known criminals. Once a child is stigmatized by the name-calling of others, the verbal label would appear to be no less durable. Children report that name-calling is one of the most distressing and aggravating attacks they can suffer and the case studies presented in Chapter 10 show how potent a form of abuse this can become.

Our suspicions, fears and prejudices are most strong when we encounter a stranger, someone different who we have not previously experienced:

> For the most part we do not first see and then define, we define and then see. In the great, blooming, buzzing confusion of the outer world, we pick out what our culture has already defined for us and we tend to perceive that which we have picked out in the form stereotyped for us by our culture. (Lippman, 1922)

The power of abusive name-calling is noted later in this chapter in the context of racial abuse among children.

Our library of stereotypes has been built up for us even before our birth from the heritage of opinions held by our parents and transmitted to us in the form of nursery rhymes, myths and legends as well as direct comment. We inherit our prejudices from our ancestors. We have ready-made templates in which to fit our new experiences and these determine our tolerance levels (Goffman, 1968). Goffman offers what he believes to be the template held of young American males: 'a young, married, white, urban, northern, heterosexual Protestant father of college education, fully employed, of good complexion, weight, height and a recent record in sports'. This, he claims, is the perspective all look out from. Many young men must harbour feelings of inadequacy and failure. There do seem to be indications that many of those who bully feel that they fit their own accepted social template – they are confident and powerful – whereas the victims do not. Goffman notes that once the victim to be stigmatized has been chosen, that person rapidly becomes isolated and, therefore, unprotected and even more vulnerable.

It is not yet clear whether bullying children seek out those who have a 'stigma' or mark, such as red hair, glasses, a stammer or other noticeable feature. The wider literature would suggest that possibly less venom is directed towards those who are unable to do anything about their so-called 'stigma' (e.g. those with an obvious physical disability) as opposed to those who, in the eyes of the attacker, can (e.g. obesity or poor coordination and clumsiness) (Goffman, 1968). I suspect that the victim is chosen for reasons other than obvious physical features but, once identified, the red hair or glasses become easy targets for provocation and harassment. The case study of John shows how a confident gregarious boy was able to overcome a deviant physical feature (see Chapter 10).

The process of labelling

Trends and changes in any one discipline often match a groundswell, a climate of opinion, in several other areas. The study of the phenomenon of labelling emerged from various sources simultaneously: anthropology, sociology, psychology and the law, among others. The catalyst group of labelling theorists, ironically given that label and so falling foul of their own hypothesis, put forward the view that allotting a label to a person or an event could have complicated and far-reaching repercussions. The reaction of the target person to the label in itself could have a more profound effect than the initial cause. It becomes a process of social reaction and interaction. Labelling, whatever form it takes, creates secondary problems (Becker, 1963): 'The critical variable is the social audience and not the individual actor' (Erikson, 1967).

In general terms, the process of labelling is considered by theorists such as Lemert (1967) to take the form of a downward spiral which takes place in stages:

1. Initially, the target child displays factors perceived subjectively by others as being removed from the norm.
2. Having been identified, the factors are commented on unfavourably.
3. The subject is now more aware of these characteristics causing the adverse comments and, subsequently, tension and anxiety result in them becoming emphasized.
4. The subject is punished by the labellers for the unacceptable characteristics or behaviours.
5. The behaviours intensify and the punishment increases.
6. The subject accepts and begins to believe in the label with a resulting lowering of self-confidence and -esteem.
7. The subject is isolated and vulnerable and unable to call on support from others and fully accepts the role which has been allocated to him/her.

The case study of Mark, who was given the name 'The Martian' because of his uncoordinated movements, shows how devastating the effect can be on an already vulnerable child.

Hargreaves (1967) suggests that there are four conditions which determine whether or not the child accepts the labelling: the frequency of the labelling, whether or not those doing the labelling are perceived as significant to the labelled, the support those allocating the label have in the group, class, school or street, and whether or not the labelling has been done publicly. If these conditions are present, the label is more likely to be accepted and, Hargreaves proposes, can come to engulf the person. The target child has only three options: to conform so the label cannot apply, to use a strategy to try to neutralize the situation, or to accept the label as part of their identity.

The theory of labelling does not go unchallenged (Ackers, 1968). Labels in themselves, it is argued, cannot create deviant behaviour. Attention must not be detracted from those features which caused the behaviour to emerge and which drew the unwanted attention in the first place. In removing the label we are only taking the first step in remedial action. As with Mark, removing the label 'Martian' was only the first step in the remedial programme. Other strategies were required to be implemented before he was able to integrate fully within the group.

The power of identification and labelling can begin in the very early years and have both long-term, perhaps permanent, and pervasive effects. In the early days of toddler rough-and-tumble play fights, children learn how to function in the group, who they can challenge and who can challenge them – those who cannot cope are quickly identified, pushed to the side lines, and if they are unable to change their low status, they run the risk of being allocated the role of victim and are thus isolated. Once self-confidence is lost it is difficult to regain.

The labelling of a vulnerable child may escalate the situation in another way. The first attack on the child may perhaps be over very quickly, the bully moving on and forgetting the incident. If others observed the attack, whether it be verbal or physical, they themselves are able to allocate the label and role to the victim so that a general and diffuse bullying situation arises which can last for several years without there being any leader. The victim, unfortunately, continues to be the butt of low-key punches, kicks and jokes.

It is critical that such patterns of escalation are observed and identified by staff so that the sequence may be broken in the initial stages. As with all aggressive and disruptive behaviour, the key skill lies in recognizing the critical moment to intervene (Pik, 1981).

Finally, it must be mentioned that the labelling of the power-less by the powerful occurs in a variety of contexts: world politics, the judicial system (Tutt, 1981) and the classroom, where the teacher labels a pupil disruptive or deviant. The greatest danger, perhaps, is that we need to be sure we know where our own social ideals, ambitions and values lie. We need to be able to recognize our own prejudices and biases and we need to be able to identify our own perspective because, once initiated, by accident or intent, there would appear to be an inevitable escalation of the situation.

Racial bullying

Those children who perhaps receive most labelling in society are those who are identified by their race as being different from the majority. Racism is too complex an issue to be subsumed under the heading of bullying, to be mentioned as a mere insertion, but it is pertinent because it most often takes the form of bullying – be it social, psychological or physical in nature. An example of play-ground bullying is given by a child in a middle school in Norwich:

> They are bullies and there are about five or six in my class only and at playtime there are many bullies from other classes. They kick me and call me 'black', 'chocolate', because of my colour and they don't like us because we are Indian. (Akhtar and Stronach, 1986)

This quiet erosion of identity and self-esteem by respectable whites, it is suggested, begins as early as 4 years of age. Kureishi (1986), who wrote the book which was made into the popular film of the same name, *My Beautiful Launderette*, writes: 'I reckoned that at least every day since I was five years old, I had been racially abused.'

One of the most hurtful and damaging, yet most used and pervasive forms of racism, is name-calling. A 17-year-old girl describes the pain: 'I think it's worse than being hurt physically, because physical hurt heals quicker than being called names' (Cohn, 1987). Name-calling is more difficult to spot and check than physical bullying. Perhaps we do not take it seriously enough? Children are told to ignore it and to shrug it off. Davey (1983) describes how children are attracted to name-calling as a provocative tool:

> the convenience of ethnic classification will prove irresistible tools for children in their attempts to order and simplify their social world, unless there is a considered and coordinated drive to introduce them to the potential fluidity and interdependence of human groups and to promote inter-group acceptance and friendship.

Allport (1954) wrote of 'labels of primary potency', which refer to physical features and, once adopted, tend to prevent any alternative or cross-classification. In one group of 13- to 17-year-olds, it was found that over half the name-calling that occurred referred to racist names and that over 60 different abusive racial terms were used – the under-13s used over 40. The next highest category for the older group was 11 names for sex- and gender-based name-calling. The danger has long been recognized (Cohn, 1987):

> Words which are highly charged with emotion, taboo or distaste, do not only reflect the culture which uses them. They teach and perpetuate the attitudes which created them. (Schultz, 1975)

A survey of the attitudes of children showed that black, Indian and white children all wished to be white, but that in play situations they chose playmates according to their gender and that this was the prime reference over colour. There was a strong bias towards own race group, which was higher in the home environment than in the school class or playground. The parents of all groups felt bewildered by the issue of discrimination and looked to the schools for advice, expertise and help (Davey, 1983). Perhaps schools can encourage multi-ethnic groupings by offering cooperative and problem-solving learning situations which demand mutual dependence.

It is of interest to note the responses of headteachers to requests from parents for help with this problem. They parallel exactly the common response for requests for help with other bullying situations:

There is no problem in the school.

There may be a problem but it is not a racial problem.

The parents and children are over-reacting (Akhtar and Stronach, 1986).

All children and parents in this study felt that there was a serious problem. It is possible that one of the key factors perpetuating the problem is the conflicting and vague expectations we hold of these children. On the one hand, they may be regarded as colourful and exotic, yet on the other, they may be expected to hold the same values and to behave as middle-class whites. The educational and influential political systems, at both the national and local levels, still rely heavily on the views of highly educated, successful middle-class whites. Black children and their parents are outside this framework, without any direct access to make their views known. Even where the black community has representation on committees, it is of interest to note how little shift in actual power has taken place and that consultation alone could lead to further frustration (Gibson, 1987). As with other disadvantaged groups, goals are offered but nobody is able to identify the path to take to achieve them (Tomlinson, 1987). Schools alone cannot combat racism. It must be seen in the full political context. Schools can, however, escalate or de-escalate the situation by the attitudes and practices at work within the school. One tutorial lesson a week will change little; it is the quality of all daily interactions throughout the school day which will be influential in bringing about a more positive situation. Social attitudes are man-made, they are the result of schooling in prejudice; therefore, if a positive attitude is presented throughout all aspects of the school day, then some inroads can be made to counteract the current situation which appears to be characterized by an uncomplaining acceptance that prejudice is a widespread and commonplace feature of contemporary life in Britain.

The crux of the matter is that there is an implicit consensus in our society as to where the various groups stand in the order of things. It is from within this consensual perspective children learn to notice group differences and how to evaluate. (Davey, 1983)

Clumsy children

One group of children identified by Olweus (1978) as being at high risk of becoming victims were found to be boys with coordination problems. Only in recent years have the emotional and social problems of these children been more widely identified and appreciated. The emphasis of the earlier work lay in the effect such difficulties had on academic progress.

This is not an uncommon problem: McKinley and Gordon (1980) estimate that approximately 1 in 25 boys experience these difficulties, although far fewer girls have been identified (see also Laszlo and Bairstow, 1985). Olweus (1978) noted that 75 per cent of the boys he identified as victims had coordination problems. The problem has been severely underestimated because these children often do not appear 'clumsy'; in fact, almost without exception, the coordination problems of those children I have worked with, were not considered to be of major concern by their teachers. Rather, it was the secondary social and emotional problems which were the cause of referral. Both Michael and Mark had such problems which did not figure prominently in their initial referral, although they were most pertinent to the bullying. There are frequently so many interrelated problems that it is far easier to spot a clumsy child once one is familiar with the syndrome than to describe one in print.

There are usually fine motor control problems in evidence when the child is writing, drawing, sewing or gripping a pencil. Gross motor skills such as running, throwing and catching are often impaired. The child will most probably have an unusual gait. There is usually a confusing and jagged profile of performance skills; the one child perhaps being able to throw but not catch. The one area in which these children often fail is when two or more movements need to be amalgamated and synchronized as in riding a bike or swimming. In such skills, the upper and lower parts of the body are involved in opposing movements.

The most subtle and possibly influential process which is frequently affected is that of perception, the process that links the eyes and the brain. Perception affects balance and it is common for these children to become fearful once their feet are off the ground. The clumsy child appears to have difficulty in building up a memory of tactile skills. The hands or feet need to be in sight all the time an action is being executed, e.g. buckling shoes, buttoning a coat, combing hair or climbing stairs. There is an over-reliance on vision, which in itself causes problems such as over-balancing and slow speed of performance; also, as mirror images in themselves cause problems, tasks such as cleaning teeth can seem quite complicated.

When we realize that other, seemingly unrelated, skills are often affected – such as sequencing and the organization of actions; that there may be enunciation difficulties, and intermittent hearing loss, perhaps resulting in specific learning difficulties – then it becomes abundantly clear that many of these children suffer numerous and pervasive hidden problems. If their difficulties remain unidentified they can be confusing and frustrating to teach. Most often they are urged by parents and teachers alike to try harder, yet their problems are such that without specific help, by trying harder they just make matters worse by exaggerating an incorrect action. The effort these children need to put into their school day may make them over-tired and irritable. The constant urging to work harder and faster can make them tense and anxious. They may, on the other hand, choose to withdraw.

Once the clumsy child enters his/her peer group as a toddler, social difficulties may arise when the other children rush round on their bikes or, in later years, go swimming and play team games. The slow, uncoordinated child may be pushed to one side, never chosen in a game, or left alone while the others play. If the child has confidence and determination the social repercussions will be minimal. If, for whatever reason, the child lacks confidence, he/she may become solitary, later perhaps preferring books, computers, videos or hobbies to attempting friendships. These interests frequently become an obsession, since being occupied with solitary pursuits, they avoid risking the rebuffs, taunting and bullying of their peers. Sadly, clumsy children do appear to have mannerisms which encourage bullying and the jibes and nicknames of the group, as was the case with Mark, who was called 'The Martian'. This is often due to the presence of attendant movements. For example, while writing with one hand the fingers of the other may move or there may be very slight but noticeable body movements when the child is excited. All these are due to the child being unable to make totally discrete movements with just one part of the body.

Once identified, there are programmes available to support these children, but the most crucial parameter is the confidence of the child. Compensatory success not only raises the self-esteem of these children but improves their status within their peer group. There may well be one area of sport in which they can succeed; with practice and confidence, swimming is often such a sport because the water supports the body. If a skill can be found and sensitive encouragement offered, the foundations can be laid for the development of friendships and group acceptance.

Victimology

One of the reasons why it has been difficult to help victims of bullying is that there is little information available to those who wish to help the victims. An immense volume of literature has accrued about crime and criminology but we still know relatively little about the criminal and far less about the victims of crime. The National Crime Commission Report (1967) stated 'One of the most neglected subjects in the study of crime is it's victims.' As long ago as 1948, von Hentig drew attention to this other side of the established school of criminology, but as recently as 1981, Haward noted that after half a century of concern shown exclusively for the criminal, at last some degree of interest is being directed towards the victims. There is a theory that the relationship between the perpetrator of the crime and the victim is more intricate than previously thought. This may be true in face-to-face crime. In a study of rape victims it was found that the discriminating factor between those attacked and those who were not was the submissive posture and deportment of the young women who were raped (Nelson and Menachem, 1973). It would seem that the attitude of the victim of a crime immediately prior to attack is of crucial importance. There are perhaps a few critical seconds when everything hangs in the balance, when the victims may ward off or precipitate the crime by their actions. Schafer (1977) writes:

> Crime is not only an individual act, but also a social phenomenon. It is far from true that all crimes 'happen' to be committed; often the victim's negligence, precipitative action, or provocation contributes to a genesis or performance of a crime.

This emphasis could be open to misinterpretation in the case of child victims. There are, without doubt, those who appear to provoke attack from others, and such children may be in greater need of our help than would perhaps first appear, but most victims of bullying are passive victims (Olweus, 1978). As adults we may perhaps need to be more responsible for taking the preventative actions advocated by the police to protect ourselves, but we cannot expect the most vulnerable of our children to be able to work out for themselves how to avoid attack if we have not first taught them exactly how this is done and ensured that they are able to cope. If there are a few critical seconds when the posture, verbal and non-verbal signals may initiate or deflect an attack, it must be our responsibility as adults, parents or teachers, to offer this information and training to those young people at risk.

Emotional effects

The victim of a bullying situation may have been subjected to a number of attacks of unknown intensity over a prolonged period. In consequence, they may be suffering from a sense of degradation, humiliation and shame, in addition to intense anger and fear. The victims rarely seek help from adults or their peers. Some of the reasons why this could be have already been mentioned. The cognitive changes which seem to take place in many victims of bullying perhaps need further emphasis – they begin to believe in the abusive name-calling, thinking perhaps that names such as 'baby', 'wimp' and 'idiot' must be true, for otherwise they would have been able to cope with the bullying. Their inability to cope proves that they are inferior. A gradual but pervasive erosion of self-esteem takes place. As they are ashamed of being so unpopular, in their own eyes, and of not being able to cope, they may well become more adept at hiding their suffering so that this too could be a reason why bullying appears to continue for a very long time unless checked. It is too painful to admit that one is bottom of the social heap and so very disliked. Many victims prefer to keep their distress to themselves. Although the confusion and complexity of the emotional turmoil of the victims of crime is becoming better understood, victims of bullying in school can still find themselves, with the best of intentions, subjected to intense interrogation by parent or teacher and cajoled, persuaded or demanded to disclose embarrassing or even dangerous information on the spot.

The emotional reaction to a crisis such as bullying has been described variously:

> Crisis reaction refers to the state of upset persons in crisis are undergoing; feelings of helplessness, inadequacy, confusion, anxiety and tiredness as well as disorganisation in work and interpersonal relationships. (Halpern, 1973)

> A lowered self esteem and depression and a resultant lowering of school learning. (Lewis *et al.*, 1979)

> A crisis is seen as a period of psychological disequilibrium in the face of a hazard event which can neither be escaped nor solved with the customary problem solving resources. (Caplan, 1964)

In recent years it has been recognized that mental cruelty can be as damaging as physical abuse; an example being the current recognition of both as legitimate grounds for divorce. It could be that we continue to underestimate the distress non-physical bullying can cause.

In studying the victims of crime, Haward (1981) found that there was no evidence to support the hypothesis, tacitly held by some, that those victims suffering from some degree of trauma after their experience must have been more vulnerable previous to the crime being perpetrated. This finding dispelled any suspicion that the severe reaction shown by victims after a crime was simply due to some already established inadequacy in their coping skills. It was found, however, that the adverse effects of crime were generally far more severe than had previously been supposed. In addition, the witnessing of a crime and the threat of a crime – recognizing one's own vulnerable position – also caused severe adverse effects. Parallels can clearly be found in bullying, in that fear of being bullied affects a considerable number of children, especially those who have witnessed an attack (Davies, 1986 and Elliott, 1986). The attack may seem minor to an adult, yet it may have produced severe psychological sequelae for both victims and observers, even those who are physically and psychologically robust.

Victims of bullying do appear to be trapped in the situation, frequently over a long period of time. If they can see no way of escape, depression can result. The repeated experience of a negative event can result in a depression similar to endogenous depression. The causes of adult depression were once sought in childhood, but it is now recognized that depression can begin in childhood (Trad, 1987). It is suggested that as we are becoming more skilled at asking more pertinent questions the reported incidence of childhood depression is rising. Quite young children are now known to make serious attempts to end their lives, some as young as 5 years old (Kosky, 1983). It may be that the true suicide figures of the very young have been masked in the past by medicinal overdoses, traffic accidents and other such events (Shaffer, 1974). As yet, the research in this area is sparse and some aspects, such as the interpretation of questionnaires with young children, are queried because of the limited conceptual development and language skills of some children (Firth and Chaplin, 1987). In general terms, however, there does appear to be enough work from various fields to alert those in close contact with children that there is cause for serious concern.

Children attempting suicide appear to share some common factors; more than half had witnessed violent episodes between their parents and more than half were the victims of parental violence (Kosky, 1983). Research on bullies shows that these types of violence are present in the majority of their homes (Olweus, 1980). There is a well-established link between physically abused children and self-injury (Green, 1978). It could perhaps be that the factor which decides whether the children from such traumatic backgrounds become aggressive bullies or turn to self-abuse or even attempt suicide, may be the degree of self-confidence and physical strength that they possess. In simple terms, some may have the personality and strength to hit others and may do so, others being less strong and confident may turn their anger upon themselves.

Interestingly, males from such backgrounds develop violent attitudes and behaviours more often than females with similar experiences, who tend to become depressed and even suicidal (Kosky, 1983; Abramson *et al.*, 1987). This may be because the boys model their violent fathers, or because they have the strength to hit out at others, whereas it is less likely that girls can do the same as easily.

It is understandable that a child who is being bullied can feel helpless and not able to control the situation, believing that there is nothing which can be done to alleviate the problem. A feeling of learned helplessness could develop where the child no longer takes responsibility for the situation (Seligman and Peterson, 1986). Learned helplessness is characterized by a lack of ability to reflect accurately on the impact of an action on the environment, an inability to appreciate the general concept of causality (Seligman and Peterson, 1986). There is a poor sense of being in control, not only over immediate events, but over one's destiny. If we believe we cannot effect change we do not act to overcome problems or master the environment. Such children are said to have an external locus of control. They perceive that the point of control, i.e. the locus, is situated outside of them in chance, luck or authority (Seligman and Peterson, 1986). Their lives are thought to run on without any contribution they may make having any effect. This negative, passive perception is thought to be a strong predictor of future depression. A correlation between low self-esteem and an external locus of control has been shown (Trad, 1987).

Children who feel that they are in control of their own behaviour are considered to have an internal locus of control and to be more effective in their actions and decisions. Children who have experienced favourable outcomes to their actions will be more willing to seek out cues, to analyse a situation and to attempt to bring about positive change.

A pupil attitude factor which appears to have a stronger relationship to achievement than do all the school factors together is the extent to which the individual feels that he has some control over his own destiny (The Coleman Report, 1966).

The situation

It may be that a child who is both happy at home and at school becomes a victim of bullying simply because he or she is caught in a specific situation from which there is no easy escape, e.g. meeting older children from another school on the way home, as in the case of Tony. The victim and the offender are now more frequently being understood not only in relation to each other but in the wider social context. Crime is now considered to be a function of a mesh of social circumstances and social phenomena (Clarke, 1985). Factors such as environmental and seasonal changes have been found to affect the occurrence of crime. This ecological approach applied to the problem of bullying takes into account such parameters as the design of buildings – narrow corridors encourage jostling and pushing, dark corners and distant changing rooms provide the ideal venue for an attack. Corridors in schools, unlike classrooms, are sometimes the responsibility of no one teacher and so remain unsupervised. Narrow alleyways and isolated paths in close proximity to the school can prove to be treacherous for the vulnerable. In considering crime in general, there is now far more emphasis on prevention than was previously the case, and parallels may be drawn when preventative work in schools is considered in the context of bullying. To remove opportunity is the keyword for the preventative action taken by the police in their bid to combat crime (Mayhew *et al.*, 1976). As more women now leave the home to work there are more homes empty during the day and more daytime thefts are committed. The increase in expensive, yet portable possessions such as videos and televisions, has intensified the rate of housebreaking. Crime appears to increase relative to opportunity. There is little empirical evidence to support a displacement theory in this context, i.e. if the changing rooms in schools were well-supervised, then children would deliberately look elsewhere to bully (Clarke, 1985). Rather, opportunity stimulates crime, so that sound supervision helps to prevent bullying because delinquent behaviour is not necessarily an innate characteristic of the individual, but occurs as a result of the interaction between the individual and the environment.

If there is this correlation between opportunity and crime, it behoves us to make extensive and exhaustive efforts to pinpoint the places and circumstances in our schools where bullying and other deviant behaviours occur, and to direct our financial and personnel resources to the planning and supervision of them for the safety of all.

Handling a crisis

As yet there appears to be no well-established taxonomy of behaviour for handling crisis situations, although it makes economic sense to prevent rather than repair. Little has been done in the past to prepare pupils for the interpersonal crises they may meet either at school or in later years. Perhaps the crisis situations encountered by most pupils may be grouped under the headings, developmental and situational.

Developmental crises

At certain stages of development, it is common for there to be vast differences between children of the same age, e.g. at puberty. Not only are there differences in physique which can cause obvious problems in bullying situations, but differences in emotional maturation can result in the vulnerable youngster being isolated and ridiculed. The difference in emotional age between pupils in the same class may easily be overlooked. Puberty itself is an example of a time when pupils are vulnerable; the age is characterized by mood swings, embarrassment, insecurity and low resilience. Boys and girls are often highly conscious of their appearance and any rude comment is taken to heart and brooded over. Girls may experience premenstrual depression of which we still know amazingly little. Few pupils face this time of emotional and physical change with equanimity.

Situational crises

It is now widely recognized that any transition, e.g. moving house or changing jobs, can be a stressful event. A study of 4-year-olds who were starting school found that those who were unable to cope with the adjustment, whose personalities did not immediately match the demands of the situation, soon developed psychosomatic illnesses (Faull and Nichol, 1986a, b). The stress was just too much for them to cope with. The stress of changing from a primary to a secondary school is now well-documented and many schools are working closely to provide good links (Youngman and Lunzer, 1977; Galton and Willcocks, 1983). Several studies have found that the fear of being bullied when entering secondary school worried children far more than anything else (Davies, 1986). This gives some indication of the effect merely witnessing bullying or hearing of it happening can have on many children.

In helping children cope with such crisis situations as bullying, it is necessary to have a prepared methodology, but there needs to be some recognition of the individual child. A blanket response for all will not meet the needs of each child. Immediacy and flexibility are both considered to be important to responding to crises, because intolerable stress can quickly turn into self-injury, temper outbursts or even the tragic suicides which have occurred.

It is perhaps advisable to build on the effective strategies used in the past, while also identifying and re-examining those that were ineffective, rather than becoming involved in time-consuming innovations. One strategy is to concentrate on the situation, for this, in the case of bullying, removes the emphasis from the personality of the victim, who may be feeling that it is due to his/her own failure as a person that the bullying has taken place. By keeping any intervention as far as is possible impersonal, the confidence of the victim can more easily be restored. It is important to stress the normalcy of the situation, that it happens to most people at some time or other – even adults – and that it is a difficult situation to resolve alone, because the child may feel inadequate at being unable to cope.

To restore the child's confidence in his or her own coping skills is perhaps the best prognosis for the future, whereas a poorly resolved crisis bodes ill. Recognition of the achievement of the child in resolving the problem, in overcoming the seemingly insurmountable hurdle, can go a long way in restoring a somewhat battered self-image.

4
Family factors

Research on bullying would seem to indicate that family factors are of considerable significance in the development of the personality of the child who bullies others and the child at risk of being bullied. Olweus (1978) considers these factors to be the most significant of all. Mitchel and O'Moore (1988) found that 70 per cent of the bullies they studied had a problematic family background and Stephenson and Smith (1988) found that one-third of those involved in bullying, both victims and bullies, had difficult family backgrounds. Other studies have found that these problems are common to both victims and bullies. Research from other areas, such as child abuse or delinquency, has emphasized the long-term impact family dynamics may have on the young child (West and Farrington, 1973; Pizzey, 1974).

Family members are interdependent, the interrelationships and internal dynamics meshing to form a family unit. At any one time an individual member may throw the whole unit into disarray, one person finding his/her own solution causing a problem for another. Behaviour within families is not always described best in terms of a simple linear model of cause and effect; sometimes a circuitous or reciprocal pattern is more apt. It need not be necessary for family members to live under the same roof for the reverberations of the actions and attitudes of one member to affect the others. A parent or sibling living away from the family home may, in fact, be the most significant person, for better or worse, in a child's life.

The constant adjustments and readjustments which need to be made daily by all family members in response to each other have been described by Cottle (1981) as 'living family data'. Hoffman (1981) compared them to 'the small movements of the balancing pole making an acrobat steady on the tightrope'.

Parental attitudes and behaviour

All parents are educators, whether good or bad, and the family has specific functions to perform in the process of making the child ready to meet the demands of the world. The family prepares the child for entry into his/her social group by offering appropriate social norms and by interpreting the child's tentative and crude actions. Parenting can be good or bad regardless of socioeconomic status, an obvious fact that is perhaps sometimes overlooked. Material trappings do not ensure security, emotional warmth and sensible disciplinary control. It is clear from a wide area of research that some children have a more positive attitude towards the use of aggression, in all forms, than the majority of their peers (Olweus, 1987). Extensive research has been undertaken from various disciplines and standpoints looking at child/parent interactions, parental relationships, discipline and management practices, and the effects these factors have on behaviour both in childhood and in adult life (Patterson, 1982, 1984; Patterson and Stouthamer-Loeber, 1984; Patterson et al., 1975).

As yet, however, it remains unclear how interdependent these factors are. Although it would appear that an antisocial pattern of behaviour is learned in the home, whether to a greater or lesser extent, it is not yet certain under exactly which conditions this takes place (Patterson, 1982, 1984; Patterson and Stouthamer-Loeber, 1984; Patterson et al., 1975). The research specific to bullying indicates that the following factors are of significance (Olweus, 1987; Roland, in prep.):

1. A negative attitude between parent and child, especially mother and son.

2. Over-punitive, physical discipline, or inconsistent and lax control.
3. The use of physical aggression which is seen as socially acceptable.
4. A negative relationship between the parents.
5. The temperament of the child.

Negative attitude between parent and child

As all children are weak and dependent at birth they strive to make their mark by trying out their abilities and by making challenges on those nearest to them, usually members of the family. If these attempts are met with understanding and tolerance they are able to generalize this to relationships with others (Pringle and Clifford, 1965). If they are shunned, criticized and repeatedly meet with a negative response, they quickly lose confidence in themselves and may become withdrawn and anxious (Pringle and Clifford, 1965). On the other hand, compensation may be sought by degrading others through physical or verbal attack. Children with low self-esteem may seek ways to prove that others are even worse than the perception they have of themselves (Adler, 1943). Similar familial experiences could result in one child becoming a bully, as the case of Tom shows, whereas another smaller and weaker child could become the victim, as was the case with Simon. The discriminating factor in the case of these two boys, both of whom were rejected by their fathers, was that Tom was strong and energetic, and Simon was the reverse.

An infant needs to feel safe enough to openly display the feelings of frustration and anger appropriate to all young children (Pringle and Clifford, 1965). If the home cannot offer an atmosphere of security and support, the young child may feel too insecure to allow any demonstration of anger. These negative emotions may then be turned inward, or unleashed upon others, in the form of aggressive behaviour and in situations where the child does feel confident. Early experience does appear to determine how normal aggression is handled in later life (Jamieson, 1984; Klein, 1960).

If the child has been brought up in an atmosphere of support and acceptance, by mid-childhood an emerging realization of their own strengths and weaknesses should be in evidence. This awareness is accompanied by an acceptance of themselves, with a parallel acceptance of others, and an associated assertiveness and confidence. The previous acceptance and support received from the primary caretakers, of all aspects of the emergent personality of the child, is the cornerstone of this development (Pringle, 1971).

The attitude of a mother to her son would appear to be of particular importance. A harsh, cold and rejecting attitude on the part of the mother, referred to by Olweus as 'silent violence', is considered by both Olweus (1980) and Roland (in prep.) to be correlated with the bullying behaviour of the son. Roland found that the more the mother rejected her son, the more the boy bullied others. The negative attitude of a mother to her daughter, or a father to his son or daughter, were all found to have an adverse effect, but it was the mother/son relationship which was found to be of greatest significance.

Discipline practices

An over-punitive, authoritarian, rather than authoritative, style of family discipline could result in the child becoming hostile and aggressive. Children growing up in a coercive environment commonly develop into coercive young people who, in turn, rear children likely to repeat the pattern (Pizzey, 1974 and Straus, 1980).

The reverse is also possible in that a hostile and punitive parent could sap the young child's confidence so that he/she becomes anxious and fearful. Such children sometimes develop nervous habits, self-punitive actions, or disturbed bodily functions such as bedwetting, all of which could result in them being unpopular and a target for the jibes and taunts of others. I would suggest that those from such a home background with a robust personality and physique could become attackers, whereas the small, frail and timid could become the attacked. The latter may, of course, bully in situations where they feel confident. Mark was a child who experienced a harsh and punitive relationship with his father, although no physical punishment ever occurred; however, the damage done was pervasive and long-lasting. Parents using harsh, physical discipline are using a modelling process by displaying to the child that this is an effective way of controlling others and getting one's own way (Bandura, 1969):

> The motivation to inflict pain is rooted in the child's exposure to behavioural and cultural norms which indicate that the infliction of pain on others is an appropriate response to be made to pain. (Feshbach, 1970)

This could be specific modelling, because the strong and powerful parent is, in fact, bullying the weaker, vulnerable child. By witnessing an aggressive parent, a boy could replicate this behaviour in the company of younger siblings or more vulnerable children. This could explain, in part, why more boys than girls bully others physically. It is fathers who are usually more violent in the home and who, to the watching child, appear more successful. Parents may give crossed messages to children, e.g. when they are told that they will be smacked if they hit other children. This indicates to children that a powerful adult can hit weaker children but they themselves must not hit others. The modelling process, therefore, may occur in a variety of ways.

Sadly, perhaps, families tend to be insular and children from very punitive homes may think that all families behave in this way. They themselves may grow up thinking that there is only one way to rear children, i.e. the way in which they were brought up themselves. Child care is not an innate skill, and it needs to be taught just as any other skill does, otherwise maladaptive methods can continue. There appears to be a need for training and tuition for both older pupils and young parents. There seems to be some sort of a cycle of abuse, e.g. women entering an Aid Centre, having been beaten by their husbands, were found to be more prone than others to beating their children. Pizzey (1974) describes it as husbands beating wives, who beat their children, who later assault their parents. Mothers who have witnessed violence in the home as children, are four times as likely as others to abuse their own children (Straus, 1980). It is not rare for the physical abuse of children to be carried over three generations (Straus, 1980).

Newson and Newson (1976) studied the normality of violence in homes and found that over 50 per cent of the parents interviewed smacked their children for disobedience, most once a week, 8 per cent daily, and that more boys than girls were punished in this way. Perhaps this too helps to explain why boys tend to use more physical violence in bullying than girls. In a different study, Pizzey (1974) found that boys who either witnessed or were the target of violence in the home became aggressive and destructive, whereas girls grew more passive and withdrawn. A study of abused toddlers found them to be twice as aggressive towards their peers as other children, and a similar result was found among adolescents (George and Main, 1979; Monane et al., 1984). The violence may, however, be turned inwards in the form of self-mutilation, depression or suicide, which may only develop in more obvious ways in the adult years. We need to remember that more people are maimed, beaten or killed at home than elsewhere, and that we are less safe with 'our loved ones' than on the inner-city streets (Jamieson, 1988).

The interactions between abusing mothers and their children have been studied closely. Normal mother–child contacts have been described as a kind of ping-pong game, where the move by one partner is a reaction to the other (Shaffer, 1974). The responses of the abusing mothers to their children's needs seem to be inconsistent, even haphazard. They appear unable to identify and respond appropriately to the young child's signalled needs. They over-estimate the baby's abilities and pitch their demands and expectations too high, misread the messages from the young child, and misunderstand the impact of their own actions on the frail and vulnerable child. Rather than there being a cruel and sadistic intent, there would seem to be a misunderstanding of the concept of an appropriate relationship between mother and child, perhaps because it was outside the mother's own childhood experience.

The parental style of discipline may be punitive and harsh, but it would seem that the factor which makes the relationship a damaging one is the lack of empathy and warmth (Olweus, 1987). The child's own perception of the situation is important, because if there is a feeling of care and concern, of interest and acceptance, then the child seems able to accept more easily the discipline of the parent. Not all parents who have experienced a difficult childhood fail to offer their children a satisfactory one. Gareth's mother was brought up in care, but he had the advantage of a warm and rewarding maternal involvement.

Physical aggression seen as socially acceptable

Within any given family there could be a situation where each member may be warm and supportive, and satisfying the physical and emotional needs of the child, yet the values, standards and goals of the family unit be so different from school and authority that the child has to cope with a dual standard of expectations and behavioural codes. There may be a cultural difference in training children to be, or not to be, aggressive. The home and neighbourhood may prize such skills – kudos may be earned by demonstrating a quick wit and a slick response when confronting authority figures (Hamblin, 1978a). The yardstick for success in the home and neighbourhood may be very different from that of academic and intellectual prowess perhaps held by the school. Achievement may, therefore, be measured on a value scale, with the school and society at large at the opposite ends of the spectrum:

The ability to perceive, learn, think, and reason in a culturally approved mature fashion cannot be effectively learned if he lives and functions in some isolated subculture in which one is not imbued with the values of the dominant culture and where its limitations on freedom of will cannot reach him. (Schafer, 1977)

There can be no doubt that some parents allow, even encourage, their children to use aggression in settling quarrels and achieving their goals. One theory proposes that there are two main groups of parents who condone the use of aggression by their children. One group is defined as 'diffusion parents' who are lax and permissive, nagging but not willing or able to carry out their threats. 'Selective diffusion parents' attempt to train their children in social behaviour but continue to allow aggressive behaviour (Patterson *et al.*, 1973). Such parents are genuinely bewildered by the complaints of fighting and scrapping in school that their children are involved in. They may overtly claim to discourage aggressive behaviour, but in confidence defend the aggression in a belief that all children fight and must learn to 'stick up for themselves'. In my own experience I have found that this attitude is often translated by the child into a belief that this is an acceptable way of controlling others. They develop a social image of masculinity which they equate with physical strength and the overt demonstration of this power.

An aggressive personality pattern is the result of the child with a strong need for self assertion and dominance being allowed to believe that a positive attitude to violence is acceptable. (Olweus, 1978)

There is a danger in stressing cultural and socioeconomic differences, because in my own experience I have found that there are almost as many differences, on all indices, within localities and socioeconomic groupings, as there are across boundaries. Parenting skills are not solely determined by economics or by any social class structure. Donnie was a child from what could be considered a privileged background who attended a private school. Regardless of family circumstances, it would seem that family attitudes to the use of aggression, in whatever form, influence the behaviour of the child.

Behaviours do not occur in a vacuum. Within the family, or any other situation, there is a nexus of rewards and punishments. Experiences which have been rewarding in the past are more likely to be repeated; unpleasant experiences lead to the behaviour being extinguished (the Premack Principle – see Wheldall *et al.*, 1983). The child's repertoire of behaviour is constantly regulated, reinforced and maintained by the feedback received. In this way, the child learns which behaviours are acceptable and when to use them appropriately. Even preschoolers (Patterson *et al.*, 1967) found that their aggressive behaviour was being rewarded: children under attack cried, yelled, withdrew or gave up the coveted toy, thereby leaving the aggressor rewarded in some way. Adults often have high expectations of children, but most only comment on failure and antagonistic and annoying behaviour (Wheldall *et al.*, 1983). What they should learn to do is praise routine achievement and sustained effort.

It may be noted here that teachers are in an extremely influential position in which to help children deal with aggression, whether as perpetrators or recipients. How they themselves exercise their own control over their pupils may have considerable bearing on how children handle aggression. Children may attempt to control others by coercion so that non-aggressive skills and socially acceptable behaviours need to be taught. The catharsis hypothesis, of letting aggressive children rid themselves of their negative emotions, is disputed by Bandura (1973a), who suggests that this only provides and allows a rehearsal of the aggressive behaviour. It would seem better to avoid conflict and confrontation if possible, as entering into a coercive cycle may only accentuate the aggressive temperament.

A negative relationship between the parents

There is a general consensus of opinion that a negative relationship between parents may have some adverse effect on the child. The research specific to bullying indicates that this is so (Olweus, 1987). A high proportion of both victims and bullies experienced a background of conflict. It would appear more important that the atmosphere in the home be secure and stable, rather than the parents remain together in a state of conflict (Rutter, 1971). The long-term effects of marital conflict are evident in the case of Mark. Rutter (1971) states that 'Hostile marital relationships seem to have more reliably negative effects on child development than does divorce and the absence of one parent.'

The quality of the relationship between parent and child, its context and interactions, are considered to be more important and to have greater predictive value of future attitudes and behaviours than mere contact hours. If the conflict is violent the repercussions may be quite far-reaching. One of the key discriminating factors between violent and non-violent delinquents was found to be whether or not they had witnessed conflict in the home (Millham *et al.*, 1978). All members of the family may become enmeshed in the marital conflict and be fighting for survival, but children are often the weakest unit, the least physically strong, least articulate and most dependent and vulnerable.

In studying bullying, Roland (in prep.) found marital hostility to have both a direct and indirect influence on the child. A hostile marital relationship reflected on the child by weakening the relationship between the mother and child, resulting in a lack of empathy and warmth. In this way the child suffers two-fold: directly from the effects of witnessing the marital conflict, and indirectly from the associated lack of maternal warmth. This in turn is strongly correlated with the bullying behaviour of boys, i.e. the more a mother rejects her son, the more severe his bullying behaviour is likely to be.

The temperament of the child

Mention has already been made to the temperament of the child in Chapter 2 and details of the temperament of both bullies and victims are given in Tables 1–5. It must be stressed that family factors, although considered to be highly influential, cannot account for everything. There does appear to be more recognition in recent years of the differences in temperament of individual children, whether due to environmental or inherited influences, and the emergence of a more sympathetic climate towards those parents of children with a more demanding temperament. An example of such a child can be found in the study of George who found it difficult to control his volatile responses. Peter Ustinov described parents as being 'the bones on which children sharpen their teeth'. Historically, the emphasis has been on the influence of the behaviour of the mother on the child. More recently, the mutuality of the situation is beginning to be examined. An irritable child may influence the mother's behaviour adversely, and even siblings may be caught up in a coercive situation (Bell and Harper, 1977).

Family dynamics

It has been noted already that a high proportion of both bullies and victims have been found to have problematic family backgrounds (P. Stephenson and D. Smith, 1988). Factors such as divorce, alcoholism, poverty, lack of maternal affection and inconsistent discipline have been cited in relation to the bullies by Mitchel and O'Moore (1988). Many of these factors are associated with adult depression in one way or another. As yet no research has considered family factors in relationship to depression, but I consider that it could be a contributory factor in the interaction between parents and their children which could result in the latter becoming bullies or victims. The labile personality of the depressed adult could result in inconsistent discipline and management practices. This in turn may result in the child developing a state of learned helplessness as a result of being unable to build up a repertoire of appropriate behaviours. Michael's mother was depressed and unable to offer him the support he required to counter the difficulties he met in school. A child in this situation will not have had the experience of matching behaviour to consequences and so will be unable to build up a pattern of predictability. Without the ability to predict the consequences of their actions, a state of bewilderment may ensue. In this confused state the child could believe that he or she has been responsible for the violent, or other less drastic punishment, or that these things happen regardless of one's own behaviour (Seligman and Peterson, 1986). It is easy to see how difficult it could be in such circumstances to develop any sense of responsibility for one's own actions. Stephen believed that his poor behaviour had been a contribution to the break-up of his family. This was untrue, but his mother had often used the threat of leaving home when he misbehaved. It was his father who left the family, but Stephen still felt guilty and blamed himself.

Family scapegoating

Perhaps the saddest case of bullying is that of the family scapegoat, because, until the child is old enough to live independently, there is little chance of escape. In my own contacts with parent groups I have found a considerable number of adults who, in retrospect, feel that they were systematically bullied by siblings throughout their childhood years. At the time they did not really see it as bullying – rather more like being bossed around – but the intensity of the memories, and the resultant damaged relationships with those siblings in later years, have brought them to realize that it was bullying.

Research has shown that a surprising amount of bullying takes place between siblings (Elliott, 1986). The bully may perhaps be a younger sibling. Toddlers are able to knowingly use teasing or conciliatory behaviours; they are able to appreciate the feelings of others and so understand the annoyance they can cause with their taunts. It has been shown that younger children are twice as likely to provoke quarrels as older siblings, but that the latter are twice as likely to be blamed if they retaliate (Koch, 1960). Boys, it would seem, are twice as likely to fight outside the home as girls, but girls fight equally as much with siblings at home (Newson and Newson, 1976).

Sibling rivalry encompasses anything from 'mild bickering to a shattering intensity' (Jersild, 1966). Poor sibling relationships between 3- to 4-year-olds was found to be a sound predictor of disturbed behaviour 4 years later (Richman *et al.*, 1982). As 80 per cent of children grow up with siblings it is perhaps of importance to consider carefully how influential siblings can be in shaping each other's behaviour (Dunn, 1983). It has been suggested that the effect of sibling behaviour contributes to the individual differences in personality within a family of children (Rowe and Plomin, 1981). There are strong indications that there is a considerable stability within the relationships of young children over a period of years (Stilwell and Dunn, 1985).

There are, undoubtedly, cases of particular children being scapegoated by their parents. These children are the recipients of a severely negative attitude and become 'blame-oriented', as the families are unable to view the child's behaviour objectively (Wahler *et al.*, 1986). In some families displaying a high incidence of aggressive behaviour, it is only this child who is labelled as aggressive, and he/she will receive up to three times as much punishment as his/her siblings (Patterson *et al.*, 1975). The interactions between family members are both complex and pervasive and require detailed analysis before any rash judgement can be made about any one individual.

Child abuse can be seen in this context, because the victim is undoubtedly being subjected to one form of bullying behaviour. A further example of distressing family relationships, but one which is not discussed openly yet, is that of teenage violence in the home, where adolescent or even younger children bully their parents to get their own way. There are parents from all cultural and economic groups under severe pressure due to being physically bullied by their adolescent children. There are support services available but, as in most bullying, until the problem is brought out into the open, these parents may not receive the help they need.

The catalyst

The child may have an active role in maintaining a status quo in the family dynamics. Children are not necessarily passive pawns in the complex manoeuvres of the total unit, but may have a critical part to play. The symptoms of the child – aggression, deviance or phobias – could be the catalyst holding the family together. The child and the other family members may be unaware of this function but there could be one key person who is actively supporting the situation. An example of this is the child who refuses to go to school claiming to have been bullied. On investigation it might be discovered that the mother is depressed, and has let the child become aware of this, to the extent that the child feels a need to stay at home to protect the parent. Wendy was a child caught in this situation. Children frequently find it difficult to cope in school after a prolonged absence, so in such cases claims of bullying attacks, real or imagined, on their intermittent return visits to school are common.

Events external to the family may have a traumatic and resonant effect on individual members. Life events encompassing dramatic change, such as sudden death, divorce or unemployment, can have an overwhelming effect on a child even in a caring and supportive family (Hamblin, 1978a). In the case of sudden unemployment, the material change may be obvious, but the need of the child to accommodate a distressing and disturbing change in the personality of one or both parents may be overlooked. Children from more materially comfortable homes may find the experience of failure extremely difficult to cope with as there may be a considerable discrepancy between their academic achievement, for example, and parental expectations. Families who experience such difficulties are often more reluctant to seek help from outside agencies (e.g. teaching staff) because they feel this labels them as 'problem families'. This might put even more pressure on the child to cope alone.

Bringing about change

Families do change; family dynamics alter. Even in the most disadvantaged circumstances individuals do manage, not only to cope, but to improve their situation and make a better life for themselves and their families. The picture is not necessarily pessimistic. It is possible to increase a child's resilience or to change his/her behaviour to a slightly more acceptable level, both for their own comfort and those around them.

> Pupils are not determined by their past . . . They are not victims of an earlier childhood. Pupils are more than their backgrounds. (Schools Council, 1968)

In another form, 'experience is what you do with what happens to you' (A. Huxley quoted in Jamieson, 1984).

The prime criterion to consider, often overlooked in our haste to help, is whether or not there is a genuine wish and commitment to change among all the family members. Families with a multiplicity of problems were found by McAuley (1982) to be less motivated to change. The main aims are two-fold: to change parental behaviour and to bring about a concomitant change in behaviour and adjustment in the child. The three main areas into which parental programmes fall are parental education, therapy and training. A high percentage of families of delinquent children fail to engage in any intervention.

Wahler (quoted in McAuley, 1982) suggests that the following were factors common to families resistant to change:

- low socioeconomic status;
- low educational attainments;
- single parent;
- frequent contact with police and courts;
- frequent contact with helping agencies;
- isolation in the community;
- frequently in the company of kinsfolk and professionals;
- high percentage of past interactions reported to have been aversive or unpleasant.

Topping (1983) showed parent training to be one of the most economical and effective ways of bringing about change in the behaviour of difficult children. There still remains, however, a confusion as to which factors are most important in working with families, i.e. exactly which offer the best outcome for change. Within the specific area of discipline and management procedures, the following have been found to be influential in bringing about positive change (Patterson and Stouthamer-Loeber, 1984):

- parental use of appropriate controls and firm but fair discipline;
- close parental monitoring of the whereabouts of the child;
- encouragement of positive social behaviour in the child;
- the training of the child in problem-solving techniques.

All of the above were found to be important and parents encouraged to use the techniques were able to bring about a reduction in the antisocial behaviour of the young people in the study. Of the four factors the most influential were found to be:

- firm, consistent discipline given in an atmosphere of warmth and positive involvement; and
- close monitoring of the whereabouts of the young child.

In a study of football hooligans, Dunning *et al.* (1988) note that many, having been socialized on the streets from an early age, with minimum parental oversight, will have had little opportunity to model appropriate social behaviour.

In summary, the family unit is made up of a mesh of

interacting factors. No member exists in a vacuum. It is, therefore, nearly always necessary to look for change in both the family
and child simultaneously. As studies such as the extensive work of
Patterson have shown, once the child's behaviour is appropriately
managed, and in consequence the child is able to manage a
repertoire of behaviour for his/her self, then the family can have
fun together which is, perhaps, an underestimated but worthwhile aim.

5
Social behaviour

Lonely

Being lonely all the time
Just sitting in the old, cold house,
Nothing but the telly talks
The News, pictures,
But I just sit in my chair
No one to speak to, no one to hear.

I see my friends come to my house
But they are far away now,
My old friends at my old school.

Who were my friends?
Brian, Paul, Simon, Tony, David
My friends seem to come but fade away,
I look down along the motorway
Waiting for them to come.

One day I must return to see my friends
I have other friends now but I don't know their names.
I just wait in the chair
All alone by the fireside, waiting.

(Terence Ryan, aged 10 years)

In my own work in schools I stress that, in my opinion, bullying is not a discrete phenomenon which needs to be, or even can be, considered out of the context of normal social behaviour. It is a social interaction whether between groups or individuals, which has gone badly wrong because appropriate social behaviour has never been established or has broken down. I propose that it is only by looking at the problem in the context of the daily social interactions in the group and in the school that any understanding of the problem can emerge and remedial action be taken.

Popular children

We can learn just as much about the complexities and interactions involved in a negative behaviour such as bullying by taking an obtuse approach, by studying which factors contribute to some children being robust and successful and well supported by their peers. This may be especially so in the case of bullying as the problem is usually covert, well hidden from adult scrutiny and analysis. We need to understand the attitudes of the 'silent majority' who witness the attacks and why they are seemingly unwilling or unable to help.

Those who are popular remain so despite any change in the situation and, unfortunately, those who are unpopular retain their sad position. Rarely do the social stars, isolates or neglectees change position in the popularity stakes (Moreno, 1953). Friendships do change over time as new interests emerge. Dramatic changes are sometimes seen, e.g. a gregarious, sociable child may become withdrawn and shy in adolescence. Altered circumstances, such as a change of school, can also bring about marked differences but, overall, various research suggests that those who are rejected and ignored may remain so for a number of years if they do not get support.

The following factors contribute to some children being more popular than others (Jersild, 1966; Ginsberg *et al.*, 1986):

1. Children, like adults, choose those who have a similar background, social values and interests as themselves.
2. A general air of attractiveness appears to influence both boys and girls.
3. A good physical appearance, athletic competence and energetic temperament, plus an ability to organize and participate fully in a range of games and activities.
4. Names seem to have a bearing on selection.
5. A confident, independent presence, the ability to win the trust of others, an ability to take responsibility for self and others.
6. A cheerful, sensitive and flexible disposition, the self-control to be able to handle their own negative moods and those of their peers.
7. A gregarious personality showing rapport with others, the wish to seek out, establish and enjoy friendships.
8. The ability to de-escalate conflict situations, to offer alternative strategies and to resolve disputes, to ward off trouble and ignore provocation, to cope without blaming others.
9. An ability to manage and control peers without aggression, to

resolve conflicts verbally and rationally, providing acceptable alternative solutions for a better outcome.
10. An understanding and appreciation of friendship skills.

It would indeed be an extraordinary person who possessed all the above – child or adult – but children who are popular do possess a reasonable balance of a variety of these characteristics, no one to excess. In summary, not only do social skills come into play, but a wide range of cognitive and linguistic abilities.

Popular children are unlikely to involve themselves in bullying others because they are confident and secure in their interactions, therefore having no need to resort to coercion to impress or dominate their peers (Duck *et al.*, 1980; Duck, 1984). Whether by inclination, or as a result of training or self-control, they are unlikely to use aggression to settle differences because they are able to assert themselves in an age-appropriate manner.

In contrast, unpopular children were found to be more restless, talkative, boastful, volatile, lethargic, unkempt, unimaginative, shy and attention seeking than their classmates. In their relationships the confident were found to blame, ridicule and threaten their peers, so that even if they joined in a group they were unable to sustain the relationship.

Children with low social status were found to have probably witnessed parent conflict and to have a stressful relationship with their parents (Allen, 1975). In one study, the parents of unpopular children expressed more dissatisfaction with their own lives and their parenting skills than other parents. It may be that in some cases these children are unpopular even with their parents and so are not receiving the family support they need (Allen, 1975).

Lonely and unassertive children often allow others to dominate their actions and attitudes, becoming even more submissive and apologetic. This timid presentation encourages the more thrustful and powerful to dominate them more vigorously. The socially unskilled rate themselves as having low self-esteem, considering themselves failures and unwanted, yet unable to do anything to resolve the situation (Michelson and Mannarino, 1986). There is a risk that such children begin a downward spiral, which only compounds their problems. However, not all children with a low rate of social interaction have severe social problems: solitary play may be by choice and mature in character. A superficial observation could lead to an erroneous judgement.

One study considered those factors which led children to decide whether or not to go to the assistance of another in trouble. In general, children tended to choose those they thought would help them if they themselves were in trouble. Younger children chose those most like themselves and those they liked the best, whereas the choice of older children seemed to be determined more by need and circumstance, with both moral and intellectual factors coming into play (Eisenberg and Pasternack, 1983). Such research is of inestimable value in helping those who are vulnerable. The peer group is able to learn how to identify those children who are in need of support and how this may be offered. In addition, children without friends can be helped to see ways in which they are able to amend and adjust their behaviour so that they are in a position to elicit group support if necessary. There is still perhaps an expectation among adults that any child will learn to make friends given the opportunity. Many children do appear to learn appropriate sub-skills by a process of imitation and observation, but there are those who, because of an innate disadvantage, unfortunate past experience or environmental frustrations, require direct instruction and practice. Several studies clearly show that the neglected and rejected child remains so regardless of a change of class or geographical location (Moreno, 1953).

Friendships

Making friends is a demanding and highly complex skill. Children, when beginning to make a new friend, must 'coordinate their efforts with all the virtuosity of an accomplished jazz quartet' (Gottman, 1986). A high degree of sensitivity is required, and subtle techniques and strategies come into play with even very young children. There are specific rules pertaining to friendships and children work hard to start a new friendship and then sustain it (Gottman and Parker, 1986) unaware of the skill they are using. The informative and entertaining work of Erving Goffman (1974) shows how adults engage unwittingly in a complex network of norms, rules and expectations in daily social interaction. We only become aware of these parameters when we have broken through them, often with painful or embarrassing results.

Friendships differ from more ordinary interactions between acquaintances in the degree of time, effort, resources and concern invested by all parties. Sullivan (1953) separated friendships from relationships by suggesting the former required some element of cooperation and reciprocity.

When studying friendships it is necessary not only to look at social behaviour but also to explore sociolinguistics and cognitive skills, because these play a major role in the ability of a child to form and sustain friendships (Garvey, 1984). The most effective and enjoyable way to develop these wide-ranging and complex skills is to be in the company of other children. It may be that children learn best from their peer group – those equally as inexperienced as themselves, those having a similar lack of social skills – rather than older children or siblings (Lewis *et al.*, 1975). However, a child with a severe problem is often able to benefit from the companionship of older pupils who are more tolerant and astute in discerning his or her needs. Such a strategy is only used until the child in question is able to enter into rewarding social interactions within the peer group. Only in recent years have friends been chosen predominantly from the peer group; historically – and still in some cultures – this was not deemed important. It may be that only with someone the same age and at the same stage of development is it possible to sort out individual similarities and differences, the very foundations of a friendship.

Friendships are a two-way process – not only do they require a myriad of skills, but they are also essential for all-round cognitive, social and emotional development (Janes *et al.*, 1979). Gottman and Parker (1986) refer in detail to research findings which indicate that friendships are important to the development of academic and cognitive ability, adjustment and maturity, self-perception and the comparison of self to peers, linguistic skills, moral development, mastering aggressive impulses, appropriate sex-role behaviour, and school attendance.

The isolated and friendless child is at a severe disadvantage: not only is he/she at risk in the current situation but also in later life. It was found that children experiencing difficulties with peers (e.g. the bullies and the bullied) were more likely to develop psychiatric problems in adult life:

> Childhood peer adjustment variables under some circumstances may even distinguish disordered from nondisordered adults when many other intellectual, behavioural and demographic variables do not. (Cowen *et al.*, 1973)

Janes *et al.* (1979) also found that 'failing to get along with other children' was frequently related to negative adult adjustment:

> poor peer relations serves as an ominous sign for future adjustment . . . a teacher's perception that a child was not getting along with other children could have served as a warning light for diverse adulthood problems.

No other teacher-rated behaviour was as robust a predictor of future trouble or distress.

One point which I consider is sometimes missed is that it is difficult to overestimate parental concerns about childhood friendships. Parents interpret their children's friendships as giving signs of social achievement, social competence and robust mental health (Cowen *et al.*, 1973). If their own child is isolated, bullied or aggressive to others, the feelings of failure and shame experienced by parents, i.e. that their child is so unpopular with others, may make them hesitate to seek help from either the school or other parents. After the toddler years, we do not perhaps as parents seek out frequently enough the unpopular and lonely child, assuming that once in school a child will meet other children and therefore make friends. The more research we gather the more we realize that not only is this not so, but that to leave these children on the sidelines as passive observers of life, is to put them at risk in the future.

In considering intervention it is important to remember that knowing how to act in a situation is no guarantee that the appropriate behaviour will be executed in the crisis situation: knowing we should take faulty goods back to a shop does not give us the courage to do so! Not only do we need to teach social skills and to rehearse them, *in situ* if possible, but the parallel techniques, e.g. resilience to provocation, need to be taught in as practical a fashion as possible.

The skill of choosing friends is perhaps an area in which some children require support. It may be that only towards the end of the primary school years are children able to cope with the concept of all the individual personalities of the children in a large class (Jersild, 1966). To choose and select friends appropriately may be a more subtle and complex process than some children realize; they could perhaps benefit from low-key support. Many simply opt for those from their own neighbourhood. In a large secondary school, it can be very much a hit-and-miss affair, with the non-gregarious and timid – those with fewer of the characteristics of popular children (i.e. the very children who would benefit most from peer support and friendship) – remaining on the sidelines or being actively rejected. The case of Simon illustrates this point well (see Chapter 10). He was trying to break into a group and was being rejected. As adults we are able to use subtle signs and cues to discern whether or not our approach is welcomed or rejected, and we learn that we can only make friends with willing parties. Children sometimes need help to understand this rather complex process of trial and error, advance and retreat.

Proximity and opportunity play a part in the selection of friends at any age. Not only does experience help in making friends but it also improves the quality of the relationships children can offer each other (Rubin, 1980, ch. 2). Translated to the classroom it has been noted that when pupils are given the opportunity to discuss and work together on a task there is a better understanding of each other's point of view, of consolidating the relationship and of generalizing the contact to a friendship off the task. When pupils work together in couples or small groups a more even distribution of popularity across the class has been found to emerge (Schmuck and Schmuck, 1971). If this social mix is the prime aim, the goal needs to be planned and progress evaluated, because generalization from work relationships to social friendships may not always happen as a matter of course. The school can, it would seem, play a valuable role in facilitating friendships for the lonely, isolated and vulnerable child. In an even more direct manner, it has been found that pairing a victim of bullying attacks with a more robust or older child has not only helped shield the isolated child from attack but also helped the target child to learn how to win approval and acceptance from others. Being seen in the company of more influential or older pupils also has very positive effects. The bullying child can also learn how to interact with others more appropriately and successfully from such informal contact (Furman et al., 1979).

An arrangement such as this requires diplomatic oversight – the target child, whether bully or victim, perhaps being unaware of the match. Where pupils at risk are learning and assimilating skills by direct or indirect contact with more successful pupils, they are in a more normal learning environment than when being directly instructed on any social skills programme offered by adults.

The developmental stages of friendship

There are broadly based developmental stages of friendship which are bound up with developing cognitive, emotional, moral and linguistic abilities. The process of friendship may perhaps be more cumulative than discrete, with behaviour at one stage being called upon later. Friendships may wax and wane as more specific needs and preferences emerge but, throughout all stages of development, there is a strong and pervasive bias to form social relationships (Rubin, 1980, ch. 1).

Toddlers

Children as young as 14 months show a preference for particular friends (Rubin, 1980, ch. 2). Throughout these years there emerges a growing preference for friends of the same sex, with the choice usually biased, perhaps by necessity, to those in their own neighbourhood. It is based more on opportunism than selection. If taken to other situations they are able to widen their circle of playmates.

At this age children play in parallel, alongside another child, rather than fully interacting, and an increasing use is made of verbal play. There is a dependence on the adult caregiver and, the more secure that relationship is, the more competent the young child will be in moving towards interacting with peers. The play activities are a series of single episodes, so adult support is needed for any prolonged interaction.

The onset of self-knowledge and classification begins – name, age and sex are used to identify self from others (Rubin, 1980). As children move from parallel to cooperative play, more opportunities arise for squabbling and bickering. Conflicts are brief, lasting only a minute or so, and the encounters are quickly forgotten (Jersild, 1966). Healthy preschoolers need to be able to defend themselves and what is important to them. It is possible at this early age to spot those who need to assert themselves over others.

The infant years – ages 5–7

At this age children tend to define friends as those they play with rather than by individual characteristics, although stronger relationships are developing with increasing maturity as a clear preference can now be expresssed (Rubin, 1980). With emerging cognitive and emotional powers, games can be remembered and sustained for longer periods. Advanced language skills allow imaginative and fantasy themes, a skill which is highly prized by others and is influential in the selection of friends, so there is less need to rely on purely physical pursuits.

Cooperative play is enjoyed and the skills of recruiting and enticing others to join in are displayed. Competitive games are popular, but judgements are black and white and rules need to be explicit and adhered to (by everyone else!). Children of this age are more independent and wander further afield. They are more self-assured and boastful. The skills of taking turns, sharing and waiting are present at this cognitive stage. Conflicts can now be settled with language; previously, only physical methods were available, e.g. shouting, hitting, avoiding and ignoring. Now they can compromise and seek arbitration. Popular children, even at this age, have access to a wide variety of ploys, so requring them to rely less on aggression to settle differences (Hartup et al., 1967).

Patterson et al. (1967) found that aggressive behaviour was

rewarded at this age; the dominant child kept the snatched toy, got the attention, or made the attacked child cry. A total of 85 per cent of these outcomes were rewarding. Aggression at this stage can be symbolic, e.g. when the youngster snatches the toy to demonstrate power and dominance over those weaker but, once attained, the toy is immediately dropped by the aggressor and all interest lost. The other category of aggression is goal-oriented, where the toy is snatched for use by the aggressor.

The bullying child can be identified at this stage by a power-assertive, dominant, impulsive, and energetic style of play. It may be that such children have a higher pain threshold than their peers or, perhaps, for cognitive reasons, they are unable to distinguish between real and play fights. They do appear to possess fewer strategies to diffuse conflict, perhaps because of lack of training, impulsivity or cognitive factors. For whatever reason, they have access to a limited repertoire of appropriate skills (Olweus, 1978).

The older primary years – ages 7–11

By this age most children have enjoyed several years of friendships. There is, by now, a firm preference for friends of the same sex and age. Children of this age are able to work in, and enjoy, group activities for prolonged periods (Gottman and Parker, 1986). They have mastered the procedures for requesting and negotiating entry into groups. They are able to recognize the subtle differences of approach required, depending on whether they are already accepted or on the fringe. A wider variety of language is available to them and they are able to make adjustments, for example, in the less formal language used among close friends and in the home and the more formal language used for situations such as school. Team effort is enjoyed and it is important to be accepted in the group. There is a desire to conform to the group norms. Being conspicuous is embarrassing. Often superiority and ranking seem important and much time is spent in claiming one's family car the largest, or one's model the best.

Efforts to control others take the form of 'I'll be your friend if . . .' Rituals, rules and logic are enjoyed and become an integral part of imaginative games. Humour is greatly appreciated, especially the incongruous, unpredictable and illogical, as in, for example, jokes about elephants on buses. Along with an appreciation of the silly there is a growing awareness of technology and a developing ability to organize oneself, one's work and other people. Play can reflect anxieties and worries. There is the beginning of a self-awareness; what is good and bad about oneself and others (Gottman and Parker, 1986).

Aggressive children at this age try to show power over others. They may try to take the lead in a game, not for any organizational reason, but to dominate. Similarly, they may initiate power-associated games such as cops and robbers, war games and other media-stimulated themes. These are chosen as a vehicle for the demonstration of their power and strength over the group rather than for any intrinsic qualities (Manning and Sluckin, 1984). The case study of Donnie illustrates how, although he did not overtly bully his peers, they were too afraid to challenge him and remained submissive to his dominant personality at the expense of their own needs. Aggressive acts at this stage can be premeditated and ill feeling sustained (Manning and Sluckin, 1984). Frustration can be withheld from an original source so that the anger can be taken out on a more vulnerable target. There is a clear understanding of how to taunt and tease others, the jibes and provocation being remorseless. When criticized or opposed aggressive children can become unduly angry and resentful.

Adolescence

The physiological developments of puberty bring about associated emotional states which are often bewildering. There will, no doubt, be evidence of the remnants of childish emotions (e.g. egocentricity) which are hard to relinquish (Shaffer, 1985). These regressive periods may contribute to the self-doubts and confusions experienced by many young people.

The increasing independence from home results in a wider backcloth and a new variety of extrafamilial settings. Conflicting standards and degrees of freedom are encountered and challenging behaviour emerges in an effort to come to terms with the many conflicting demands. Dual standards are presented to our young people – they are too young to drink and drive yet old enough to earn a living and take on other challenging responsibilities. It must seem that adults throw them out of the nest, but with a piece of string still tied around the leg. Often the responsibilities we ask of young people are vague and nebulous and this lack of direction can compound their confusion.

Increasingly at this time the peer group is used as a sounding board and their values adopted. It is a time of strong views and vehement emotions, political and world affairs become issues of importance and a sense of fair play is appreciated (Gottman and Mettetal, 1986). There is a clear understanding of the concepts of loyalty, trust and betrayal. At this age girls in particular use good and bad gossip to find out where they stand in comparison to others (Gottman and Parker, 1986).

Group behaviour

Children in school are necessarily members of groups and sub-groups, whether in an active or passive role, and in so being encounter both positive and negative experiences. The importance of this type of experience has been noted many times: 'Socialization is a process by which an individual acquires the standards, values and behaviour which mark him out as belonging to a particular group' (Hamblin, 1974). The functioning and malfunctioning of groups is perhaps one of the most pressing sociological problems today: 'When a hundred clever heads join in a group one big nincompoop is the result because every individual is trammelled by the otherness of the others' (C. J. Jung quoted in Simmel, 1964). A group is not just a collection of individuals but a collective organization united by common interests and goals. Even very young children enjoy group experiences and in the middle childhood years boys in particular veer towards same-sex gangs. During the adolescent years the group becomes increasingly stable, exclusive and important, taking over some of the roles the family fulfilled in earlier years (Dunning *et al.*, 1988).

The functional role of the group changes over time depending on the needs of its members. There is always a reciprocal function between the group and individual members, so it may be important to analyse the dynamics of the group and tease out the interplay between the individuals. What is each member getting from the group? What is the group getting from each member? Needs and expectations must match and the equilibrium of the group be preserved.

What is the group offering its members?

It is important to consider what the bullying group is offering its members. It would often appear that children enmeshed in a group bullying situation, or other malfunctioning group situation, would not be behaving in this way if they were not part of a group.

1. A surrogate family

As family structures are becoming increasingly disorganized, many positive attributes – loyalty, continuity, acceptance and support – might, primarily, be supplied by the group. Some group members may have been associates since they were toddlers, and these friendships are often the most stable relationships they have, especially where parents are divorced or separated. Several studies suggest that even if this is not the case, many young people on the fringes of antisocial behaviour spend very little time at home. The bullies identified by Lagerspetz *et al.* (1982) had only tenuous links with their families. The influence of the gang may be more powerful and pervasive than any other.

2. *To offer standards and rules*

The group may have well-defined rules and a code of conduct which form a framework for personal reference. To understand the baffling behaviour of a member it may be necessary to become familiar with the rules, values and demands of the group with which the member must comply (Savin-Williams, 1980). The behaviour of the individual, of even very young children, is shaped up to a nearer approximation to the acceptable standard of the group by the other members.

3. *Self-knowledge*

Most of us are influenced, directly or indirectly, by what others think of us, and we may or may not choose to alter or amend our behaviour or attitudes accordingly, to win the approval or respect of significant others. For some young people the approval of the group is of paramount importance and the sub-culture of the group can be highly influential in affecting the self-image and self-evaluation of the individual (Fine, 1980). Peer approval is highly motivating for many adults but in childhood and adolescence it may clash with the aims and goals of school and home. Group opinion and peer pressure are powerful channels to bring about a change in attitude. If a group deplores bullying and knows that the bully is dominating a child any one of them could dominate, so that no kudos can be attributed to the bullying, these actions are seen as simply being cruel and cowardly, and the rationale for the bullying is lost.

4. *Protection*

Those who feel themselves less emotionally or physically robust than their peers may turn to the group for support. A child with low status may seek an enhanced identity – a borrowed kudos – from a high-status group if permitted membership. It is not uncommon for bullying groups to contain one member who is ineffectual and would, if not in the bullying group and protected, be a prime target themselves for attack.

5. To offer an identity

On initial formation groups may introduce identification devices to give themselves an added cohesion. Some of the more popular are:

- name: Cosa Nostra, Ku-Klux-Klan;
- uniform: clan tartans, Salvation Army, sports teams;
- password: Masonic, cubs.

These identifying practices enhance group solidarity.

6. To offer friendship

The group can offer support and acceptance. Groups may be used to test out ideas and hypotheses about the confusions of the world, such as issues relating to sex and adult behaviour. Fears, insecurities and anxieties may be voiced in a supportive group, perhaps more acceptably by jokes and innuendoes. The information elicited in this way runs parallel to that gained from more orthodox sources and is assimilated in an attempt to try to make sense of the world. Groups sometimes amend their language to protect their privacy, as in the use of prefixes or suffixes or substitute syllables, to make their conversations incomprehensible to outsiders. In some cases a different terminology is used – a 'slanguage' – a method found in several cultures in the world to avoid adult interlopers (Fine, 1980).

7. To serve common aims

Groups form most readily when prospective members are aggrieved, experiencing low morale, or offered a strong leader (Hemming, 1983). Adult examples of this are the early socialist movements, the Jarrow Marchers and the Luddites. Any strongly authoritarian system which forces upon subordinates an inferior status often generates violence in some form. Groups in school challenging authority may win twice over by winning the challenge and also by the kudos attained by being seen to win. Even if unsuccessful, there is the danger of the challengers achieving a 'glorious victory in defeat'. A class may respond as a group to support a disruptive faction if they are all disaffected with the school or the behaviour or attitude of the teacher (Hargreaves, 1967).

The feeling of group support was used in the cases of Stephen and George (see Chapter 10) where drama was the medium chosen as a tangible and experiential way of eliciting the somewhat abstract quality of group support to help someone in need. From the concrete dramatic examples the group feeling eventually generalized into better group relationships. In addition, this method also facilitated group cohesion and identity.

Membership of groups

By including and excluding candidates for membership the group boundary is established and identity confirmed.

1. Inclusion

The following factors are considered to be relevant to inclusion and acceptance for membership: shared aims, interests and attitudes, age, proximity and familiarity (Cartwright and Zander, 1960). Group members become like one another through a process of strong pressure to conform, implemented by the use of group laws and accepted standards of behaviour: 'The link between group solidarity and similarity is so prevalent as to approach the status of a universal law of social behaviour' (Rubin, 1980). This process of conforming to group demands was noted in the behaviour of two contrasting teams at a summer camp. One group prized the 'he man' image, the other chose a humanitarian ideology. Both groups quickly got members to conform by using silence and reprimands until the chosen mode was well established (Sherif, in Rubin, 1980). Left to themselves it would appear that many young people are able to use quite sophisticated behavioural techniques to a level many professionals would envy.

2. Exclusion

Even preschoolers are sensitive to being excluded from the group. Young children, it would seem, prefer to play with those they dislike rather than play alone (Jersild, 1966). Girls in particular use social exclusion, ostracism and malicious gossip as a bullying strategy (Roland, in prep.).

Those children most in need of the experience of being attached to a group, for both support and the social learning experience, may be afflicted with self-doubts and insecurities and be afraid of rejection and ridicule if they try to enter. It would seem that prospective members do amend unacceptable behaviour to gain entry to groups, but isolated children are perhaps those who are unable to adapt. Some members may over-conform at the expense of losing their individuality. Perhaps more could be done by adults to encourage respect for differences as well as teaching young people how to conform.

3. The leader

Within the two major categories of democratic and authoritarian styles of leadership there are many personality differences. The leader may be energetic, voluble and a good communicator or, perhaps, aggressive and coercive, or resourceful and imaginative. There are many functions a leader can play within the group and the leader can quickly lose his or her position and be replaced if the needs of the group are not being met (White and Lippitt, 1960). The leadership may simply be task-oriented and the group disband when the task is completed. The leadership of even the most informal group is not static and the leader must continue to gain credit and show leadership skills to retain his or her position (White and Lippitt, 1960). An effective way of breaking up a bullying group is to challenge the aims of the leader, to unobtrusively bring the group round to see that the actions they are being led into, or simply supporting, are cowardly and foolish (Hamblin, 1978a). One study conducted some time ago shows how a group may have leadership without any realization as such (Savin-Williams, 1980). Girls at a summer camp declared their group to have no leader, but within the group there were found to be maternal leaders, some antagonists, and the majority who were described as the 'Amorphous Miss Average'. One small group were classified as 'clingers'. These girls openly recognized the dominance of the others; they were overly compliant, the most physically immature and the worst athletes. They were picked on by the others and slept nearest the staff for protection. They were quite clearly being bullied.

4. Cohesion

Groups with a high level of cohesion have been found to exert a powerful influence on the attitudes and behaviour of their members (Schacter, 1960). Measures of cohesion include the level of demands made on individuals, the degree of conformity, the degree of support offered a member under attack from outside, the strength of rebuffal of intruders, and the difficulty of the initiation. Counting the number of mutual statements made within the group has been one way used to measure the level of cohesion. The suggestion is that the more 'We' and the less 'I' statements made indicates the level of group feeling. The 'We' statements confirm the boundary: 'We are in the group, you are out' (White and Lippitt, 1960). The case of Stephen (see Chapter 10) shows how he was excluded partly because of his skin colour which was different from the others in the class. This gave the group a rationale to unite more firmly together in order to exclude Stephen.

The interactions between group members are obviously very subtle and discrete – such measures as we have used to date offer little insight into the covert and intuitive mechanisms at work. Adults are particularly unsuccessful at penetrating these groups, presumably one reason being that the rationale for many of the groups is to exclude adults and offer an alternative to their power structure.

5. Group malpractice

Group solidarity makes the behaviour of its members inflexible and unreparative. The guilt experienced by members of a group would appear to be divided by the number of individuals concerned and the amount of cruelty and violence to be multiplied (Hyatt-Williams, 1983). The replacing of individual identity by group identity means a loss of responsibility and guilt. Mobs do things with mutual support one member would not do alone. The group offers protection from retaliation and also from investigation and detection. There may also be the hope of a more diffuse punishment being meted out; if not, at least there will be companionship in suffering the penalty. It is, therefore, usually advisable to tackle each individual alone in the group when challenging bullies and to make clear each has been fully responsible if only by watching and condoning.

The group may not be established prior to the deviancy; it could be that in a case such as bullying, the aggression had been dormant. The arrival of a leader might act as a catalyst and so cause a group to form through the process of group contagion. Once the excitement level is raised, meeker observers may drift into the group to become active. Those needing prestige and borrowed kudos may be incited to join, as proposed in 'magnetic field theory' (Hyatt-Williams, 1983). This is one of the dangers of media publicity, because groups such as Mods, Punks and any current equivalents, form an identity simply through a label allocated to them by others.

There may be a cognitive change once the group has formed and is able to draw on mutual support, in that the group may come to believe that the victim of the attack, be it a child or a nebulous authority target, is deserving of the violence. The main aim of the group could be to prove that group members are acceptable, whereas those who are attacked are obviously inferior: 'We must be OK because you are not.' The group can have a powerful influence on the behaviour of an individual and many interesting accounts of experiments, formal and informal, illustrate this process. Zimbardo *et al.* (quoted in Kidder and Stewart, 1975) found that two groups of students – role-modelling prisoners and prison warders – had to be removed prematurely because they took over their roles too realistically. The work of, for example, Goffman (1974) contains many readable accounts of the behaviour of individuals in the presence of groups.

If the group is challenged without careful planning, an increase in hostility may result and the deviant behaviour might continue but in a less visible form. Resentment and revenge might also fuel further incidents and add to group cohesion. The group activities may be entertaining and reinforcing so that it could be difficult to offer equivalent alternatives. A simplistic attack on the group could add prestige, glamour, mystery and subsequent power. Weak and ineffective measures could add to the conspiratorial atmosphere and infuse an heroic element to the leader or group.

If, however, the group is not challenged, this might be viewed as weakness and as giving tacit permission to the group to continue. In a bullying situation the dyad of bully and victim is central and, unless this is resolved and unscrambled, the group will reassemble and reform at a later date (Hyatt-Williams, 1983). In the novel, *The Deceivers* (Masters, 1952), the Thugs, followers of the goddess Kahli, prove difficult to eradicate because the central figures remain in role, ready to reform elsewhere. One of the primary aims must be to detach the catalyst from the group or, at least, from the role of leader. Hamblin (1978a) suggests that it is important to deglamourize the group by pointing out the infantile and immature aspects of the group's behaviour and to deflate the heightened prestige with humour if possible, because this is one of the most powerful, acceptable and effective deterrents. Once a bullying problem has been openly discussed, I have found that it loses much of its potency, so that the exposure in itself is often enough to ward off further attacks.

Communication skills

Communication skills are of paramount importance in determining the success of a child's interactions with his or her peers. Research on bullying indicates the importance of these skills. The specific skills deemed necessary for the building of friendships are:

● being able to detect the norms and expected behaviour in a situation so that appropriate conversation and behaviour is used in context;
● the ability and desire to display warmth and empathy so that relationships are cemented;

● the wish to share common interests, information and activities (Rubin, 1980).

There would appear to be a correlation between poor language skills and antisocial or disturbed and difficult behaviour. An inarticulate child has little resource to the wit and humour many use to deflect trouble from adults and peers alike, and to release any inner tensions. A build up of frustration can lead to an eruption and violent confrontation (Hamblin, 1978a).

There are specific processes of communication which help friendships to gel. Even young children use a distinct pattern of speech to build up a relationship, a social sound play where an alternating set of phrases is used in a rhythmic manner to establish empathy and rapport. An example is given by Garvey (1984) of two youngsters trying out their language and friendship skills simultaneously.

I have a dadda.
I have a dadda too.
I have a real dadda.
I have a dadda too.

This ritualized play patterning of speech serves the nonspecific function of the greetings adults frequently use:

How are you?
Fine. How are you?
Fine.

No specific information is required, the exchange is simply to reinforce mutual interest and to confirm empathy. Children who are shy and withdrawn may not be able to consolidate their relationships in such informal ways. Some children may not have assimilated the information that this is the effective procedure to take.

Entering the group

Members of a group of young children quickly rebuff outsiders, perhaps because of an innate resistance to the disruption of the status quo or a fear and rejection of strangers. The onus is on the newcomer to indicate quickly and appropriately the contribution he or she can make to the group (Corsaro, 1979). If the first attempt is unsuccessful a further effort may succeed: 'We don't like you today' can quickly prevent any shy and anxious child from risking further rejection by making future attempts at socialization. It may be preferable to choose the role of passive

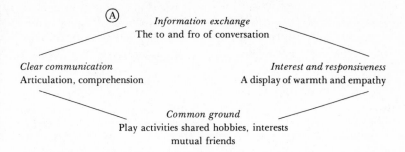

Figure 2 The four factors influencing the success of an initial approach (Gottman and Parker, 1986).

observer. If this is so, the shy child will fall further and further behind the peer group as the others benefit from the invaluable experience of social interaction with their peers. Gottman and Parker (1986) provide a model for the initial approach and suggest four significant factors concerning how children make friends (see Fig. 2). If the advances break down, a return to A will be necessary. Modifications may be required but unskilled children may simply repeat the unsuccessful process over and over again. The cohesion of the group and the popularity of the newcomer may be measured by the number of entry bids required (Corsaro, 1981).

Popular children use specific strategies in that they do not draw attention to themselves but hover quietly in close proximity to the group, perhaps copying the group activity. They make specific verbal entry bids: they are complimentary, they make no comment about themselves, they ask relevant questions, and do not make suggestions until asked. In other words, they attempt to build up a shared frame of reference (Cosaro, 1981). If rejected they note the criticisms, make modifications and bounce back. In addition to all this, a cluster of non-verbal skills are brought into play: facial expressions, posture, gesture and eye contact. The intricate patterning of speech is effective in obtaining acceptance such as affirmation, pauses and inflection. All in all, a vast battery of skills are synchronized and used intuitively by even young children. It is only by examination of the process when it has failed that we get any idea as to how accomplished children are in their social behaviour. As adults we would appear to find difficulty in assessing accurately the social status of young children in a group. Even when we try to measure the social interactions we encounter difficulties due to the developmental limitations of linguistic, perceptual and other cognitive factors. Photographs and drawings of children in the class group have been used successfully to elicit information about friendships from young children. Children inside a friendship group use language in an informal manner, but in such a way as to confirm the positive group feeling:

- the statements of others are openly acknowledged and confirmed (yeah, hmm);
- the use of linking words confirms attention is being paid and gives the speaker encouragement to continue (and then? when?);
- phrases are repeated with slight modifications (I've built a castle. You've built a castle) (Preece, 1987).

Young children playing together, unsupervised, invent elaborate conspiracies and pretend shared deviances such as running away from home or poisoning others (Gottman, 1986). To be able to offer and share in imaginative play, the ability to communicate a theme, to entertain, to negotiate an idea and translate it into a successful game, are all skills highly valued and contribute to the popularity of some children (Rubin, 1980, ch. 5).

Communication between child and adult is a two-way process; it is vital to understand what the child or young person is not saying in addition to listening to the verbal exchanges. It is sometimes impossible to put complex concepts and emotions into words and yet we ask many questions of children who have had little such experience and possess few sophisticated linguistic skills. Pikas (1987a, b) believes poor and inappropriate communication contributes to many social conflict situations and stresses that children need practice in communication to avoid confrontations. In his workshops for teachers on bullying, Pikas emphasizes listening and speaking skills, giving and receiving verbal and non-verbal messages and asking critical questions. In addition, symmetrical communication is advocated where both speaker and listener reciprocate time and effort – if we expect others to listen to us, we must expect to listen as carefully to others.

Quarrels and conflicts

Few friendships run smoothly. Quarrels may have a positive problem-solving role, e.g. when a hurdle occurs each participant is required to assimilate or reject the view of the other and to adjust their own perception. Through the bickering and squabbling of childhood the needs and opinions of others begin to be understood and in this way the world of the child evolves. A casual observation may be misleading, because the closer the relationship, the greater the probability of quarrels (Green,

1933). To judge the relationship the ratio of positive to negative interactions needs to be analysed. A simple count of conflicts could give a distorted picture. One very highly regarded skill, although not consciously regarded as such by children, is the ability to resolve disputes amicably. Those who can deflect aggressive situations are prized as companions (Shantz, 1987).

In summary, by looking at the complex, interacting facets of social behaviour, noting carefully successes and hurdles, not only strategies for help in crisis situations may be drawn, but the study could also identify a vast array of strategies to offer for remediation.

PART TWO

WHAT TO DO ABOUT BULLYING
A practical guide and checklist for teachers

6
The role of the school

Back in the Playground Blues

I dreamed I was back in the playground, I was about four
    feet high
Yes dreamed I was back in the playground, standing about
    four feet high
Well the playground was three miles long and the play-
    ground was five miles wide.

It was broken black tarmac with a high wire fence all around
Broken black dusty tarmac with a high fence running all
    around
And it had a special name to it, they called it The Killing
    Ground

Got a mother and a father, they're one thousand years away
The rulers of The Killing Ground are coming out to play
Everybody thinking: 'Who they going to play with today?'

       Well you get it for being Jewish
       And you get it for being black
       Get it for being chicken
       And you get it for fighting back
       You get it for being big and fat
       Get it for being small
       Oh those who get it get it and get it
       For any damn thing at all

Sometimes they take a beetle, tear off its six legs one by one
    Beetle on its black back, rocking in the lunchtime sun
    But a beetle can't beg for mercy, a beetle's not half the
       fun

    I heard a deep voice talking, it had that iceberg sound
    'It prepares them for Life' – but I have never found
    Any place in my life worse than The Killing Ground
                      Adrian Mitchell (1984)

What are the factors which discriminate between children of similar age, ability and background so that one child is predisposed towards bullying, another to being bullied and the majority not to be so heavily at risk?

The profiles presented earlier indicate that a problematic home background could be common to both victims and bullies (see Chapter 1). In my own work I have found that although both groups may have, for example, witnessed or been the recipients of violence in the home, or been rejected by a significant adult, it is the victims who have suffered a loss of confidence and self-esteem and, in doing so, become vulnerable to the attack of others.

This becomes even more significant when put in the context of the other factors which appear to discriminate between the two groups (See Table 1–5). A combination of such characteristics as a good level of energy, a well developed physique and communication skills would allow the bullies the confidence not only to attack others, but to talk their way out of impending trouble. The smaller, weaker and less energetic victims, being unable to defend or perhaps express themselves adequately, are more likely to become submissive and vulnerable and experience a rapid loss of confidence.

I would propose that it is this confidence factor which subsumes all others. Not only do the bullies have the confidence and the ability to dominate other children, but research indicates that their socialization within the home and street culture may have taught them, from a very early age, to regard a display of power over others to be an acceptable measure of kudos and social success (Dunning *et al.*, 1988). It must be added that although some bullies may lack confidence, and it is this which could cause them to bully others in a bid to compensate, it is only within a group where they do feel powerful and confident that they use their bullying techniques. The categories of victim and bully are not mutually exclusive. A child who is victim in one situation may, among weaker, younger or less able children, find the confidence to bully. Conversely, the child who is a bully in one class may be the victim of older pupils or siblings in a different situation (See Chapter 1).

From an overview of research specific to bullying and related areas, a picture begins to emerge of those children who are at risk of becoming involved in a bullying situation in school. It must be emphasized that any child could be caught up in a bullying attack by being in the wrong place at the wrong time. Such an unfortunate experience could happen to anyone and be traumatic for the victim at the time. However, many children involved in a bullying situation, both victims and bullies, have some characteristics which predispose them to risk. Some degree of socialization problems may have been noted by parents or teachers previous to the bullying. Rather than the problem being solely one of bullying it is, I would suggest, especially in the more prolonged cases, one of inappropriate social behaviour which predisposes these children to attack or to be attacked.

The school has, without doubt, a most important role to play in helping these children with their social behaviour in a variety of ways. The most effective way of helping such children could be to look to the multiplicity of strategies which could be implemented throughout the school day, available to all staff, rather than simply concentrating, for example, on a social skills programme which would be a less natural way of bringing about relevant change.

Why should the school help?

Children lacking confidence in themselves and their own ability, for whatever reason, may cease to make any effort to succeed and, therefore, withdraw into themselves. Feeling hopeless failures, they do not believe that they have the ability to change their circumstances and, therefore, a state of learned helplessness develops where there is a drift towards apathy, lethargy and depression (Seligman and Peterson, 1986). Children who feel they have no valid place in school, or perhaps society, can turn to aggression and conflict in a bid to alter their situation. These children benefit from the expertise and experiences to be found in schools to show them how they are able to take more effective control over their own lives.

Adverse social experiences may leave some children unwilling to make any attempt to involve themselves with others. They may claim to prefer to be alone, but this could result in them becoming even more vulnerable as, in this way, they preclude any of the valuable social experiences which could make them more robust. The school could be the only effective channel for change because the parents may feel helpless to alter the situation. The parents of a younger child are able to provide more friendship opportunities, whereas the parents of an older, resistant teenager may have no idea how to help.

The family may have been contributory in some way to the development of the problem, so there may be little support available, even if the parents wish for change and are willing to try to alter the situation. The environmental props which once supported children in society, such as family stability, neighbourhood communities and religious practices, have gradually been eroded away, so that there is now less access to help from these other sources. Professional agencies might be able to help, but some families are reluctant to turn to them in time of need because they regard the use of such agencies as an admittance of failure.

For some children the lack of family stability could mean that within the school community, among their teachers and friends, they experience their most stable and longest known relationships. They may have grown up with the peer group since they were toddlers, so that it is the most stable factor in their lives.

Finally, children are in school for a large part of their waking lives and are in daily contact with some teachers who are, therefore, able to use their expertise to watch over them closely for a number of years. These teachers are thus in a prime position to identify difficulties and to offer support through times of emotional turmoil in a friendly but expert fashion, something which is available to very few other professional workers.

How can the school help?

There can be little doubt, therefore, that the school has a vital role to play in helping children involved in bullying. Primarily, the school needs to ensure that there is little opportunity for bullying to occur, but, equally important, is the long-term work a school is able to offer to children with socialization difficulties. Without this two-fold approach I feel that there is a risk that the problems will recur. Simply to resolve a crisis, or only to prevent the eruption of bullying, is to tackle only one-half of the problem. Children at risk – both bullies and victims – need to be identified, and helped towards a happier and more effective social adjustment.

The most effective and economical way a school can deal with the problem of bullying is by evolving a school system which, to as large an extent as possible, precludes it ever occurring, not only by removing any opportunity, but also by offering children the quality of support, training and education which can, hopefully, attack the root causes of the bullying behaviour. Rather than an individual teacher having to try to resolve a problem, and any further ramifications, it is more effective for the school to be organized in such a way so as to prevent problems, by looking not only to the daily functioning of the school but, in addition, by looking to the long-term objectives of all aspects of the school.

The school as an organization

In recent years there has been some move away from focusing solely on the resolution of individual problems, such as case work with individual children, to taking the wider perspective of considering the school as an organizational complex which, as a result of specific and alterable factors within itself, can escalate or de-escalate social and antisocial behaviour (Burden, 1981). The school as a whole is seen to be partly responsible for any maladaptive behaviour if the necessary preventative work has not been thoroughly investigated and adopted. This perspective of the school as an organizational system has been drawn, in part, from the behaviourist approach which focuses on observed behaviours and the environmental contingencies maintaining the behaviour, rather than looking to distant sources and causes not present within the current interaction between school and child. The emphasis is on the here and now (Bandura, 1969).

Behaviours within such a framework are viewed as being the product of a dynamic system, so that problem behaviours could be considered useful in that they are highlighting any gaps or weaknesses within the system. Putting these difficulties right involves helping all those within the organization by bringing about more widespread and permanent changes rather than helping just one individual child. The focus, therefore, moves from considering what is wrong with the child to looking at what is wrong within the organization. In this way the school shares in the responsibility for the problem behaviours rather than blaming some other source, such as society, the family or the child.

This model can be criticized as being too impersonal and simplistic, taking little note of the complex familial and societal undertones to many problems. It would appear, however, from diverse studies, that the school as a whole can often be influential in preventing difficult behaviour regardless of the family and environmental factors which may have contributed to the problems in the first place. In the past there appears to have been a commonly held assumption that schools, to some extent, had a blanket effect on all pupils. Any variation in outcome was thought to be largely due to differential intake. Evidence would now suggest that specific school variables may exert a higher degree of influence on outcome than the social balance of pupils. Schools with similar catchment areas produce widely differing outcomes and statistics indicate that outcomes may correlate more with over-all school factors than the internal psychological make-up of the child (Mortimore *et al.*, 1988). In other words, some schools appear to make the drift towards deviant behaviour such as bullying difficult, in that mechanisms within the system in some way protect the pupil, whereas other schools leave their pupils at risk.

Bullying would appear to be a multifaceted problem with roots in a variety of interrelated processes: the temperament, social behaviour, physical development, communication skill, level of self-esteem and self-confidence of the child, in addition to family, sociological and school influences. If this is so, it would seem to be logical to have available, in the school, a multidimensional preventative approach, a wide spectrum of well-planned and -prepared skills and responses from which to draw in time of need. In parallel to this, in advance of any crisis, almost all aspects of the functioning of the school would need to be addressed in the context of preventing bullying. Forward planning is more effective and economical than crisis management.

The whole school system should be organized to support all children and staff so that no one child or teacher is left alone to try to resolve a bullying problem. Sound, well-planned preventative work, frequently revised and updated, should result in an atmosphere that is non-conducive to acts of bullying. A network of preventative strategies should be laid down well in advance, and supported by sound protective work.

Several areas of school management and functioning appear relevant to the problem of bullying. The evaluation of the Norwegian National Campaign (in prep.) is to consider a constellation of school factors such as teaching style, size of classes and relationships between teachers and pupils. The results have not yet been published but, even on publication, there may be cultural differences which prohibit a rash generalization of the findings to the problem elsewhere.

The suggestions offered in Part Two of this book are culled from the work I have found to be effective in working with schools to resolve bullying problems, and from strategies which have been successfully implemented by others to cope with other difficult behaviours which I consider would be relevant to a preventative approach to bullying. They are offered in staccato form, without apology, as a series of lists designed for the busy classroom teacher, but they are fully informed by the issues explored in Part One of this book.

7
Prevention

Preventative work in schools

1. School policy

The most effective preventative measure a school can employ is perhaps for all staff members and the local education authority to establish clearly that bullying in school, in any form, will not be tolerated and, indeed, will be dealt with firmly. The weight of the whole school establishment should fall in behind the school rules and policy statement. A document should be drawn up by the school and be made familiar to all: pupils, parents, staff, governors and local authority figures responsible for education. The statement, perhaps incorporated in a larger document, should make clear the school rules as well as the action to be taken when the rules are contravened. This may include notifying parents, school governors and other responsible bodies if deemed appropriate. This, in itself, could deter all but the most determined or deviant.

2. Local authority responsibility

The local authority and the governing body could offer support to a school policy designed to prevent bullying. The efficient execution of this would depend on good supervision which, in turn, would depend on adequate staffing and funding. Supervision should be required for bus queues, bus journeys, outbuildings, changing rooms and other isolated areas, plus possible timetable adjustments. Supernumerary or auxilary staff may be necessary. If adequate supervision is genuinely impossible, even with a full commitment from all existing staff, and perhaps some support from willing parents, then those responsible should be made aware, whether it be the member of staff in charge of the duty roster or the official in charge of the financial budget.

3. Architectural design of buildings

The supervision of all pupils at all times should be taken into account at the architectural stage in the building of schools. We have now come to realize that this is necessary in the case of vandalism and theft. A commitment is required from those in charge of finance at the initial stage. A good design would include well-lit corridors, plenty of window space, mirrors and glass-type doors to offer good visibility. In addition, the avoidance of isolated areas and satellite buildings is essential unless the cost of adequate supervision is taken into account at the design stage.

Measures such as these would contribute to sound preventative work and help to avoid many disruptive and deviant behaviours in addition to bullying. Parents and governors could find that they are in a more powerful position than the school staff to bring pressure to bear on those in charge of financial affairs. Vandalism and theft may be costing national and local bodies increasing amounts of money, but the protection of our children must be of the highest priority and adequate finance should be apportioned accordingly.

4. The school as a community

One of the most effective ways of preventing bullying is perhaps to look upon the school as a community where the aim is for each member to be responsible for his or herself and for the well-being of all others. The school is often viewed as preparing the child for life, but the daily routine of school may hold joys and terrors as powerful in their effect as anything a child may meet in later life. It could be argued that with age we learn to avoid, deflect and confront, whereas in childhood we have little previous experience to help us cope.

School life is, then, very much in the present for those who attend daily. Hamblin (1978a) describes it in terms of being a vibrant living community with its heroes, villains, triumphs and tragedies of which each child is a part. The school should, perhaps, reflect the community outside and represent the democratic process more than is evident in many of our establishments at present. Society at large is composed of overlapping groups requiring cooperative input (e.g. work, leisure, family and neighbourhood groups), yet, although among the most prominent institutions in our society, and one of the few compulsory activities, schools are least characterized by cooperative activities. Dewey (1966) noted that although it is essential for humans to learn to live together cooperatively, little evidence of this could be found in the classroom. There has been, in recent years, some moves to offer pupils more opportunities to work together on work programmes, but in many cases these have been biased mainly towards academic learning experiences rather than towards social development. A cooperative learning situation in class could involve pupils working in a democratic manner – socially as well as academically – towards a mutual goal, be it to solve a curriculum query or to resolve an emotional problem. Cooperative learning styles, however, may not lead automatically to cooperative behaviour. Generalization from the academic to the social situation may not occur as a matter of course. This needs to be perceived as a separate goal and the programme of work designed and evaluated with this in mind.

The experience of cooperative learning could be lost if the structural base of the school is hierarchical and competitive. This would be out of synchrony with the aims of cooperative education. Hargreaves (1984) has referred to the school as ideally being a community, rather than an aggregate of pupils, and that it is within the choice of curriculum matter and the mode of presentation that this ethos is embodied; a highly competitive, impersonal and bureaucratic atmosphere being counterproductive to the aims of community education.

There is a clear distinction between cooperative and competitive learning. In the former, the goals are so linked that everyone sinks or swims together; in the latter, if one swims the others must sink. Dewey (1966) described the aims of his Just School as a community demanding a common culture and giving fair and equal opportunity to all. Central to the ideology is the concept that through joint discussions and analysis of problems a higher stage of moral judgement and deliberation may be achieved within such a community than by the individual alone.

5. The ethos of the school

The term 'ethos' is used to cover the individual identity of a school and was given currency by Rutter *et al.* (1979). Dancy (1980) has described it as 'the values, aims, attitudes and procedures of a school which interrelate and which remain a relatively permanent feature of the school'. There have been attempts to use the ethos of the school as a community to prevent bullying among pupils. One school, in a disadvantaged inner-city area, has been referred to as the 'Telling School', as the headteacher impresses upon all new pupils that they have the right to attend school without fear of being bullied (St John Brooks, 1985). It is explained to the pupils that the rule that it is unacceptable to tell was invented by the bullies. Fearful pupils are visited in their homes and every support possible is offered to them. Bullying, racism and other such issues are discussed openly in class, and boys taking a pride in their 'macho' image are made to confront the reasons for their swaggering and bullying behaviour.

I have myself been involved for several years with a school which has a similar ethos but which uses a different approach. The pupils, all with severe emotional and behavioural difficulties, meet together several times a week to thrash out their problems with the staff and each other in a meeting of the whole school, staff and pupils together. This has proved to be highly successful for over two decades. The school is admittedly small, but the model may well be adaptable to tutor or registration groups even in a large school. In this atmosphere conflict is handled constructively. To avoid conflict is to deny development. To encounter it naturally, to work out a solution amicably, and to learn to see the situation from the perspective of another, could be one of the most valuable experiences we can offer our young people.

A similar procedure is described by Laslett (1982) in his article about a children's court, although in the former example all positive aspects of school life were aimed along with concerns and anxieties. The meetings were not merely a punitive procedure.

An example of an attempt to establish a community ethos in most difficult circumstances is the Carimeela Project in Northern Ireland. Children from the varying religious, political and cultural backgrounds meet together, in a relaxed environment away from the troubled areas, so that they can have the opportunity to learn about and from each other.

6. Management

One of the most pervasive factors influencing the quality of life for all in a school is perhaps the style of management at all levels. This is what enables the ideology of a school to be translated into effective practice. As can be seen from the case studies in Chapter 10, a teacher can initiate a wide variety of far-reaching strategies to help a child who is involved in a bullying situation, whether it be as victim or bully, but the support of a good management team to aid the implementation and coordination of the proposals is essential, especially in a larger school. The clear communication of aims and goals, a consistent policy understood by all, seems to be the parameter of prime importance. A united and cooperative team would seem to be able to achieve almost any goal, whereas the best of policies will fail if the staff is disgruntled, fragmented and out to sabotage. Being able to lead a team in an authoritative rather than authoritarian manner, allowing for the personal development of individuals within the team, and offering clear and attainable goals, would appear to be the important criteria of effective management.

7. The teacher–child relationship

One factor which would appear to be of great significance in the development of any pupil in school is the quality of the relationship between teacher and child. No methodology in itself can offer optimum learning. The impression made by a teacher, for good or for bad, could be of lasting importance, as teachers may be remembered with a greater degree of clarity than the material they taught. They may be viewed in a heroic light or even as surrogate parents. The effect of this daily interaction in school cannot be underestimated because teachers fulfil a variety of roles.

In discussing the role of the teacher in preventing bullying, Roland (1988) suggests that a teacher should develop a special relationship with each child in the class if at all possible. This should be built on something that they alone share, such as an interest, a skill, a pet, a hobby or knowledge of a family member. A topic of mutual and genuine interest shared with a teacher offers the child an individual identity which counteracts the feeling of being just a face in an anonymous group. Each child, no matter how large the school, can have an empathic and rewarding relationship with a teacher.

Teachers are models for the young in their care who note details of their attitude and behaviour. There is a hidden curriculum at work in schools as young people are highly sensitive to picking up and assimilating cues on how to conduct themselves. Young people may look to the adults in school for guidance and a code of conduct which could influence the way they themselves treat others. Quite young children are able to discriminate between preaching and practice and they register strongly patronizing and demeaning remarks made in their presence. Adults need to be particularly clear and unequivocal in their communication with the young as they could be misinterpreted, especially by those pupils who may previously have encountered negative relationships with adults.

A strong and stable relationship with an adult outside the family has been suggested as being a powerful discriminating factor between those young people from severely disadvantaged backgrounds who eventually succeed and those who do not (Quinton and Rutter, 1985b). A positive relationship encourages self-esteem and -confidence and these are prerequisites to the development of a belief in one's ability to alter circumstances for better or worse (Rotter, 1966). To believe in one's ability to bring about change and to be in control of one's own life must surely be one of the main aims of education.

One aspect of school life which is underestimated is that many pupils look to teachers to provide a safe and stable environment in which they may develop. I suspect, from my own observations, that in some of the most disadvantaged areas the truancy rate may be lower than one would expect for, in many of our schools, children find a quality of relationship unavailable to them at home.

As can be seen from all the case studies presented (see Chapter 10), the work implemented and carried out to help the children has, almost without exception, depended on one teacher with the necessary high level of commitment being available and willing to help. No other individual or agency has the same opportunity and access to as wide a range of responses as does the teacher who is familiar with the child.

8. The curriculum

Mitchel and O'Moore (1988) and Byrne (1987) found a far higher proportion of bullying in remedial groups of children, in both primary and secondary settings, than in other classes. As yet it is unclear as to why this should be, but it may be relevant to note that a correlation has been found between those children who feel that they have failed academically and the emergence of behaviour problems (Rutter et al., 1979).

If the school is looking to build up the self-esteem and confidence of the pupils, one of the most effective ways of doing so is through the design and presentation of the curriculum. Conversely, the confidence of students may be eroded by a poorly designed curriculum (Hargreaves, 1984). The major part of the curriculum in many secondary schools is focused on the large percentage of young people following a public examination syllabus (Bird et al., 1981). Those who are not doing so may question the time and effort allocated to their own requirements. Their perception could be that being academic failures they deserve the ignominy of low-level streaming, low-status subjects, temporary staff or those with little specialist training. They may feel that they have no place in an establishment where kudos is gained through academic success. There may be exciting new initiatives for these young people, but perhaps they defeat their purpose if they carry titles indicating low attainment and do not have a similar permanent financial input to other parts of the curriculum. Even the identification of pupils with special edu-cational needs may be fraught with danger if carried out in an insensitive manner so that pupils with difficulties are highlighted in return for very little extra help.

One study found that of the pupils in one secondary school, 50 per cent claimed that the curriculum was boring (Raven, 1979). It is illuminating to track a pupil or class for a day or week to test the curriculum diet. Pupil pursuit studies can also throw up such phenomena as the number of lessons in a day which are based on the ubiquitous worksheet. Disaffected pupils may only attend school because there is little else to do, rather than having any definite aims or expectations; others may vote with their feet and truant, some disrupt lessons to make things more entertaining. The curriculum needs to cover as many learning processes as possible and students themselves welcome and respond positively to opportunities to collaborate in the design and delivery of the curriculum and in evaluating their own progress. If the curriculum appears to be boring and inappropriate to their needs the students might take matters into their own hands: 'People don't grab for prestige in socially useless ways until they have lost confidence in their ability to gain prestige in socially useful ways' (Adler, 1943).

If the curriculum is not able to offer pupils opportunities for self-development, a sense of personal worth and access to the goals society promotes, they could use any of several forms of deviant behaviour, including bullying, to express their rejection of the aims of the school. The curriculum may be seen as promoting the view that the middle-class white culture is the 'right one', to the exclusion of others, and, as such, be forcefully rejected by those unable or unwilling to fit the mould. Older pupils have the intellectual and physical development to lend potency and power to their challenge.

It may be relevant to the problem of bullying to consider the differences in the way boys and girls challenge the school system. Boys appear to do this more overtly by conflict and confrontation. The position of girls may be slightly different. It could be that girls have an equally strong but alternative system which runs parallel to that of the boys as well as that of the school. Girls use their maturity to confront by wearing earrings, make-up, ignoring the dress code and flaunting their sexuality (McRobbie and Garber, 1976). A parallel gender difference in bullying behaviour has been noted by Roland (in prep.): boys were found to use overt physical aggression more than girls who chose the covert tactic of social ostracism. In the secondary school years young people may need to encompass two lives, functioning as an adult out of school yet being treated as a child within. This encourages them to resist a system with which they feel uncomfortable.

Not all pupils who confront and challenge in schools are

from the disadvantaged groups in society, whether academic or social, nor is problem behaviour unique to our time. These theories need to be seen in the perspective of other sociological and historical contexts.

9. Discipline and disruption

The well-being and safety of all pupils in school entails a commitment to sound and consistent disciplinary procedures being enforced. The way in which this is carried out may have long-term effects on the pupils. A custodial and over-rigorous style, in conjunction with negative expectations of the pupils, has long been acknowledged as counterproductive:

> But ye hem them in on every side with terrors, threats and stripes so that they can get no liberty whatsoever; wherefore, being thus indiscretly afflicted, they put forth a target of evil thoughts like thorns. (St Anselm in Coulton, 1967)

Not only can harsh and punitive discipline be ineffective but it can be interpreted by pupils as violence, and so offer a model for their own aggressive behaviour. To them it may seem that the message is that the powerful can dominate the subordinate. It is easy to see how this could encourage a bullying attitude in some children.

Several studies on disruption have made mention of bullying in the group of behaviours classified as disruptive, although a connection between the two has not been supported as yet by a body of research, although at least one study has found a correlation between the two (Riley, 1988). Disruptive behaviour can clearly be classed as bullying if there is a repeated and deliberate intent to humiliate or denigrate a teacher, who, for whatever reason, is powerless to prevent the assault. Few careers expose adults to such risk of ridicule and insult, much of which is suffered in isolation and privacy. Disruptive behaviour has many parallels to bullying in that the teacher may feel humiliated, angry in a futile and ineffective fashion, or even blackmailed, i.e. a disruptive pupil 'messes about' in class because the teacher is afraid of the repercussions if sanctions are imposed; there may even be aggression and violence expressed towards the teacher. It could perhaps be of value to look at teachers experiencing a high rate of disruption in the context of victim behaviour. Are there lessons to be learned from the general study of the preventative and response behaviour of victims, their posture, confidence, humour, conformity, etc., which could help in such situations?

I have noted when teaching or observing classes where

disruptive behaviour is likely to occur, that the more vulnerable pupils are often taunted and scapegoated by the more confident in order that they may take their possessions, or simply provide them with a source of entertainment. The less physically robust and fearful children may be under a great deal of tension and stress in a class where disruptive behaviour breaks out. This may not be regarded generally as bullying but there are many similarities between the situations. It would appear that most children appreciate good supervision and the subsequent air of stability and security (Hargreaves *et al.*, 1975). As research indicates, I would suggest that children put bullying at the top of their list of fears; indeed, children may be more afraid of other children than the deviant adults we so often warn them about (Galton and Willcocks, 1983).

One simple way of eradicating a common cause of discipline problems and of avoiding constant acrimony and confrontation, is by taking a whole-school approach to the rules. Rules may vary from class to class, without reason, so offering opportunities for challenges and confrontation. In specific work areas there will be a need for particular rules, but there will also be a need for general rules throughout the school and for these to be adhered to by all staff. Pupils soon spot areas of weakness and laxity and these are treated as such. Pupils need to be able to predict the standard of conduct expected and the sanctions to be imposed for failure to comply. To avoid a confrontational manner rules could be couched in positive terms: 'Walk' rather than 'Don't run', 'We do . . .' rather than 'I will not allow. . .'. Clear and explicit rules compiled and agreed upon by all staff, and pupils if possible, well posted and kept to a minimum can contribute not only to preventing trouble but also to establishing an atmosphere of stability and security throughout the school.

The attitudes of individual teachers influence the challenging behaviour of disruptive pupils. Teachers appear to be chosen, ranked and targeted, according to specific aspects of their behaviour, although the process of selection may not be a conscious one (Cicourel and Kitsuse, 1968). The rules seem to centre around pupil expectations of teacher behaviour. Pupils grant legitimate authority to each teacher on merit. This cannot be a matter of insistence, for it is impossible to enforce respect. Those teachers who do not abide by the universal but unstated rules, who offend the code of conduct in the eyes of their pupils, offer, in their perception, justification for disruptive acts.

There would appear to be several ways in which teachers may offend these unwritten rules: by being too authoritarian, straightlaced, humourless, anonymous, distant or boring. Making personal remarks about such things as the appearance, physique, dress, race or family of pupils is taboo. The most common complaint against teachers is perhaps the accusation of being unfair. To scapegoat one child, or to apply rules in an inconsistent manner, means that the teacher is not abiding by the universal rules and their power system could be open to attack. This selection is a constant and dynamic process, so that any shift in personnel or circumstances requires the re-establishment of relationships. Few disruptive pupils are disruptive all day with all teachers so that it could be profitable, in some cases, to seek out the areas of dissonance between teachers and situations in an attempt to bring about change. If done in a crass way this could prove threatening, for to keep order in class can be regarded as the major way a teacher can gain peer status. Teachers can be bullied by others in the staffroom; to admit to problems may be to admit to failure.

It has been suggested that there is a spectrum of disruption from severe to mild attack (Knoff, 1983). Once the severity is ascertained and the true target identified – to annoy the teacher or another pupil, to stop the lesson, to release pent-up emotions or, as seems often to be the case, simply to have a laugh and some fun – then there is a greater possibility of altering the behaviour. Disruptive behaviour is usually tried out on one or two friends before spreading through the whole class if a good response has been received from the first audience (Knoff, 1983). As in other forms of bullying, the response of the teacher in the initial moments is critical. A firm but good humoured, prompt reaction from the teacher can prevent any escalation of the problem and does not result in one party losing face. There are a great many subtle interactions going on concurrently in a teaching situation and a great deal of personal investment may have been made by both the teacher and the other pupils. All could be lost, for the time being at least, so it is not surprising that a great deal of stress is engendered by disruption in class.

It must be stressed, however, that teacher behaviour is not the whole picture. Some children act in a disruptive manner regardless of the person in charge, as they bring their problems into school from home or elsewhere. In such cases, teachers have to take the brunt of the child's powerful feelings of anger, revenge, disappointment or anxiety. The target teacher could simply trigger memories of other significant adults. On the other hand, quite simple factors could be at play. One example of this is that it would appear that non-examination subject lessons are prime targets, for they are ranked as having a low status by some pupils (Bird, 1980). If this is so, the school can consider ways of allocating a higher status to these subjects.

One aspect of classroom interactions, perhaps less frequently emphasized than others, is the perception teachers hold of their own career and life. A bored, disillusioned or aggrieved adult is less likely to offer a stimulating and rewarding input to pupils. According to their own perceptions, teachers may each have a different response to an individual child. Even the most problematic of pupils may be seen in a positive light by some members of staff.

10. Supervision

From an inspection of the case studies in Chapter 10, it can be seen that some instances of bullying emerged, or escalated, as a result of staff being unpunctual or failing to be on duty or supervise carefully. These examples could be subsumed under the heading of professional practice. Factors such as these have been identified as contributing to the level of effectiveness of a school. Several other aspects of practice have been identified such as quality of wall displays, prompt marking and feedback of work, specific use of praise, thorough preparation of lessons, and a high level of tidiness and cleanliness in the building (Mortimore *et al.*, 1988). These factors, in my opinion, are the more tangible indicators of a deeper process, i.e. the commitment of individual teachers to their pupils.

Good supervision coverage is one of the most efficient and economical preventative strategies which can be applied in schools to prevent bullying. Passive supervision is not always adequate to cover such problems as bullying as it is nearly always hidden. It is a sub-curricular activity in that it goes on underground in that 'curriculum' organized by the pupils themselves which runs parallel with that offered by staff and which can, at any one time, be the more important to the individual child. As staff rarely see or hear anything untoward – for the victims rarely complain – active, vigilant supervision is required to spot incidents in the initial stages. To ignore incidents could be interpreted by the bullies as condoning and giving tacit approval to their behaviour and thus reaffirms the suspicions of the victims that they must try to cope alone.

Good supervision need not imply a heavy presence of teachers shouting orders around the school. Constructive supervision can provide a positive input to the school day. An informal and friendly atmosphere at breaktimes and between lessons with staff in evidence chatting to pupils, or among themselves, while keeping a keen but friendly eye on the happenings around the building, is of great importance. There is a growing interest in more structured playtimes and lunchbreaks, because it is becoming more widely recognized that the quarrels and conflicts which erupt in the playground, instigated by the more volatile children, spill over into the lessons, perhaps affecting everyone for the rest of the day. Involvement in extracurricular activities sometimes affords valuable insights into pupil attitudes and behaviour which are not accessible through the normal curriculum programme. Part of such work can, perhaps, be organized by older pupils, thus offering them a variety of valuable learning experiences not easily gained in other ways.

In a busy school day it may be arduous for a teacher not on duty to find time to check a cloakroom or toilet when passing or call in an out-of-the-way library or work area. Corridors are often overlooked as, unlike classrooms, they are not the responsibility of specific teachers. A spotcheck, however, is a very powerful deterrent, for such intermittent reinforcement is a most powerful psychological mechanism. A couple of minutes spent in this way could save a long investigation at a later date, because problems do seem to arise to fit the opportunity. High-risk areas and times could be identified by small-scale research undertaken by staff or pupils. By tracking a class or a pupil for a day or a week, a teacher is able to identify high-risk areas on the school grounds and anomalies in the timetable.

An unsupervised class, for whatever reason, could result in vulnerable children feeling trapped and at risk. To alleviate the boredom of waiting, some pupils indulge in the thoughtless taunting of others. This can easily become a habit and, if several others join in, it can get out of hand. Even if the victim braves the jeers of the bullies and is able to leave the room, the scene has already been set for future attacks. Those in authority should ensure that the timetable arrangements enable staff to be punctual and that standards of professional practice are kept acceptably high.

11. Children alone out of school

There are times when children will be alone and therefore at risk of attack from bullies, e.g. the journey to and from school. The school bus requires adequate supervision because, once on the bus, the victim has little chance of escape. At school entry and exit times, there is an unbalanced proportion of children to adults using the local transport so that, similarly, the local bus may offer little protection. Certain routes home, such as secluded pathways, parks or passageways in proximity to school, are all likely target spots. A survey can identify these areas. Children arriving unusually early or late to school, or suddenly altering their regular route, could be experiencing problems. Spotcheck supervision is enlightening, economical and worthwhile. Staff may not feel directly responsible for children off the school premises but parents worry about reports of bullying and rumours spread and influence the reputation of the school.

It is, in my experience, the quality of supervision, ideally conscientious and friendly, which can often discriminate between those schools which experience a high level of difficult behaviour such as bullying and disruption, and those schools in the same locality which do not. If the staff work amicably together as a team and all take responsibility for all pupils all of the time, not only on duty days and not only on the school premises, a stable and controlled atmosphere conducive to fruitful work and leisure pursuits and positive social development may be achieved.

A high level of commitment not only contributes to sound educational practice, but indicates clearly to the pupils that they are considered worthy of the time and effort spent. There is evidence that pupils appreciate good supervision and see it in terms of their own protection (Hargreaves *et al.*, 1975).

12. Communication

Effective communication is considered by Pikas (1987a, b), a Swedish psychologist, to be the key to resolving conflicts. Pikas proposes that a breakdown in communication is often the factor of greatest significance in many conflict situations, not only in the specific situation of bullying in schools, but also in the wider context of environmental issues and world politics. Pikas has studied the problem of bullying for several years and has organized many workshops on communication techniques which are designed to train teachers to help pupils communicate more effectively in conflict situations. An outline of the approach used in the workshops is given in the following section. One particularly pertinent aspect of this work is the emphasis Pikas places on careful listening. As adults we are sometimes guilty of not attending carefully to what is being said to us in a busy classroom. Brandes and Ginnis (1986) make this point and urge that we give children 'the gift of our attention'. One way of boosting the self-esteem and -confidence of children is to show them that they are respected and worthy of individual attention.

In recent years more emphasis has been placed on pupils of all ages communicating with each other in all areas of the curriculum. There is now, perhaps, as much importance allocated to the process of learning, the generation and discussion of original ideas and opinions, whether in oral or written form, as to the reproduction of prescribed material. Teaching methodologies such as the problem-solving approach, cooperative learning styles, initiatives such as the National Oracy Project, studies of the language and style of questioning used by teachers, even the content of some public examinations, all reflect the current climate of emphasis on effective communication.

Poor communication may lead to subtle yet potent misapprehension. There are cultural differences which are mirrored in the challenging behaviour of some black pupils which could be misinterpreted if unfamiliar. An example of this is that in some sectors of both black and white cultures there is much emphasis on display of masculinity. For white males this is said to imply physical strength and the will to use it in defence or attack, in addition to the ability to consume large amounts of alcohol or other substances. Black males are said to prove their masculinity in their reputation for style and maturity which is centred around dress, music and girls. They go to school to chat with friends as well as to learn and because this continuous dialogue is a highly prized skill, time in school is allotted by them accordingly (Coard, 1971). This is frowned upon as time-wasting by some staff. It becomes easy to see how some young people come to believe that they are being unjustly criticized due to poor communication causing misunderstanding.

It is not only within pupil interactions that good communication is relevant to preventative work. Fast and efficient lines of communication need to be laid down before bullying problems arise, so that incidents can be dealt with quickly before any secondary problems occur. The clear and effective transfer of information is essential to the satisfactory resolution of a bullying problem. From an examination of the case studies in Chapter 10 it is clear that, although a key person is necessary to form a strong relationship with the children concerned, the quality of the collation and dissemination of information to all interested parties is crucial, not only at the time of crisis, but to prevent any further occurrence. A variety of viewpoints may be necessary to complete the picture, because small but relevant details can be missed if the incidents are viewed from only one angle.

Parents need to be encouraged to contact the school to communicate any anxieties in the initial stages before crises develop. A brief word to the relevant member of staff could prevent a full investigation at a later date.

Workshops and discussion groups should be held for parents and for older pupils, who are the parents of the future, as a routine event to alert them to issues such as bullying. The Norwegian National Campaign (in prep.) included workshops for parents as well as teachers. As well as helping their own children to avoid or cope with bullying incidents, parents can also explain to their children the role that everyone can play in preventing bullying by encouraging a sense of responsibility for the welfare of others. Children can be encouraged to alert adults to another child in difficulty and to develop an understanding that this is not telling tales but acting responsibly. Advice on how to do this appropriately will be needed to be given to children, for otherwise they too could put themselves at risk.

Schools can play an important role in alerting other agencies to such issues as bullying. Social workers, general practitioners and health visitors, for example, are all in an ideal position to spot common warning signs such as truancy, undiagnosed illness and emotional difficulties. Once alerted, these agencies can use their particular perspective to identify children at risk and halt a problem in the earliest stages.

13. Liaison work

The jump from primary to secondary school can prove a traumatic experience for some children. One study found that over 50 per cent of the children entering a comprehensive school were more apprehensive of bullying than anything else (Davies, 1986). This degree of anxiety is unfounded but real to the pupils concerned – even adults find mixing with 1000 or so others each day a tiring and demanding experience. Many new initiatives are now being introduced in many schools, but there is a danger that once the introductory period is over vigilance will be relaxed and, therefore, problems might go undetected.

A full profile can be compiled identifying specific social needs and alerting the new school to any risk factors. This information is valuable to have to hand when groupings and timetable arrangements are being made.

14. Children alone in school

The child most probably at risk from being bullied is perhaps the child alone in school. Neighbourhood friends, acquaintances and relatives all offer physical and moral support, and their importance might perhaps only be recognized when they are absent. Confident and gregarious children cope but others run the risk of being left on the periphery of groups. The shyness or confusion of such children can lead to them being thought of as stupid or, in some cases, disobedient. Liaison work with feeder schools should identify these children so that they may be monitored and, if possible, helped to be accepted into a group or a friendship could be encouraged. Thoughtful pairing with compatible others will help initially. Friendships cannot be made but opportunities for them to develop abound.

Children with established friends often find themselves at risk if separated from supportive colleagues for option subjects or

other activities during the day. Walking alone between lessons is a
real ordeal for some pupils. In a well-supervised class it may not
come to light that they regularly face a barrage of verbal or
physical abuse as they make their solitary way to the playground
or next lesson. Simply being ignored, or left to sit alone in class,
may be excruciatingly embarrassing for these children.

15. Induction work

Many schools run a programme of introductory activities in the
initial weeks to help new pupils to settle, because it is a critical time
for the building of friendships and the development of confidence. Shy or withdrawn children may find it difficult to
approach staff or peers for help. Their confusion and uncertainty could turn to anxiety in the large anonymous system.
Those with friends will remind each other of important and
relevant information and pass messages to and fro. The lonely
child will need to be self-reliant and -confident to succeed. It is,
therefore, imperative that all pupils are able to find their way
around school, that they become familiar with staff immediately
and that they are allocated a key teacher with whom they feel
confident and comfortable.

16. Research

Large multidisciplinary teams may be necessary to formulate new
ways of analysing school systems and to find effective ways of
disseminating these findings. One of the most economical and
rewarding ways to evaluate aspects of school life, however, is to
undertake small-scale action research work which can be carried
out by practising teachers within their own classrooms and
schools. The growing interest in this type of *in situ* evaluation
reflects how pertinent and enjoyable such low-key research can
be. There are many small-scale topics which can be undertaken by
pupils as part of the curriculum. In this way, the many aspects of
school functioning which relate to the social behaviour of pupils
can be studied to the advantage of all concerned. This work needs
to be carefully and sensitively designed so that any surveys or
sociograms do not relate directly to bullying, or highlight the
friendless state or unpopularity of any specific child. Valuable
information can be gained in an oblique way, for example, by
older pupils taking a survey to find what was most difficult for
newcomers to cope with in the first weeks and then offering
suggestions for change. A list of hints and tips should be
published for new entrants, preferably couched in humour,

which could be included in the introductory booklet many schools now send to intending pupils.

17. Personal, social and moral education

One of the most obvious channels through which schools are able to help children with their social behaviour is through such curriculum programmes as Personal, Social and Moral Education. Schools have always aimed to promote the social development of pupils in a variety of ways but the traditional approach, other than by religious input, has perhaps been diffuse and pervasive rather than being allocated a timetable slot.

If the ideology is not to be lost the school itself must be a pastoral system. The sharing of ideas, the encouragement of supportive comment, the suspension of judgement, a respect for the opinions of others, and a cooperative rather than competitive approach to success, will be far more effective than a timetabled lesson used without expertise or commitment. One weekly session does not compensate for any frustration and failure experienced throughout the rest of the school week – the destruction of dignity which academic failure can bring, the shame and embarrassment a poorly coordinated child may feel in a games lesson, or the denigrating remarks thrown at those of different race or accent.

It is important to be clear about the aims of the programme because there are many types of pastoral work undertaken by schools. The choice of emphasis will reflect the true goals of the school:

● *Child-centred:* aims to enhance the emotional, social and physical needs of the child.
● *Pupil-centred:* to develop academic skill.
● *Discipline-centred:* to control and manage behaviour.
● *Administrative-centred:* to fit in with the timetable slot.
● *Subject-centred:* intrinsic in the curriculum subjects.

It can be salutary to remind ourselves that our goals are cultural concepts and not unchallengeable facts. In Japan, for instance, the aim is to encourage children to be good group members, obedient, compliant, submissive and cooperative, so that there is a repression of pronounced individualism (White, 1987). In our own schools we encounter children from different cultures, and thought needs to be given to the conflicting demands which they face in the home and school environments.

As pupils mature, they need to be able to grapple with the basic questions of 'Who am I?' and 'Who do I hope to become?', while the school needs to consider 'What kind of children do we want them to become?' There would appear to be a primary need for us to understand ourselves and our behaviour. We need to be able to examine and account for our own attitudes and actions. Adorno *et al.* (1950) note that it is only by understanding ourselves that we can understand the world around us. Parallel to knowledge of the self is a need to understand others. Children need opportunities to develop the ability to transmit and interpret appropriately both verbal and non-verbal signals and communications, to develop insights into their own behaviour and that of others, so that they are able to understand the emotions, needs and aspirations of others as well as themselves. Hamblin (1978a) suggests that it is necessary to understand others and their emotions so that it is possible 'to get into another's shoes and if they pinch, then you feel the hurt'. This feeling of reciprocity seems to be essential to appropriate social interaction at any level. Through the curriculum and the pastoral ethos of the school the essential change in attitude can be brought about, so that victims no longer need to suffer alone. Group and individual counselling is a strategy that can be used to support this work.

Many pupils who cause concern in schools seem, for whatever reason, to find difficulty in discriminating and identifying the fine nuances involved in communicating with the wide variety of people they come into contact with throughout the school day. They misread signals and seem unable to draw on a sufficiently wide repertoire of responses to maintain rewarding relationships with others. By encouraging the development of feelings of empathy and reciprocity pupils may be helped to take responsibility not only for themselves but for the welfare of others. This seems to be an important stage in any attempt to alter the behaviour of a bullying child. If, as it would appear, children develop self-respect and responsibility for others in response to their experiences, it is essential that the school offers situations in which the child experiences success and opportunities to practise taking responsibility, preferably not only through a specific curriculum input but through the daily functioning of the school.

There may be criticism of the inclusion of Personal, Social and Moral Education on an already overcrowded curriculum, on the grounds that it may not be sufficiently intellectually stimulating, having the low status of a non-examination subject. This criticism would perhaps apply only if the syllabus depended on following a prescribed low-key lesson plan. If the work is centred around problems pertinent to the current functioning of the members of the group, then a wide range of intellectual processes could be engaged. When bullying has been used as a topic for this work there has been, in my experience, a most stimulating intellectual input from the pupils. In this way, the language of problem solving, of describing emotions and social difficulties, could be introduced. I suspect that some young people appear hesitant to discuss important issues simply because they do not have a sufficient repertoire of language to describe the vast array of emotions they are experiencing. The skills of reasoning and logical thinking, problem solving, the weighing up of alternatives and consequences, analysis and decision taking, premeditation and reflection, are but a few of the skills necessary for sound social interaction, and they can all be encouraged through the present-ation of specific and relevant problems presented as a dynamic social framework. If viewed only as recipients of good advice the pupils will be understimulated and understretched. If asked to generate their own solutions with unity of purpose and mutual support, these same pupils will develop more quickly. The main aim must be to encourage maturity of response rather than to find ways of over-protecting vulnerable children.

Summary

No matter what strategy, technique, teaching or learning style, or level of sophisticated curriculum input is introduced in the school, attempts to enhance the level of self-esteem, -confidence and social functioning of any child must fail unless supported by an organization which offers respect and recognition to each individual pupil. Children need to be treated with consideration if they are to show consideration to others, and respect if they are to allow others feelings of self-worth. Teachers are powerful role models and are on the spot when young people are passing through the most critical stage of their social experimentation. They are in a prime position to encourage the optimum social development of all pupils, especially those in need, such as children caught up in bullying – whether victims or bullies. A unified approach by a committed team of highly experienced professionals, could, in countless ways, facilitate the emotional, social and academic growth of young people in school and, in so doing, help prevent the occurrence of problem behaviour.

Preventative strategies in schools

1. A school policy known and supported by teachers, pupils, parents and governors.
2. Those in charge of finance need to allow for and support adequate supervision.

3. The design of school buildings needs to be considered, with priority given to visibility and access for supervision.
4. The school as a community. The school should offer the experience of working and interacting in groups. The structure of the school needs to reflect the community ethos. There have been successful attempts to use a community ethos in the resolution and prevention of bullying problems.
5. The style of management can facilitate or impede the implementation of the ethos.
6. The relationship between the teacher and child is significant.
7. An ill planned curriculum can erode the self-esteem of a child. If the curriculum is boring, it might offer few opportunities to develop a sense of self-worth or access to the goals society promotes.
8. The style and quality of discipline may be influential. Being over-punitive may offer a model for aggression, whereas lax discipline might leave pupils at risk. Disruptive classes may put the teacher in the role of victim and also put at risk the vulnerable pupils. Rules need to be uniform, consistently applied, few and well known. Teachers can encourage disruption by their own behaviour.
9. Supervision. All staff need to be responsible for all pupils at all times. The quality of supervision needs to be conscientious yet friendly. Problems arise to fit the opportunity! Active supervision is necessary because bullying is often covert and hidden from staff. Spotchecks are very effective because they may save a long and complex investigation at a later date. If bullying is not spotted and stopped immediately, this might be interpreted by bullies as a go ahead to continue.

Supervisory tactics

(i) Changes in circumstances can lead to unfamiliar companions or isolation:

● a change in home location;
● new travel arrangements or routes chosen;
● end-of-year class changes;
● new groupings, as in option subjects, etc.;
● quarrels with usual friends.

(ii) A desk diary, graph or other record of details of all reported or suspected incidents may show a pattern, a gap, or weakness in the supervision:

● do incidents occur at a certain time, day, place? Why?

- are there times when there is too much stress on staff or pupils? Why? What could be changed?
- could entry, exit or playtimes be altered or staggered to reduce numbers, avoid pupils from another school?
- could these times be better supervised?

(iii) Are staff available and prepared to deal with an incident during their preparation or free time?

(iv) Are staff willing to help each other in class to observe and analyse the interactions e.g. a second teacher in class on a pretext?

(v) High-risk areas are the toilets, cloakrooms, changing rooms, libraries, showers, etc. The layout of buildings may invite attack, e.g. long secluded corridors, satellite buildings and ill-lit stairways. All these should be identified in red on a map and placed next to the duty roster to serve as a memory prompt to encourage spotchecks.

(vi) Older, more responsible pupils can help with routine supervision.

(vii) Playtimes and breaks should be supervised constructively because any conflict could spill over into the rest of the day:

- games, activities, hobbies, clubs, books, could be offered;
- traditional skipping rhymes, songs and games could be taught;
- a project on play could be an exciting and informative learning experience;
- observation work including video could be enlightening;
- dinner supervisors, etc., may benefit from training.

10. Situational factors. These factors concern situations where there is no direct adult supervision. Work in school needs to be attempted in the following areas:

- long-term change in attitude, so that the pupils realize that it is their responsibility to ensure the safety and welfare of all, that they are not telling tales;
- effective supervision at all times will decrease the risk of attack;
- fast, well-used lines of communication between staff, pupils and parents need to be established or reviewed.

    (i) *Journey to and from school*. Children arriving unusually early, late or by a different route may be experiencing problems.

- *The school bus:* this requires adequate supervision because, once on the bus, there is little chance of the victim escaping or of using avoidance tactics.
- *Local transport:* at school entry and exit times there may be an unbalanced proportion of children to adults using the transport. Adults witnessing worrying situations should be encouraged to alert the school.
- *Routes home:* any little used or secluded pathway or area is a possible target spot. Surveys by pupils or staff could identify these areas. Those nearest school are most likely to be selected, so occasional spotchecks by staff, older pupils or paraprofessional staff such as 'lollipop' or other traffic personnel, auxiliaries, parents or any willing helpers could decrease the risk of incidents.

(ii) *Unpunctuality of staff.* Children waiting in class for staff to arrive are trapped with little possibility of escape. Thoughtless or malicious taunting, started to alleviate the boredom of waiting, could quickly escalate and group attacks may occur. Once the victim is picked out in such a situation the process of labelling and scapegoating can quickly develop and be maintained.

(iii) *Subject groupings.* Older pupils may be placed in groups away from their friends. Even confident and popular children can find themselves in a vulnerable situation walking alone from class to class. Sitting alone or being ignored can be an embarrassing experience.

(iv) *Change of school:* This can be a difficult experience for children. Play and dinner times are often the most worrying, especially if the child has to mingle with a vast number of others. Fear and anxiety make children even more vulnerable and less likely to make friends. Those most in need may be left to cope alone.

(v) *Children alone in school:* Relatives, neighbourhood friends and older acquaintances all offer physical and moral support. The importance of these may only be fully appreciated in their absence.

12. Liaison work. Children and staff could exchange visits. In some schools, primary groups are offered introductory lessons in the secondary school before the start of the initial term. There is a danger that once the introductory period is over a more relaxed attitude might ensue. Vigilance needs to be continued.

13. Identifying children at risk. A profile should be handed on from school to school, or teacher to teacher, to identify those pupils at risk. This helps when groups are arranged and timetabling is finalized. The net for information could be cast wide to several professionals. Susceptible children include those who are:

- without friends or acquaintances;
- unusually tall, small or stand out from the crowd;
- shy, timid, withdrawn and socially passive;
- poorly coordinated and lethargic;
- poor communication skills;
- volatile, sulky, tearful i.e., those who would react badly to provocation;
- prone to psychosomatic illnesses;
- school refusers;
- of ethnic origin, from a different area or with a different accent;
- from out of the catchment area;
- from a family unpopular in the area.

14. Induction work. The initial weeks may be critical for building friendships, developing confidence and assuring success.

   (i) *Mapwork*:

   - Maps can be drawn to clarify the confusion of buildings, rooms or areas, many of which have unfamiliar or technical names. Routes to specific places can be plotted and coloured in, e.g. the way to the dining hall, games block or music room. Key places can be identified with appropriate drawings placed on the map, e.g. clothing drawn in the lost property area, typewriters in the main office, etc.
   - Key subject rooms can be located on the map and lists of necessary equipment which pupils need to take to the lesson marked in:

     Design and Technology: pens, compasses, set-squares, etc.;
     Cookery: apron, recipe book, pencil, etc.

   - In larger schools approximately 80 staff might be encountered in the first few weeks. Line drawings of relevant faces might be placed on the map – secretaries in the office and year tutors in their rooms, etc. A gallery of subject teachers can be displayed and cartoons of hierarchy figures can be drawn by older pupils and displayed. Children always poke fun but rarely at those who can laugh at themselves. Notices, photographs and posters all help a shy child find their way around.

(ii) Some schools have tried a befriender system where older, reliable pupils are paired with young rookies. This works best on a volunteer basis where the older pupils offer a commitment for the first two weeks, each being responsible for a few new entrants. Those new pupils most at risk should be allocated to the most suitable older pupils. A planned programme can offer opportunities for older pupils to talk in small groups to younger ones about problems such as being bullied.

(iii) Older pupils can be surveyed, by each other, to identify what they found most difficult to cope with in their early weeks in school. Suggestions for change can form the basis of a programme of helpful activities and tips and hints, preferably couched in humour, and can be included in the introductory booklet most schools send out to intending pupils.

(iv) *Friendship support.* Friendships cannot be made but careful pairing of children in class and for leisure activities might help. Proximity and familiarity offer fertile ground for friendships to emerge.

15. Communication

(i) Good lines of communication need to be laid down well in advance of problems occurring:

- teachers with teachers;
- teachers with pupils;
- teachers with parents;
- teachers with all other agencies.

At inaugural meetings parents should be encouraged to contact the school if they are aware of any child at all in difficulties. Some children will tell their parents about others being bullied but not break the taboo on telling tales in school.

(ii) Communication skills can be developed in school in many ways. Pikas (1987a, b) believes that better communication contributes to better relationships and interactions. He proposes seven steps:

(a) Creating motivation. Pupils need to realize that they can solve their problems if they communicate better.

(b) Agreeing upon the value of communication. Pupils discuss how they can improve their communication skills.

(c) Practice. Groups of three are formed – a sender, a receiver and an observer:

- the sender speaks to the receiver;
- the receiver repeats the message back to the sender;
- the sender corrects the version if necessary;
- the observer comments on the exchange.

(d) Discussion:

- How can bad communication be improved?
- How to listen to others.
- Discussion of the role of non-verbal communication.
- Discussion of the role of incomplete communication and the difficulties this can cause.

(e) Discussion of how to put forward an opinion without upsetting others.

(f) Communicating in conflict situations.

(g) Pupils try out the strategies on their own without a teacher present.

(iii) There are many other opportunities for enhancing communication skills:

- The National Oracy Project offers encouragement to schools to consider the value of oral communication.
- Problem-solving work and cooperative learning programmes offer scope for discussion.
- More emphasis is now being placed on the language teachers use in the classroom, e.g. how the quality of questions posed by the teacher can encourage or cramp the learning process.
- Teachers are directing their own role more to listening than talking.
- There are many games and activities which encourage clear communication. Recent initiatives include mediation where a peer helps restore a conflict by listening and feeding back to the antagonists what they are really saying to each other.

16. Research. Small-scale research can be undertaken by pupils or staff to identify:

- high-risk areas and times;
- major anxieties and concerns;
- timetable difficulties.

One way of observing the functioning of the school from the perception of the pupil is by undertaking a pupil pursuit study. One or more pupils are followed, with their knowledge, for a day or longer. The experiences they encounter with the curriculum, in the playground, or waiting in corridors, can prove enlightening. Any work of this kind needs to be sensitively designed so that surveys and sociograms, for example, do not relate directly to bullying or highlight the friendless state or unpopularity of any child.

17. Community work. Pupils may develop the skills of responsibility, empathy and reciprocity from working in the community and offering their services to those in need.

18. Training. Training in child care is offered in some schools to the older pupils, both boys and girls. Workshops for parents can prepare them for problems such as bullying and offer strategies for them to use to help their children. Parents can be enlisted to encourage their children to take responsibility for others.

19. Within the classroom situation. Is the teacher in full control of the class? In a disruptive situation the teacher may be the victim and other more vulnerable pupils be at risk from bullies. Confident staff will readily admit to frustration but an inexperienced teacher may feel too defensive to admit openly to disciplinary difficulties.

    (i) *School support.* Teachers under stress could be offered support through:

    - timetable rearrangements;
    - an alteration in the composition of groups;
    - a withdrawal system for crises operated by senior staff;
    - in-service training to offer new insights;
    - an observer in the classroom on a pretext could discern and analyse the social groupings, relationships and reactions even if the actual bullying remains unseen.

    (ii) *Deflect and diffuse.* It may be necessary to confront a bully but it is usually advisable to do this in private. Incidents need to be acknowledged immediately, otherwise it may seem that the teacher is condoning the bullying, but by deflecting the attention of the group or diffusing the crisis with humour or firm comment, the class could be deprived of the free entertainment they may have been anticipating, even encouraging. With no feedback from the group the bully may lose motivation for the attacks. If low-key verbal abuse or physical provocation is allowed to continue the bullying could become an established habit.

(iii) *Classroom organization*. Recently there have been conflicting views about classroom organization. If the aim is social grouping, interaction and collaboration, then proximity of work areas, tables, the sharing of books and equipment is ideal. For maximum concentration on task and work output well spaced out desks are deemed preferable by some educationalists. It is often worthwhile experimenting with the seating arrangements so that the pupils are best placed for the task:

- windows on either inside or outside walls are distracting;
- wide aisles give unimpeded movement;
- good visibility of board and equipment helps concentration;
- it is easier to scan the room from the back;
- the allocation of desks can prevent arguments at the start of each lesson, and can provide opportunities for compatible children to be placed next to vulnerable classmates. This could encourage a friendship and distance those at risk from the bullies.

(iv) *Routines*:

- The class could be met at the door. The old technique of pupils standing behind their desks until the teacher is ready gives an opportunity for all to calm down and offers a transition period between playtime and lessons.
- A clear signal that the lesson is to begin gives cues about the behaviour which will be expected.
- A routine for dismissal can avoid a stampede in the corridor.
- If a class regularly enters in a difficult mood it may be beneficial to note the previous activity – a lesson or a playtime – and consider whether a timetable adjustment or a buffer period or activity would help to calm the class down.
- The physical position of the teacher could be influential. Walking around the room and speaking from the back and sides not only helps give a feeling of cohesion to the group but also puts the teacher in

a position to spot trouble at the outset. Standing beside a pupil can be a calming influence. This does not disturb the pace and flow of the lesson.

● When a teacher is standing, he or she is in a position of command and some pupils prefer this because it lends an air of security and control and indicates a commitment and involvement.

● A technique which is practised by experienced teachers is the skill of indicating with a tilt of the head or brief eye contact that they are attending to an individual child while they are keeping a firm eye on the rest of the class.

● Both the teacher's and the pupils' books and materials need to be to hand. Fumbling in desks and cupboards loses eye contact, pace and control.

(v) *The delivery of lessons.* Good subject matter can be ruined by unprofessional delivery. Posture, gesture, voice articulation, range and expression are all important and can add interest and an air of confidence. Instructions should be simple and brief and varied i.e. written, spoken, diagrams, recorded on tape or video. Each phase of the lesson should be signalled and appropriate behaviour requested. Work should be in keeping with the needs of each pupil and texts checked for readability levels. Presentation should be varied and demands wide-ranging.

In summary, there is a great deal of accumulated teaching experience in schools which could be collated and used through supportive work undertaken in staff discussion groups.

8
Protection

Self-protection

Any child can be at risk from bullies. It is best to warn and advise them on how to cope well in advance:

1. To be alone is to be vulnerable; stick with the group and never be last to leave, especially isolated buildings or rooms.
2. Stay in sight of peers and adults when possible.
3. Crying, yelling and running away gives free entertainment. Look the bully in the eye, stand up straight and try to look confident. Walk quietly and confidently away.
4. Try not to show any temper reactions. Stay calm.
5. Speak slowly, clearly and firmly.
6. Think about arriving earlier, later or choosing a different route.
7. Leave expensive items at home, and do not brag about possessions or money. If you are asked to lend someone an expensive item try to make an excuse, e.g. say that your parents check you take it home. If it is forced from you or you feel you cannot refuse, do not fight to get it back. Tell an adult the truth and ask for help.
8. If you have a nickname you hate or you are called names try to get used to it. Do not be afraid to laugh at yourself. Try to make jokes and shrug off casual taunts. If you are amusing you may become popular.
9. Are you being provoking? Could you alter your behaviour in any way?
10. If you are being bullied ask a friend to accompany you. This may break the habit.
11. Always tell someone, preferably an adult. Explain carefully if you are afraid and ask for help. This is not telling tales. If the bully is not stopped a younger person may be the next victim. Lots of small incidents may get you down so tell the adult how long it has been going on and exactly what is

happening. Most people have been bullied at some time so do not be ashamed.

12. Rehearse walking away, keeping calm and laughing off taunts at home.

Warning signs

Children being bullied could be under considerable stress and indicate this by behaving in a way which is out of character. The following are some common warning signs of anxiety or stress. If several are present it would be advisable for parents to approach the school, or for the school to contact parents, to express concern.

Anxious children may show the following signs:

- bed-wetting;
- nail biting;
- nervous tics;
- night terrors;
- sleep walking;
- flinching, jumpiness, forgetfulness, distractibility;
- underachievement;
- personality change – snappy, withdrawn, tired, indications of not sleeping, weepiness, outbursts of crying, loss of appetite;
- demands for extra money;
- school refusal;
- wish to change routines, routes to school, school bus;
- lack of confidence, withdrawal from social activities;
- temper flare-ups, abusive language, impulsive hitting out;
- late for school, hanging back, staying behind late at school;
- 'mislaid' books, equipment, belongings;
- torn and damaged clothing and belongings;
- bruises and cuts;
- fear of the dark, of sudden noises, of physical contact with others (bullied children may even cross the street rather than approach any group of people);
- avoidance of specific lessons or days, e.g. games, swimming;
- psychosomatic illnesses, non-specific pains, headaches, tummy upsets.

Analysis

Is it really bullying?

The first thing to establish is whether or not the problem is one of bullying or whether the cause lies elsewhere. There may be quite a different problem underlying a false accusation of bullying.

1. A child who is reluctant to attend school, or shows other signs of stress, may claim to have been bullied in order to draw adult attention to some other worrying situation. Bullying is a label familiar to all and could be used by a child to label some indeterminate anxiety. Young people sometimes find it difficult to identify and discuss emotional problems and concerns such as parental disharmony, social rejection or fears of academic failure. The feelings of confusion, bewilderment or shame may be too diffuse for a child to pinpoint. The desired attention from adults may be gained by false claims of being bullied.

2. Children claiming to be afraid of attending school because of bullying may have no realistic concerns about what lies in wait in school but be intensely worried about the home situation. Rather than being afraid to go to school, they are afraid to leave home. This may be because of a parent threatening to leave home, illness in the family or jealousy of a new sibling.

3. Concerns and anxieties of all kinds may make a child more vulnerable to the normal rough and tumble of school life. Trivial incidents may be blown up out of all proportion by a worried child who has misread a situation while under stress.

4. Individual, trivial incidents, perhaps not in themselves severe enough to be classed as bullying, if reported frequently, should not be ignored or hurriedly dismissed, because the provocation over time could build up into a distressing climax.

5. Adults may be unaware of the effect on a child of such sweeping threats as 'We're going to kill you', or be unaware of the significance of taunts relating to the subculture of the group. Such threats may assume alarming proportions when the child is in bed, alone at night. The child may intellectually know that this is an unrealistic threat but still react badly on the emotional level. Even the victim may be unaware as to how traumatic the experience has been until the emotional repercussions indicate the level of stress engendered.

It is important to consider not only whether the reported action warrants the label bullying, but to try to estimate the effect it has had upon the child. If not taken to task the bully could continue, unaware of the effect of the seemingly trivial acts upon a vulnerable child.

The dangers of false accusations need to be explained to any child making them for whatever reason. It could mean that help is not forthcoming in the future when there may be genuine need and the social implications of falsely accusing others needs to be explored. If bullying is suspected:

1. Look for the warning signs (see p. 132).
2. Ask all staff to supervise carefully because the incidents may be occurring in specific situations.
3. Is the child isolated? Sociograms could identify this.
4. Contact parents and unobtrusively seek information from classmates.
5. Have an observer in class situations where bullying is suspected on a pretext.
6. Seek information widely: local shops, traffic personnel, school bus personnel.
7. Contact the previous school and other agencies, such as the education welfare officer.
8. Many cases come to light in discussions in class on the topic of bullying (see pp. 119–21).

Who, what, why, where, when?

Ingenuity and detective work may be required to unearth the details. The victims may not tell because of:

● fear of reprisals;
● the shame, humiliation, degradation suffered;
● an inability to perceive how to go about changing the situation due to low self-esteem and feelings of helplessness;
● an unwillingness to publicize their unpopularity;
● an inability to explain due to emotional or intellectual constraints; perhaps too confused, afraid or upset;
● an inability to perceive actions such as teasing, extortion, social ostracism, intimidation as bullying;
● by seeking help it will confirm the taunts of being incompetent, a baby or stupid, and so they will lose the respect of parents and staff by their inability to cope;
● the bully may claim it is only a game but it must be stressed that *a game is enjoyed by all participants!*
● victims may feel this is their lot in life, especially if they have little self-esteem;
● no confidence in the adult's ability to help.

The peer group may not tell because of:

● fear of reprisals;
● wariness of attracting the unwanted attention of the bully to themselves;

- the unwritten code about telling tales;
- an insensitivity to the distress the bullying is causing, because any one child may only witness an occasional incident;
- even the peer group may be unaware of what is happening;
- a previous experience of adults being unwilling or unable to help.

Analysis of the group

A diagram of all collated information could be useful to find out who is bullying who:

- a group bullying a group;
- a child bullying a group;
- a group bullying a child;
- a child bullying a child.

Who is the leader if it is a group?

There may be a hidden leader, a provocateur, whereas another child may erroneously consider him/herself as leader and take the blame. Is the leader using the group as a smoke screen to avoid identification or punishment? It may seem like a group activity but in reality be the intent of only one child who is covertly manipulating the group. I have identified hidden leaders when videoing classes for other purposes. Older children may volunteer information in general discussions about school life.

Analysis of the pattern of events

A record of days, lessons, exit and entry times and break times could indicate a pattern. Consulting the timetable could throw light on the incidents because a change in programme could have resulted in the targeted child being without supportive friends in class or when walking alone between lessons. An investigation of routes to school, travelling companions, etc., may offer clues. There may have been a trigger incident which has resulted in the attacks.

Contact with home

Information should be sought concerning family affairs which could be relevant. The net for information may need to be cast widely and parental permission sought to contact such agencies as the family doctor, education welfare service, or social worker. Information from such sources may previously have seemed irrelevant until viewed in the context of bullying. Parents need to be assured immediately that the matter is being taken seriously and an investigation is in progress.

Observation work

Has the whole of the incident been observed and understood? It is easy to misperceive an incident of bullying, both in the observation and the understanding. Teachers in charge of large, busy classes may not see the whole of a bullying incident, their attention being drawn only to the latter part, the retaliation of the victim to a previous attack:

- the victim could have been subjected to an onslaught of thumps, his/her equipment snatched or books damaged;
- the bully may have made a premeditated attack by carefully choosing a moment when the attention of the teacher was diverted;
- the surprise or stress of the provocation may have elicited a spontaneous reaction from the victim, such as a yell or retaliatory attack.

The teacher and the rest of the class are more likely, therefore, to witness the spontaneous retaliation than the original provocative act of the bully. The primary provocation being premeditated goes undetected, but the spontaneous secondary reaction is observed. If the victim is chastised this could encourage the bully by adding to the fun. The victim, however, could become labelled as provocative and annoying due to misperception and erroneous judgement, although there may be some justification for this opinion in some cases.

The role of the teacher in such cases is to observe carefully and try to identify the antecedent behaviours to the reaction.

A child subjected to prolonged bullying can develop a defence strategy to cope, but may use one which is maladaptive and causes further difficulties:

1. The victim may try to hit out first before others get the chance to attack.
2. In a bid for help, or in distress, self-mutilating acts may be adopted – pulling out hair, severe nail biting, scratching skin, or clothing and equipment could be destroyed.
3. A supportive gang could be enticed to aid and abet the bullying of those who are even weaker.

In this way the victim could be considered the bully, whereas, in fact, the child remains vulnerable. Any bullying needs to be seen in the full context of the home, school and neighbourhood environments, in addition to the past social behaviour of the child.

Identifying the rationale for the bullying

What is it in the interaction between the bully and victim which has triggered or is sustaining the bullying?

The role of the victim

1. Many victims are popular within their group and are socially well adjusted, but are targeted simply because they have been in the wrong place at the wrong time.
2. Some children seem to set out deliberately to provoke the bullying, accepting this behaviour in preference to being ignored.
3. The bullying may stem from mild teasing which has been in the spirit of fun but then got out of hand without the victim realizing it.
4. The victim may have encouraged the attacks in order to get the bully into trouble so that, in reality, they are the bullies.
5. Provocative children may allow this behaviour so as to gain the sympathy and attention of the rest of the group in an inappropriate bid for acceptance.
6. A small group of children have emotional problems such that they experience feelings of guilt which require them to be punished.
7. There may be a stoical acceptance of the role.
8. Children who are small, weak and lacking in confidence when with their peers, may gain the confidence to bully when in the company of younger children. This could depend on their own attitude to the use of aggression.

The role of the bullies

1. Many bullies appear to adhere to a code of conduct which allows the use of aggression, in whatever form. This is acceptable within their own circle of family and friends. They may have witnessed violence at home or been bullied themselves.
2. Some bullies may be using their bullying as a means of gaining some degree of prestige to boost their poor self-image and -confidence.

3. These children may not intentionally set out to cause distress to others but do so due to inappropriate social behaviour.
4. Bullies feeling on the periphery of the group may make an over-boisterous and forceful approach to gain entry, which could be frightening to those who are less robust.
5. The distinction between leadership and dominance is subtle so that children may erroneously consider themselves leaders when, in fact, they are simply dominating the group. Such children may not be disliked by the majority, they may provide fun and entertainment, and may be encouraged by others to escalate the bullying, but this could be at the expense of those less popular.
6. The antics of the bullies, the wit and sarcasm which may be used, may be entertaining for the group and gain desired acclaim and kudos for the bullies but leave the target child humiliated and distressed.
7. From the early days children, especially boys, tussle and tumble about in play fights. These experiences offer a realistic assessment of physical skill and prowess. Later, this extends to academic, social and sporting success. This competitive attitude may be taken too seriously and cause distress to others.
8. The bully may be receiving encouragement from the group.
9. The bullies may be identifying and targeting those who display similar failings to themselves, the rationale being that this puts their own faults into perspective. By doing this they are able to show that their own deficiencies are common to many and, by convincing others that the victim has even more pronounced faults, their own failings become minimized.
10 The bullying could stem from a thoughtless attitude on the part of the bully to whom the attacks could seem trivial and inconsequential.

Once the victim is identified

● the victim is identified as vulnerable;
● this becomes public by the intent of the culprit or by others witnessing the futile attempts of the victim at self-defence;
● the role of the victim is firmly allotted;
● this gives permission for anyone to make a casual attack of any kind;
● the situation is then open for mobbing to occur;
● those who would have supported the victim drift away;
● the victim is pushed further onto the periphery of the group, so becoming more vulnerable to attack.

From a careless, insensitive action on the part of the bully, a victim can quickly be reduced to a prolonged period of attack, attacks from a number of children and a constant fear of mobbing, all of which can add up to intolerable stress. The original attacker may have left the situation and be quite unaware of the trouble left in his or her wake.

The response of the teacher

Staff need to examine their own responses to bullying incidents, or the suspicion of such, with care, because any indication of a lack of support to the victim could be read by others as permission for further attacks. Young people often look to adults as models and seek from them indications as to how to behave. The reactions and attitudes of teachers can subtly escalate a troublesome situation. Conversely, an over-sympathetic approach towards the victim could alienate the group and make matters worse. A child scorned by peers could find superfluous pity and ineffectual action from adults even more difficult to bear:

1. There must be a fast and unambiguous response from the staff.
2. A harsh or over-punitive response could result in the bullies modelling the behaviour or becoming vindictive towards the teacher or victim.
3. Incidents of bullying may come to light while the class is in progress. These can be dealt with by confrontation or by deflection. Incidents need to be dealt with, because to ignore them may be interpreted as giving permission; however, confrontation best takes place after class when the teacher is well prepared. Unnecessary confrontation in front of the group may offer free entertainment to the class and encourage the bully. Provocation and taunts may become habitual and need to be stopped promptly, but it is better to diffuse the situation in class first and tackle the issue later.
4. Staff who are not teaching, perhaps in their preparation time, could help in a situation where bullying is suspected by observing and analysing incidents in class. An observer in the room, on a pretext, could analyse the social groupings, relationships and reactions even if the bullying remains hidden.
5. The problem must be brought out in the open because it thrives on secrecy and often fades when discovered and discussed.
6. If the teacher has a good rapport with the pupils, class discussions, held in registration time or within the Personal,

Social and Moral Education curriculum, on the problems of personal relationships could be one way of bringing about the necessary changes in attitude. Peer disapproval can be potent and the opportunity can be taken to ensure that everyone in the group understands that they have a responsiblity to each other.

7. Relaxation techniques can help both the bully and the victim.
8. One of the most effective and economical ways of bringing about changes in behaviour is by working with parents. The home situation can offer many rewards – watching TV, extended bedtimes, favourite food, etc. There are usually more opportunities for rewards to be taken at home than in school, so that a reward system operated in conjunction with home, with the support of the parents, could be to the advantage of all concerned.
9. Opportunities for working and interacting with other pupils should be encouraged. Children who have been isolated for some time may need strong incentives to attend group meetings – tokens, gifts, prizes, guest speakers, outings or equipment could entice them to attend. If asked to stay behind in school for an activity, care must be taken that the children are not being put at risk of attack.

Suggestions for working with parents in helping children to feel comfortable in groups are given in Chapter 9.

The unpopular victim

The victim could be a child struggling to come to terms with an emotional problem. A child in such a situation might present a variety of annoying or distressing behaviours which are associated with an insecure or compensating personality. These outward behaviours, manifestations of deeper trouble, do not always endear the child to others. Outbursts of temper, boastful and compensatory claims, aggressive or provocative moods are not engaging. These children need to be understood to gain tolerance and affection from others. These behaviours may be in high profile, aggravating and disruptive, or simple stress habits such as rocking, fidgeting or chattering.

The reaction of the teacher could encourage others to notice and poke fun or to ignore and offer support and confidence to the troubled child:

1. The teacher may subconsciously transfer feelings of irritation to the group, so giving a green light to the bullies.

2. The peer group might need little encouragement to provoke an unpopular child.
3. The anxiety symptoms may have arisen because of bullying but, in any case, further stress will cause them to escalate and the situation to worsen.
4. The behaviour, especially temper tantrums, might be entertaining to others and provide a welcome release from work. Such interruptions could be covertly maintained, the group provoking the unwitting victim.
5. The frequent cues and reprimands needed by such a child could halt the flow of a lesson. This is irksome in a well-controlled lesson but can be disastrous where the teacher has only tenuous control over the group. A more robust and dominant child could be allowed to control the troublesome victim but to allow another child to assume such a role is to exacerbate an already stressful situation.
6. The victim may be provoking others by assuming the role of class clown in a bid for acceptance. The situation needs to be examined carefully because this may be tolerated in the safety of the classroom but the victim may be at risk outside the class.
7. Intelligent children may take on a more subtle role as victim by choosing to merge with those of lesser ability in order to be considered one of the gang. This offers the protection of the gang.
8. Jokes and nicknames used by teachers may seem witty and humorous in class but be picked up and used *ad nauseam* or exaggerated cruelly in the playground.
9. Not all teachers can work with all children. Circumstances found to be intolerable need to be admitted to and altered before the situation causes distress to all.
10. A teacher may innocently assume the role of bully. Group reprimands are rarely effective, because the diluted effect is lost on the culprits, yet those least in need of chastisement may react badly and become afraid of the teacher.

Programme of work with the victim

It must be stressed that some victims of bullying may endure a great deal of taunting and aggression, yet they are able to cope. The effect the bullying is having on the victim is the important factor, and the severity of the incidents needs to be seen in the full context of the situation.

Any programme of work needs to be planned carefully so that the attitudes and responses of the group are altered, if necessary, in parallel with the targeted change in the bully and victim:

1. There are simple strategies children can learn to safeguard themselves (see pp. 131–2). Some rehearsal at home or school would be useful, such as practice in ignoring offensive nicknames.
2. The supervision of pupils may need to be tightened or reviewed (see pp. 113–14).
3. The child may be happier in another class or group.
4. To give immediate protection in free time the pupil could be offered a job or function, e.g. library work, tidying the craft room, setting up computers, sorting games equipment. It is important to ensure that the area is not isolated and is covered by adequate supervision. This type of strategy could help in a number of ways by:

● encouraging or stimulating a new interest or hobby;
● developing a skill which could help to ease the pupil into groups;
● offering a degree of acceptance or kudos within the group by demonstrating a skill;
● providing a release from a stressful situation;
● providing time for the victim to recover confidence, build inner resources and to maximize potential strengths;
● breaking the habit of provocation;
● bringing relief from a conspicuously isolated and friendless state.

This is recommended as a *temporary measure* only, because the long-term aim must be to integrate the victim into the group.

Minders

A more robust or older pupil can be cast in the role of observer or companion. This too should only be a temporary measure but can be most effective by offering:

● information about incidents;
● protection;
● a break in routine so that a habit may be broken;
● an experience of friendship.

It may be advisable for this to be accomplished without the knowledge of the victim, especially if an older pupil is supporting the child in this way.

Big brother

A similar strategy which could be used is to encourage an older pupil, one with kudos and commanding respect, to befriend the victim. Only an occasional word may be required from the older pupil to the victim, merely a greeting, but it must take place in the presence of the bullying children. It soon becomes known that the victim has 'friends in high places' which acts as a deterrent. The attention of the older pupil has designated the victim worthy of attention and confidence and self-esteem can be boosted in this way. The older pupil is merely replacing the older sibling or acquaintance many children have in school but which the victim may be lacking. If this older pupil is chosen with a genuine rationale in mind, such as a mutual interest in sport or chess, then previously unnoticed strengths of the victim might be highlighted in an acceptable way.

A similar scheme has been used in the USA by social agencies where older boys are allocated to single-parent families, where circumstances preclude the youngsters from gaining appropriate social experiences. The volunteer acts in the role of the older brother and offers a range of opportunities to the younger boys:

● to enjoy social outings;
● to increase strengths and skills;
● to increase self-confidence and -esteem;
● to model coping strategies;
● to copy social behaviour such as entering and interacting in groups.

Specific, goal-related counselling work, both individual and group work can help. Preferably, this should be offered until the victim becomes confident in social settings, not merely in the crisis of the bullying.

Assimilating the victim into the group

Once allocated the role of victim it becomes difficult for the child to be assimilated into the group even when the bullying has stopped. A carefully designed programme of work is necessary before the child is able to interact socially with confidence. The full context of the situation needs careful consideration:

1. Has the victim been maintaining the bullying for any reason?
2. What will be the position of the victim once the bullying has stopped?
3. Will the bullying be replaced by some other difficulty?

4. Was the victim functioning well socially previous to the onset of the bullying?
5. It is imperative that the programme of work is planned in two stages: (i) to stop the bullying; (ii) to ensure the child is functioning appropriately socially. Merely stopping the bullying is leaving the job half done.

The work may be most effectively carried out if a change in attitude can be brought about in the victim, the bully, and the peer group. Without some degree of change in all three in parallel there could be only superficial and temporary change. The main aims of the programme of work with the victim could be to increase confidence and self-esteem, highlight strengths, and elicit and encourage skills.

Groups

If there are several isolated children in school but no suitable interest groups already in existence, it should be possible to form an eclectic group of pupils with a variety of interests and a wide range of personalities. Each child can follow an interest in parallel with others but share supervision, space, time and equipment. Parents can contribute to supervisory duties. Children with social difficulties are offered the most support and guidance, yet they are not necessarily aware that the group has a training function. In this way there is little danger that their problems will be highlighted.

Working in conjunction with parents

It may be advantageous to work with parents who can not only support the work of the school but help in ways not otherwise available. The two parties may not work together simultaneously but share a common goal, continue reliable feedback and offer mutual support. Lonely children may be depressed and feel helpless to alter their situation. Children who have had adverse experiences with peers may have little enthusiasm for seeking new relationships. If the child has been excluded from friendships for a considerable time:

- they may be unaware of the expectations, commitments and mores of group interactions which may need to be discussed and practised;
- there may have been a simple reason for the exclusion of the child which can be easily remedied.

Parents of children who find it difficult to make friends may find that to foster appropriate friendships they need to offer:

- *time:* chauffeuring, supervision;
- *energy:* organization, entertainment;
- *money:* trips, fashionable clothes, sport, equipment;

to help ease their child into a position of acceptance. This is not 'buying' friendship but should be regarded in the same light as those parents who invest effort and money in their child's academic success.

A programme of work

The aim is to integrate the child, as soon as is comfortable, into the peer group. To push isolated children into a club or disco will only display their friendless state and social rejection to all. The programme is only an outline and needs to be adapted according to individual needs and progress.

1. *The peer group.* Social confidence and ease can be gained by children initially working alone but in communication with others: CB radio, fan clubs, correspondence (e.g. chess, penpal), voluntary work (e.g. hospital radio, library work), or working with animals or plants.
2. *Mixed group.* This could lead to a special interest or hobby which could be pursued in a group where children work in parallel rather than in full interaction with others. A skill-based group is less threatening than a social group:

computers	music	weight training
evening classes	self-defence	stamp club
craft, woodwork	dance classes	art classes
dog training	flower arranging	dress making

Such activities offer some degree of social interaction, but from a position of safety as participants may choose how and when they become involved with others. Strong structures and adult support are needed at this stage. The opportunities to be gained include:

- experimenting with safe social settings;
- the chance to practise and increase skills and techniques which could help one's self-image, -confidence and -esteem;
- companionship and friendship;
- an exchange of ideas and information.

3. *Adult groups.* Introductory groups at which parents accompany their children encourage younger children to
become members of clubs, e.g. dance, dog handling, chess, or
photography. The advantages of this are:

   (a) Once a skill is learned, confidence increases.
   (b) A new skill can increase kudos, e.g. car maintenance.
   (c) As the emphasis is on learning techniques there should be
   less emphasis on social interactions than in a casual peer
   group setting.
   (d) The adult is able to observe the social behaviour of the
   child which can be enlightening.
   (e) A shared interest between parent and child is the basis of a
   more supportive relationship.
   (f) The child can try out approach behaviours towards others
   in the supportive presence of their parents.
   (g) Children often respond better to adults other than their
   parents in a learning situation.

4. *Regular groups.* As soon as possible these children should be
eased into regular groups supported by adults: school,
church, community, disco, quiz nights. An older child may be
willing to accompany them initially if appropriate. Any skill
the child can display, unobtrusively, can be used to gain
validity of purpose within the group such as offering:

   ● *a service:* sell tickets, make coffee, keep scores, buy supplies;
   ● *a talent:* accounts, posters, music, costumes, photography;
   ● *enthusiasm:* organize trips, guest speakers, draw up rotas.
   ● *hard work:* tidy, fetch and carry, make refreshments.

5. *Public groups.* The final stage will be to attempt entry to fully
independent groups such as a public disco, party, or sports
club.

Other techniques and ideas

1. Defence classes or weight training sessions have been found
useful by some children. Isolated and vulnerable children
rarely misuse such skills, but confidence can be increased with
the acquisition of such skills.
2. A pet, especially one which would unfailingly give an enthusi-
astic welcome and demonstration of affection, may help to
boost a child's self-image and -esteem, in addition to providing
companionship and a rationale for getting out of doors. Any
pet, however, requires a commitment and, therefore, it could
be an advantage to borrow one from friends for a while to see
if it is compatible with the family life-style.

3. The school may be able to suggest a compatible child who could be invited home. Children who are without friends may be reluctant to approach anyone with an invitation.
4. An older child in the neighbourhood may accompany the lonely child to clubs or meetings, initially in the role of older brother.

In summary, neither parents nor teachers are able to make friends for an isolated child but proximity and familiarity do help, so that by providing opportunities for friendships they are supporting the child in several ways.

All parents of children in school should be alerted to the needs of those children who have social difficulties and they should be encouraged to include them in activities. Because these children are often excluded, whether they are victims or bullies, they do not gain the relevant experience to improve.

Programme of work with the bully

The bully may be a victim in other circumstances or a sad and lonely child for other reasons, but any child bullying others must first be made to understand the seriousness of their actions and attitudes. Most bullying behaviour has been learned and so the approach should centre around it being unlearned. The aim of the work with bullying children needs to be three-fold:

1. These children need to understand and accept that a code of conduct which allows aggressive behaviour, in whatever form, is not allowed.
2. Appropriate social behaviour may need to be introduced because it may not be in the exisiting repertoire of these children.
3. Attempts need to be made to alter the attitude of bullying children towards others so that a better understanding of the feelings, strengths and behaviour of other people is developed.

Rewards for appropriate social behaviour can be given – perhaps this is most effective when all the members of a group keep a record of good behaviour and all gain a reward at the end of the week. This takes the spotlight off the bully and victim and introduces peer pressure so that all group members support each other.

The work programme needs to cover two areas: supervision and sanctions, and the development of appropriate social be-haviour. The parents of children who bully others need to be informed of the situation even though they may be distressed and confused. They may have been aware of the behaviour but felt too ashamed or embarrassed to approach the school for help. Depending on their response it may be necessary to make them aware of the seriousness of the situation and possible repercussions made explicit. The position of the school and the local authority should be stressed if the problem continues after an initial warning.

At an initial meeting the school policy should be reaffirmed in front of the parents and child and possible sanctions outlined. No one should be left in any doubt that the situation will be monitored closely. The parents may have unintentionally condoned or maintained the behaviour by:

1. Optimistically hoping the behaviour would pass.
2. Over-emphasizing self-protection, which could be misinterpreted as permission to be dominant.
3. Over-emphasizing success, which could cause tension and strain.
4. Giving conflicting messages such as 'If you hit others I'll hit you', so giving a model of aggression.
5. Admiring physically dominant culture and media models which children can copy.
6. Allowing other family members to be dominant so that the child develops a subservient attitude and loss of confidence or, conversely, models the aggressive behaviour.

Parents who show concern and who are anxious for support could work in partnership with the school. Some parents are ashamed of the behaviour of their child and are eager for help and advice. They may be able to alleviate the situation through explanation and discussion. In many ways they can mirror the work carried out in school:

1. Boisterous and agile children may be unaware of how threatening and painful their attacks are on a weaker child, especially if the child is the same age or size but less physically or emotionally robust. They need to be made aware of how their actions are received.
2. Children may not consider verbal taunts and jibes or social ostracism as bullying, and think only physical attacks hurtful and worthy of complaint.
3. Bullying children may be unaware that others continue the taunting in their absence so that the victim suffers numerous attacks, becomes fearful of mobbing and demoralized or terrified over time.

4. Bullying children may have a poor self-image, which results in them seeking out a weaker child with similar problems to put their own into a better perspective.
5. Bullying children may confuse leadership with dominance and be surprised that others are afraid of their manner.
6. The bullying may only be an inappropriate attempt to secure friends or group membership.
7. Adopted media models may be discussed and more appropriate heroes encouraged.

An exuberant child should be introduced to a wider variety of sports, hobbies and interests. Modelling is a well-tried technique where a child is attached to an older child or adult so that they can copy more appropriate behaviour. This is most effective when the model is of the same sex, admired by the child and a pertinent discussion takes place throughout.

Many bullies cease their activities abruptly once taken to task and made aware of the effect of their behaviour. Any work the parents can do to expedite an end to the bullying will not only help the victim but be of advantage to the bullying child in preventing complex repercussions and side-effects from developing.

Programme of work with the bully and victim together

Bullying is a two-sided problem and, therefore, any remedy can be approached in this way. Whether this is feasible or not will depend on the attitude of the bully. A calm, unemotional, problem-solving approach may be best. Try to provide the problem as an intellectual challenge which both the victim and bully can meet, avoiding any apportioning of sympathy or blame. Aim for a solution agreeable to both parties.

Altering the behaviour

1. Elicit suggestions from both children for targets for change and a suitable programme of work.
2. Make a list of behaviours that need changing and put them in order of priority. Aim for a balanced approach so that change comes from both the victim (try to stop a sniffing habit) and the bully (be more tolerant).
3. Attempt a written contract involving both parties.
4. Reward both children for any improvement (the bullying may have been very rewarding).
5. Shape up the behaviour gradually from near approximations to the desired behaviour.

Altering the attitudes

1. Ensure the bully knows the effect the behaviour is having on the victim, if this is appropriate:

   ● the victim's constant sniffing is due to hay fever;
   ● the victim's irritating clumsiness is not due to carelessness.

2. Encourage the bully to identify and discuss the irritating behaviour.
3. Pinpoint the strengths and skills of each child. Encourage them to identify these in each other.
4. Is the bully compensating for some feeling of inadequacy? Was the bullying done for fun and entertainment?

Friendship

1. Familiarity does not necessarily breed contempt. Could the bully and victim work together in any way? (e.g. in a pair for science or on the same team in games?).
2. Never put the bully and victim on opposing teams or in competition with each other. Always give them a common goal or target.
3. Explore the possibility of parents encouraging exchange home visits, mutual activities, or joint visits to clubs where adults could offer support.

Many young people find verbalizing emotions and problems very difficult so that non-verbal techniques could facilitate communication. A silent uncommunicative child may be unable to recognize and identify emotions or find it too shameful to discuss the bullying behaviour. Cartoons, diagrams, videos and diaries may be useful for this type of work.

Work with the bullying group

It may be necessary to break up the cohesion of the group. This is best done in as subtle a manner as possible by choosing a pretext with care. It would be unwise to split the group openly or to punish the group as a whole as this could:

● offer the group an enhanced identity;
● cement the cohesion;
● result in reprisals;
● alter the attacks from physical to verbal;
● lead to a different child being bullied.

The group needs to adjust to living amicably with others. Consider why the members allowed themselves to be enlisted in this way. Who is the leader and what is encouraging the leader to bully? It may be profitable to look outside the school for answers.

Record keeping

1. Record all observations and reports of incidents to seek out a pattern of events.
2. Continue observations and supervision even after the bullying appears to have ended.
3. Seek proof that it has ended rather than passively assuming that all is well if no further reports are received. The bullying may have changed in character or be more effectively hidden. The victim may collude with the secrecy.
4. Check over a lengthy period of time because incidents may occur intermittently.
5. A different child may be targeted for the bullying.

Therefore, it is advisable to keep in close communication with all staff and the parents of the victim. The parents may still feel that the problem has not been fully resolved, or wonder if the situation in school is continuing to be satisfactory, but be hesitant to return to school.

Summary of school responses

1. Children involved in bullying may simply have been caught in an unfortunate situation, but if the bullying is prolonged it is likely that the bully and/or the victim has social difficulties.
2. The school needs to consider work on two levels:

   ● to stop the bullying; and
   ● preventative work, such as the early identification of children at risk, good supervision and help with social behaviour.

3. Bullies appear to have the strength, energy and communication skills necessary to enable them to attack others with confidence. The victims appear to be fearful and withdrawn.
4. The school needs to address the aggression of the bully, and the possible isolation and lack of confidence of the victim.
5. The causal factors would seem to be multifactorial, so a multidimensional approach is needed.

Table 7 Possible areas of work for individual cases

Changing attitudes	Behavioural work	Social confidence	Curriculum work
Changing the attitude of: bully(ies), victim(s), staff, parents, peers, the community. To develop a sense of: – responsibility of all, for all – an awareness of the needs of others – an appreciation of individual differences – an appreciation of what others can offer	Behavioural programmes can be used to support the learning of more appropriate behaviour: with the victim(s), bully(ies), peer group. Success can be reinforced by use of appropriate rewards, especially praise. Targets need to be clearly defined and written contracts, monitoring and evaluation need to be planned. A problem solving approach may be more productive than a 'blame game' but sanctions may be necessary. Sensitive support given by the peer group can reinforce any appropriate responses	A hierarchy of groups can be used to encourage social confidence. 1. Adult groups are more tolerant than peer groups. 2. Groups teaching a skill take the emphasis off social skills. 3. Structured, supervised school groups can teach a skill or develop an aptitude to encourage confidence. 4. Public, peer groups e.g. disco, youth club, party should be attempted last. It is easier to enter a group with a definite function to perform e.g. collect fees, make refreshments. School cannot manufacture friendships but many opportunities can be provided.	Input into the personal, social and moral education programme. Co-operative styles of learning could be introduced. Problem solving techniques could be used. In-service training could be used; discussions, videos, surveys, workshops. Seating of pupils re social difficulties could be tried e.g. pairing, sharing etc. Alert school leavers to parenting skills for the future. Check on effective induction programmes. Drama can be an effective medium. General curriculum areas of history, politics, social studies can be a useful resource.

Analysis and observation work	Working with parents	Supervision	Counselling
Analyse the situation and interactions where bullying is suspected. Observe – who, what, why, when, where? Use all available personnel: staff, auxiliaries, para professionals, peers and older pupils. Use covert observation enlisting the support of colleagues in class. Collect data: sociograms, rep, grids, surveys, discussions. Is remediation necessary for: – academic skills? – physical skills? – social skills?	Offer immediate support and assurance that the matter is being taken seriously. Arrange dates for feedback. Offer a co-partnership role; design a programme together. Suggest parents teach the pupil a skill, encourage an interest, to develop confidence and self-esteem. Look at column 'Social confidence'. Discuss warning signs. Discuss protective strategies. Discuss family dynamics – role of extended family, siblings. Discuss neighbourhood attitudes. Encourage all parents to support all children e.g. friendless pupils. Use parent workshops to educate parents to problems such as bullying.	Check the quality of supervision, rotas, spot checks, out of school. Examine class control and management – encourage discussion and support groups. Ensure a firm school policy is in effective operation. Ensure sanctions and controls are effective. Seek funding for appropriate supervision and school buildings. Check communication links; parents, staff, pupils. Alert staff to target pupils, target spots. Mark target spots on map kept next to duty roster. Enlist older pupils for supervision or observation work.	Suggested topics for individual, group or class work: leadership, friendship, assertiveness, tolerance, skewed perceptions, self-esteem, confidence, reciprocity, responsibility, relaxation. Consider the stage of moral development of individual pupils. Consider the level of inner restraints and controls of individuals. Is there a discrepancy between school and neighbourhood values? Older pupils could chat to younger pupils in small groups on difficulties they have encountered e.g. bullying. A variety of stimulating materials can be used – videos, cartoons, graphs, diagrams, films, literature.

6. Why should the school help?
   - children in distress are unable to help themselves effectively;
   - they may not be aware of other ways of behaving;
   - the parents may not know how or want to help;
   - there are now fewer other sources of support available;
   - teachers have daily and long-term contact with the children;
   - the relationships in school may be the most stable that some children enjoy;
   - staff in school have the expertise and experience to help.

7. How can the school help? The school may be most effective if considered as an organizational complex which, as a result of factors within, may allow or deter a drift to problem behaviour; school variables may have more influence than social, familial, academic or other factors. However, if the school is unable to stop the bullying or the attacks are severe enough to be classed as common assault, the school or the parents may consider it appropriate to notify the police or seek legal advice.

9
Parents as partners

The advantages of a partnership

1. Children may react differently at home compared with school. By putting the two halves of the picture together, a better understanding of the child can be achieved.
2. When parents and staff work together, a small detail of personality or behaviour, previously disregarded may be noticed.
3. Parents often know their child best. They are aware of their strengths and weaknesses, achievements, hobbies and any Achilles' heel. This information is useful in both understanding the current situation and in identifying any rewards or reinforcement which may be considered for progress. Effective rewards need not necessarily be sweets, money or toys, and therefore they need to be chosen with care. There is often a greater variety of rewards available in the home, and therefore it might be better to offer rewards at home (later bedtimes, extra TV, etc.) which have been earned in school.
4. Parents who are anxious are often the most eager to see change, and so they offer the most commitment.
5. Anxiety can be reduced if parents feel that they are actively involved in remedying the situation.
6. Parents should offer information about any recent upset in the family which might be contributing to the child's distress.
7. Partnerships are useful to parents under stress when:

   ● they have no access to the culprit;
   ● they have no access to the situation where the bullying occurs;
   ● their help is shunned by the victim due to fear of reprisals.

8. Because there are more rewards available in the home than at school, it might be more beneficial for parents and staff to work together on a behavioural programme.

Figure 3   Emotions that may be experienced by the parents of a victim.

Keeping close contact

Parents who know that their child is being bullied at school, and who feel unable to help, may experience one of the most difficult aspects of parenthood (see Fig. 3). In some cases the parents feel as helpless as the child to effect any change. Parents of the bullies may also experience disturbing emotions – stigma, guilt, embarrassment and bewilderment. Depending on their attitude to the situation, they might need just as much support and guidance from the school.

Parents of victims, in particular, often feel uncertain and confused about what is happening:

1. If their child has reported little to them, the circumstances may be shrouded in mystery.

2. Anxiety and puzzlement may be experienced if the child has suddenly become tense and withdrawn for no apparent reason.
3. There may be anxiety about any unexplained regression in the child's behaviour or academic work.
4. If a first approach to school has been ineffective, the parents may be reluctant to return, yet feel ineffective themselves.
5. Interaction between parents and child may be less intimate during the adolescent years because:

- there is a growing and necessary feeling of independence on the part of the child;
- there is an increasing use of peer group models for guidance and approval, so that parents are no longer the primary point of reference;
- the moods and heightened emotions which can be part of adolescence can cause tension and friction in the home;
- older children may feel ashamed of not coping alone;
- children of any age often have a room of their own or share it with a sibling – equipped with TV, computer, record player, etc. This entertainment centre leaves little time for family contact;
- parents who work, or who have extra family responsibilities, may devote less time to an adolescent, whereas they may consider this essential with a younger child.

Any combination of the above may result in an anxious child keeping his/her symptoms hidden, thus allowing the situation to deteriorate. The pathways of family communication are often subtle and can easily fall into disuse. It is useful for parents to record the amount of time they and their child spend together, and the time spent by both parties interacting elsewhere.

Depending on the school's response to the approach of the parents, their anxiety could be increased or decreased:

- they may be made to feel at fault in some way, or feel that they are being accused of being over-protective if parents of the victim or having condoned the aggression if parents of the bully;
- they may feel that their judgement has been questioned regarding the seriousness of the incidents.

It is most disheartening to have at last discovered why a child is distressed or underachieving only to be met with a dismissive or negative response from the school. Parents need to be reassured immediately that the matter is being taken seriously and being dealt with urgently. A named person should be allocated to be responsible for keeping in contact with the home.

The parent–teacher interview

There should be a forum available where all viewpoints are represented, the situation is appraised and a plan of action adopted. It may be possible for both the parents of the victim and bully to be present at the same time; however, if their views are radically different, it would serve no useful purpose.

The meeting should be kept as informal as possible and a problem-solving approach should be adopted rather than allowing room for an overly emotional response. Parents should be advised of the meeting well in advance, so that their attention and observations may be focused appropriately. A brief and informal questionnaire helps to identify pertinent information, but this should not be filled in or handed back. The purpose of the questionnaire is simply to focus the thoughts of parents who may be distraught. The following questionnaire could be used, with modifications, for the parents of the victim or bully:

Sample questionnaire for parents

1. How long have you been aware of the situation?
2. Has there been a history of bullying?
3. Who is/are responsible? What is the connection between members of the group?
4. Has there been a change in family circumstances?
5. Who were/are the child's friends? Have these changed?
6. When is the child most anxious – day, dates, times, lessons?
7. Has there been a change of mood, habit or behaviour recently?
8. What affect is the bullying having on the child?
9. What are the child's main worries, e.g. future employment, games lessons, friendships, transferring school, examinations?
10. What are the out-of-school interests and hobbies of the child?
11. Are there any other factors which could be contributing to the problem?
12. What is the attitude of each parent to the situation?

Such a questionnaire is only a rough guide and needs to be adapted for each child. The aim is simply to provide the most efficient way of obtaining relevant information so that the actual interview with the parents can be properly prepared in advance.

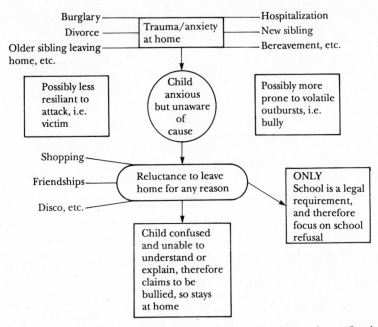

Figure 4 How reluctance to leave home is most clearly seen in a refusal to attend school.

Is it really bullying?

A sensitive interview can disclose information which disproves a child's claim of being bullied. Although a child may use bullying as the excuse for not attending school, the real reason may be due to a recent trauma or problem in the home. There may be a general reluctance or inability on the child's behalf to leave the home, but because school attendance is compulsory, it is usually here that the difficulty first comes to light (see Fig. 4).

Family structure

If the parents are willing, it is often illuminating to tease out the family structure and its dynamics. Parents may readily volunteer information, especially if they are worried. It is not advisable to ask questions which could cause upset, but other professionals may hold information which they feel could be released and which would help.

Who holds the power in the family? This is not always obvious. It is not uncommon for an absent parent or grandparent, an older sibling or relative living away from the family home who is the most influential person. This person may unwittingly hold sway over an impressionable youngster.

1. *What are the family demands, expectations?* Highly competitive parents may have unrealistic expectations which could cause stress within the family as a whole but also result in the child being over-competitive and domineering.
2. *What status does the family have in the neighbourhood?* Some families are scapegoated and shunned. Other families may cause themselves a lot of stress in attempting to hide problems from critical neighbours. The studies of both Michael and Andrew show how families may be scapegoated (see Chapter 10).
3. *Has the family placed too much responsibility on the child's shoulders?* The child may have precocious responsibilities, such as child-minding for siblings or relatives or part-time work.

The child in the family

Any stress or trauma in the home may result in the child experiencing a constellation of complex emotions.

A parent leaving home

Some of the emotions a child may experience if a parent leaves, or threatens to leave, the home are shown in Fig. 5.

Sibling relationships

1. *New baby.* A new sibling may curtail the freedom of an older child who could be pushed into a precocious maturity by being made to assume a caretaking role. Older children may shun cuddles but still need approval and appreciation, especially in private with their parents when younger children are in bed.
2. *Bullying siblings.* It is common for bullying to occur between siblings, and it is not necessarily the older child who is causing the problem. An omnipotent toddler may find attacking an older sibling fun, especially if the target child is prohibited by his/her parents from either complaining or retaliating.

Low self-esteem

A younger child who is academically or socially more successful or talented than his/her older brother/sister could cause jealousy and stress. An accepting and rewarding relationship with the parents can prevent the older child from feeling harassed by the

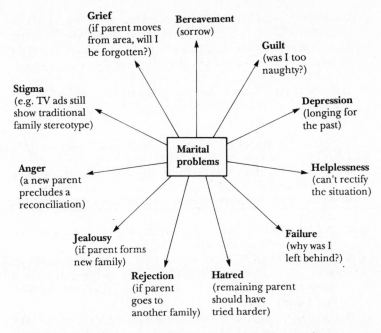

Figure 5 Some of the feelings a child may experience when a parent leaves or threatens to leave home.

younger sibling. A child may experience many rapid and frequent changes in situations and relationships at home and in school so that the aspirations and expectations of parents and teachers need to be reviewed and adjusted regularly to prevent feelings of tension or failure.

Advice to parents

Many professionals working with children have had an intensive and expensive training, but many parents have had no related training at all. Many skills can be shared with parents. Occasional workshops on specific topics should be organized by the school to help parents acquire skills before crises occur.

If your child is being bullied

1. Approach the school, but make an appointment first so that the teacher can make careful observations and contact other staff.
2. Alert the school even if the bullying has stopped.

3. Contacting school is often sufficient to stop the bullying. Once the problem becomes public the bullying usually stops.
4. Encourage the child to approach the teacher they feel most comfortable with to discuss the problem. Check they have done so.
5. If you discuss it in the family try to do so out of earshot of the child.
6. Discuss it with the child.

   ● encourage the child to talk; however, this may be very difficult for them, so be patient;
   ● sympathize, but try not to over-react and become emotional, listen calmly and try to ascertain the facts;
   ● try to avoid sensitive areas such as names the child is called;
   ● give assurances that the bullying will stop or that the situation will be changed;
   ● assure the child that it happens to most people at sometime, and that we learn to avoid it or cope and that it is not happening because there is something wrong with the child;
   ● try to help the child to use it as a learning experience, as a problem to be solved;
   ● ask the child if he/she could alter the situation in any way;
   ● teasing and taunting can sometimes be expected and prepared for, so help the child get used to a nickname, find out why it is so hurtful, and explain that it will stop if the child does not respond;
   ● rituals and initiations can often be endured but a dramatic response will encourage a repeat;
   ● encourage the child to keep a sense of humour if at all possible.

   Above all treat the situation with sensitivity, because the child may be far more distressed than you as an adult realize and may have things totally out of perspective. It is important that although you are doing all you can, as fast as you can, you appear calm and confident in front of the child.
7. Talk to other parents, if possible, to share ideas. Parents sometimes feel ashamed that their child is unpopular.
8. Encourage the child to forget the bullying when at home, to go outside, make new friends and take up new pursuits. Being outside stops the child from brooding and feeling cooped up.
9. Try in every way possible to build up the confidence of the child. This lack of confidence is perhaps underlying the bullying.

10. If the child is being bullied by those who have left school, as sometimes happens, it is possible to approach the police and discuss prosecution.
11. If the attacks can be classed as common assault the police should be informed or legal action considered.

If your child is bullying

1. Bullies are sometimes seeking attention and love. The attention gained from bullying may be preferable to being lonely. There may be a reason why the bully feels alone and lacking in confidence, and this should be discussed:

   ● a parent may have left home;
   ● a new baby may have arrived;
   ● a friendship may have ended;
   ● expectations of home or school may be too high.

2. The bully may be showing off in front of friends. It needs to be made clear that it proves nothing to hurt or distress someone unable to defend themselves, that this is a form of cowardice and proves nothing.
3. The bully may be confusing leadership skills with dominant behaviour, so needing help to understand the difference.
4. The bully may be popular with many classmates but be frightening a less robust child. A sensitive approach to explaining the effect of their behaviour has on others may help.
5. Some bullies are afraid of losing friends and so ostracize a child in class in order to gather the rest more closely around them. This could be due to a poor self-image and lack of confidence, both of which can be helped by success in any area.
6. The bullying may stem from revenge, annoyance or fun. It needs to be clear that this is not acceptable behaviour and that the repercussions are widespread.
7. Bullying for gain, money, possessions or favours can be considered a crime and the bully must be made aware of the seriousness of the situation. It is possible that the police could become involved.
8. The bully may be being bullied by others and be trying to deflect this unwanted attention towards another target.
9. Parents who know of children bullying others – by witnessing attacks or by being told of them by their own children – need to inform the school, because the bully's peer group may be too afraid to do so and it is not likely that the victim will have told either parents or staff.

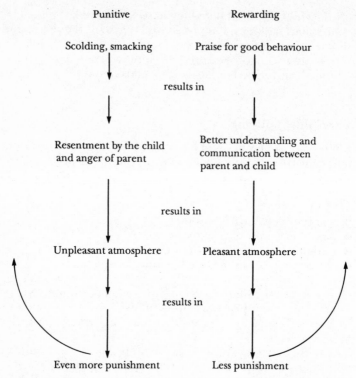

Figure 6 Two styles of parent discipline (after Patterson *et al.*, 1973).

Workshop on discipline

Research suggests that many bullies come from homes where a punitive style of discipline is used and aggression is seen as an acceptable way of settling problems. Some such families are amenable to changing the style of discipline if the alternatives are explained. A cycle of aggression may have developed where the child no longer responds to the punishment, and therefore more and more severe punishment is meted out. If only one parent uses physical discipline, then in the absence of that parent the child's behaviour can be extremely difficult to control. Patterson *et al.* (1973) contrasted two styles of parent discipline (Fig. 6). It was found that for there to be good results, the approach should be friendly, firm and consistent.

There are many schemes and books on behaviour, some written in a humorous style which could be used or adapted for workshops or recommended to parents interested in improving their discipline and relationship with their child (See Appendix).

Parents who are uneasy about using behavioural techniques need to remember that much of life is built around long- or short-term rewards and punishments. In adult life we are conscious of social stigma, acclaim or pressure. Children may need more direct sanctions and more tangible rewards.

The early years

Bullying starts in the pre-school years for some children. In any playgroup it is likely that there is one child who is more dominant and one who is more submissive than the rest. Research indicates that some children continue to experience the problem even with a change of situation and personnel, e.g. one teacher may pass on the problem to another without having alleviated the difficulty in any significant way. It is a myth that all children learn to cope. Once the roles of victim and bully are allocated, the interaction of the group would seem to maintain the situation.

Young children are dependent on adults and the interaction is, therefore, perhaps more influential than in later life. Anything that is done as early as possible to prevent bullying has the most impact and therefore minimizes the chances of secondary problems occurring. One argument, however, does make note of the plasticity of human behaviour and suggests that it is never too late to contemplate change (Clarke and Clarke, 1984).

Measures of change

1. Adults in a position of responsibility should try to identify those children at risk. This may not be easy, because as Knowles (1988) found, teachers were unable to identify the pushy, talkative child who appeared to be popular, but in fact was dominating the rest. Even with sociometric measures, it is difficult to ascertain the views of young children due to linguistic and cognitive restraints.
2. Children of toddler age do not have a wide range of language skills to settle quarrels by reason, discussion or barter. They only have available to them:

   ● *force:* to hit, push and pinch;
   ● *emotional outbursts:* to cry, shout, show anger;
   ● *avoidance:* to walk away.

3. Toddlers may not have the conceptual development to be patient, take turns, share or to anticipate anything other than immediate goals. Misbehaviour may simply be due to a lack of

understanding. Children at this stage of development need a great deal of adult support to gain the most from their social experiences.

Some areas for investigation

1. Does the dominant/dominated child continue to behave in this way even with a change of class or friends?
2. Is the child aggressive, or does he/she only use aggression in retaliation behaviour?
3. Has the child adequate physical strength and a robust personality to cope in play fights?
4. Is the child subservient and over-compliant?
5. Does the child show independence and coping skills?
6. What triggers any difficulties?
7. How does the child react to difficulties?

   - cope alone?
   - use physical strength such as hitting or thumping, or avoid by walking away?
   - become subservient and give in?
   - seek adult arbitration?
   - display distress by screaming or crying.

8. How do the caretaking adults respond?

   - punish by complaining, shouting or hitting?
   - persuade by explaining, cajoling or discussing?
   - model how to behave?
   - passively let the children try to sort it out?

9. How does the peer group respond?

   - ignore?
   - seek adult help?
   - cheer or jeer?
   - sort it out appropriately?
   - take sides?

10. What provokes the quarrels, how are they maintained, and are they quickly forgotten or revived the next day?

Parents of children with social difficulties may feel actively discouraged from attending playgroups, so that the children most in need of the experience are denied any opportunity of gaining it. Other parents can be encouraged to support those parents whose children have a behavioural problem.

Frequently, it would appear that only the problem behaviour of children is emphasized in research and discussion. One aspect of the positive behaviour of young children which has been given attention is the development of coping skills which can be considered in the context of social development. Jowett and Sylva (1986) suggest that for optimum all-round development, even young children need to be encouraged to puzzle things out, choose strategies, make decisions and weigh up the consequences of various lines of action. This style of approach encourages children to premeditate the consequences of their behaviour and possibly discourages thoughtless and uncaring responses.

10
Case studies

John

John was born with ears which stuck out at right angles from his head. When he was only a few weeks old the paediatrician mentioned that an operation to pin back his ears could be considered in a few years time.

Being a lively, energetic lad, John always found plenty to do and thoroughly enjoyed the company of other children. He was athletic and strong for his age and if anyone had mentioned his ears or had entered into name calling or bullying, John would have been able to defend himself. He also had the self-confidence to have shrugged it off. No incident ever came to the notice of his parents or teachers.

When he was 5 years old John had the operation because his parents felt that it was necessary for cosmetic reasons in later life. It was successful and none of his young classmates noticed the change.

Children with deviant features

Features such as a large nose, protruding ears, obesity, glasses or extremes of stature, may be picked out by other children and used as targets for teasing and bullying. These features, however, are not necessarily the reason for the bullying; rather, victims are often initially chosen for other reasons, e.g. their withdrawn, fearful, lethargic or rejecting personality. Only when identified and chosen for attack are the deviant features used to label the child.

The response of the victim to the name calling will influence the bully's decision to repeat the taunting or to desist. Cheerful, gregarious children, who enjoy the company of others and who can shrug off an initial mild attack, or laugh at themselves, are unlikely to be picked on for long.

The role of the teacher or parents

1. Why is the child being bullied? Why was the victim picked out?
2. Is there any truth in the taunts? Why is the child reacting so strongly?
3. Can the victim do anything about the taunts, e.g. diet, be more courageous or friendly?
4. How can the child be helped to improve the situation?
5. Can the child come to terms with the name calling? This may even carry on into adult life. Look at the nicknames of famous people, encourage the child to laugh at the name, use the name in a friendly fashion and later try to replicate the bullying in role play so the child becomes prepared for the taunts and learns how to keep calm and ignore the provocation.
6. Help the victim to understand that it is not the feature that is causing the bullying, but the reaction which is rewarding the bully.

Gareth

Gareth was a very small child of slight build. He was said to be volatile, he often destroyed his own work and that of other children, and he would try to stop others from working. The most worrying aspect of his behaviour was that, when upset, he would bring kitchen knives into school which he stole from home. The other children appeared afraid of him, but he did not threaten anyone with the knives. He used them to mutilate himself by scraping his arms or cutting his hands. He also deliberately tore and cut his clothing and had cut the coats of his classmates. The overall picture Gareth presented was that of a violent, emotionally disturbed boy, who frightened both staff and pupils.

Gareth had a difficult family background. His mother had been brought up in a children's home and so, as is often the case, forcefully resisted help or assessment in case Gareth was taken into care. Gareth's father had been a violent man and had left home. The man living with Gareth's mother had attended a school for pupils with learning difficulties, and he too resisted help in case that was to be the outcome for Gareth. Gareth was the oldest of four children, although his mother was still young. The family was in an extremely poor financial position but the relationships appeared to be rewarding and stable.

Gareth's mother became pregnant again and received regular visits from the health visitor who reported that the family lived in rather a chaotic state but that the parents were caring and supportive to all the children. My assessment of the situation in school had been that Gareth was only aggressive in reaction to attacks on him. He had been the group scapegoat for many years, and being tiny and frail, was unable to defend himself. He was extremely anxious about the attacks in the playground and the street, he experienced nightmares, was sleep walking and generally behaved in a nervous manner. The knives had been for protection, although they had not been used for this purpose.

Role of the teacher

1. The situation was appraised and the culprits made to face up to their provocative acts. The sequence of events and the build up to the incidents were identified, so that everyone involved was aware of exactly what was happening and made to take responsibility for their own actions. Bullying was discussed with the bullies and it was made clear that no form of bullying, whether verbal or physical, was going to be allowed to take place.
2. Gareth was good at art, so it was possible to build up his self-esteem by displaying his work, especially to older children, so that it was then acceptable to his classmates.
3. Individual counselling sessions were arranged to boost his confidence and self-image, but other ways were soon found to build this input into the normal school day.
4. The parents of the bullies were approached and asked for their support in stopping the attacks.
5. Extra help was given to Gareth with his work. The subsequent success boosted his self-image and the sessions gave him the individual attention he needed.

Michael

Michael was a 6-year-old boy who found it impossible to attend school. When dressed and ready to go he would stamp, scream and hide under his bed. Eventually he admitted that he was terrified of going to school. His life in school was being made miserable by older boys, as well as those in his class, for they all stood around him and laughed.

On investigation it was found that although he had no friends in school, the bullying was not as Michael had stated. Rude remarks were made about him by the other children and he was often pushed out of the way and not allowed to join in games. The main problem, however, was that he was isolated. The response from Michael's parents, who were extremely anxious and caring, was to keep him home from school and complain about the other children.

It was soon discovered that Michael was being teased about being extremely overweight. In addition, his mother had recently lost a baby and was treating Michael as a toddler, doing everything for him. Michael was not allowed out to play and, in addition, he was somewhat smothered by being dressed in clothes inappropriate for his age and the weather. Even in midsummer Michael would be wearing a coat, gloves and pompom hat.

Michael had both fine and gross coordination difficulties. He was unable to dress himself, walk downstairs without holding the handrail, ride a bike, climb or jump. The other children refused to let him join in their games and laughed at his clumsiness and timidity.

The family lived in a most disadvantaged area, well known in the town. Children from that area were stigmatized by others and even within his street Michael's family, being least able to cope, was scapegoated. The house was frequently broken into and vandalized, so the family acquired an Alsatian of which Michael was afraid, so compounding his problems.

Role of the teacher

1. Michael's mother was given advice on diet but it was found that she could not read. Therefore, a community worker was employed to take her to the shops and to show her what to buy and how to prepare simple meals.
2. The clumsiness was explained to the parents and they were encouraged to make Michael more independent by showing him how to do things rather than doing them for him. This gradually built up his confidence in his own abilities.
3. Firm advice was given concerning appropriate clothing for his age and the weather, and it was explained to his parents that this had made Michael conspicuous among his peers.
4. Michael needed a lot of help and encouragement to try out swings, roundabouts, slides and bikes. A careful desensitization programme eventually made him slightly less fearful, but he is still afraid when his feet are off the ground. This is in part due to the perceptual problems many clumsy children experience. He is improving with practice.
5. In time his parents came to terms with the loss of the baby and Michael's mother became less depressed. This led to her main goal being to help Michael. After specialist help both parents were able to take more control over their lives; go out more, clean the house, take Michael out and allow him out to play. The teacher's role was to encourage the parents

and offer positive feedback about the improvements in Michael.

6. The children in Michael's class were made to confront their behaviour. If Michael was included in their games, those children were praised. The teachers in the playground inconspicuously joined in the games when Michael was included. This stopped any rejection and eventually Michael was accepted simply as a matter of habit.

Andrew

Andrew was a 9-year-old boy who was well liked by the staff. He was quietly spoken and generous and, although timid by nature, he did have aggressive outbursts. Andrew's mother was a heavy drinker and often collected him from school in an intoxicated state. She was well known in the neighbourhood for her drinking. After a violent marriage and a similar further relationship, which resulted in two other children, she lived alone, but was frequently visited by the father of the younger children. The visits always ended in a violent row.

Andrew had witnessed the drunkenness and the violence. Most of the time his mother was extremely caring and gave the children as much as her small budget would allow. Several agencies were involved in the home but none were directly concerned with Andrew.

It soon became evident that Andrew was being provoked by the other children who called his mother names and taunted him unmercifully. Little provocation was needed to trigger an aggressive response from Andrew. Andrew had no self-esteem or self-confidence. He crept around school, keeping to the walls, and if he encountered a group he would skirt around the children, even if they were much younger. He preferred to stay in school rather than going out to play, because he was unable to withstand the provocation he met.

Role of the teacher

1. Andrew was encouraged to go out to play but, unknown to him and the other children, he was closely supervised.
2. Andrew was intelligent and able to express his feelings of rejection and loneliness to his teacher who had developed a close relationship with him.
3. Andrew was helped to predict the outcome of his temper outbursts by the use of diagrams and cartoons showing the various ways frustration may be resolved.

4. Andrew's teacher was able to get him used to teasing and provocation. He trusted his teacher and she was able to use the taunts others used and helped him to practise ignoring them and to see the humour in his overreactions. This was done in a most sensitive manner, which Andrew was able to accept.

5. Every opportunity was found in class to facilitate friendships for Andrew. Any rude remarks or unkind actions which occurred in class, whether to Andrew or any other child, were heavily chastised, and this was paralleled with a project on 'Getting Along With Others'. All opportunities were seized to share, discuss, cooperate and help others. Class games and playground activities were introduced and this was very popular with all the children.

6. The teacher, and others in Andrew's school, took every reasonable opportunity to recognize Andrew as an individual, without risking alienating the rest of the group. Andrew was given extra tuition with his basic skills to build up his confidence and he was encouraged in his hobbies. His language and conversation improved dramatically as he became more confident and he was able to speak out more without hesitation as his self-esteem improved.

7. In subtle ways this recognition of Andrew's strengths was carried over into the class. He was good at swimming and art and Andrew came to realize his own abilities in parallel with a growing recognition from others.

8. Just as Andrew was showing obvious improvements the class went to a museum and was filmed, by chance, for the television evening news. Andrew was spotlighted and was able to see himself picked out by impartial people. This fortuitous event soundly consolidated his progress and he is currently progressing very well.

Donnie

Donnie was a lively, well-built boy, 8 years of age. His family were all interested in sport, his uncles and father being extremely keen sportsmen, and Donnie was athletic and a credit to his family. All the members of the extended family as well as Donnie's father had received a private education and they were all well known as established members of the community. From influences in the home and school Donnie came to believe that where he led, others would follow. As he was independent, intelligent and physically able, it was not difficult for him to dominate his classmates and neighbourhood friends. If he suggested a game, he would ignore any dissenters – all ended up playing the game he had decided upon, simply because his forceful personality over-rode the views of others. Children who challenged his lead were left alone for days and most, consciously or not, came to the conclusion that it was easier to follow his lead than to confront him or face loneliness. Donnie was not a malicious boy but he was intent on having his own way, because he had been brought up to expect that this was his right.

Teaching points

This was a difficult case because the ideals which were considered appropriate by myself were not acceptable to either the school or Donnie's family. I was told firmly that if Donnie was dominating other children then they themselves must wish this to be so, otherwise they would have done something about it.

1. The parents in the neighbourhood tried to show Donnie that he was dominating other children and this was not leadership.
2. Games were introduced by the parents which did not centre around Donnie displaying his physical strength or agility.
3. The strengths of other children – kindness, generosity, empathy – were pointed out to Donnie in the hope that he would appreciate that all children have some abilities.
4. Only little success was achieved, because Donnie has now moved on to dominating others with his academic success.

Drama is one way of encouraging group cohesion and support. In working with severely emotionally and behaviourally disturbed children, I have found it to be a mode which has been most successful in helping one child to adapt to the group or the group to accommodate and support one child. Once the group has reached a state of cohesion it becomes possible to discuss issues, conflicts and relationships with greater success.

Stephen

Stephen was in a small class of 7-year-olds in a school for children with severe emotional and behavioural problems. Many of the group were highly volatile and disruptive. The saddest aspect of the group was that they were at each other's throats all the time, eager to see each other fail, get into trouble or be in distress. One or two of the weaker children took the brunt of the behaviour, especially Stephen, who had a darker skin and was given the nickname of Darkie.

The teacher recognized that the class needed to develop

better relationships, but nothing had come of any of the various attempts which had already been tried. Stephen was the most physically well developed but he would not defend himself; in fact he was a provocative victim in that he provoked others to bully and hurt him and this was one reason why he was in the specialist setting.

The class teacher was especially interested in drama and so decided upon this approach to develop group cohesion.

'The prince and the boat'

The drama has a simple format which may be followed in a variety of ways:

1. A prince wishes to marry a princess from a neighbouring area.
2. The king, her father, refuses his permission.
3. The prince and princess wish to steal away but they need a boat urgently, because the king will return at midnight.
4. The prince (the teacher) comes to ask the class for help.
5. Every child has a specific job to do to build the boat.

The teacher's role is to have done extensive homework so as to have the vocabulary and detailed information to hand which will lend credence to the exercise. The dramatic tension is the crucial ingredient and the teacher must regulate this so there is an urgency to finish the boat in time to help the prince and princess. It is vital that the children see that it is the hard work of all, with a common aim, that will bring about success. This must not be stated but left for the children to experience. The boat is built by midnight (just!).

'The pirates'

Many further examples can be generated by the teacher:

1. A group of sailors meet a lone sea captain.
2. Pirates have taken his gold but he has stolen the map which shows where the gold has been hidden.
3. All the sailors (all the class except the captain) help him decipher the clues.
4. Each child has a clue to solve but can ask others for help.

The success of the drama will depend on all children working to their capacity, and therefore the teacher needs to encourage their involvement. Attention to detail and careful preparation are the factors which make for authenticity.

The ethos of working together to help an independent party can quickly generate group cohesion in a short period of time.

George

George was an extremely volatile and energetic 12-year-old. Previous to attending the school he had been on drugs to stabilize his behaviour, but these had been discontinued because of side-effects. George was a well-built, attractive boy who was well liked by the staff because he was generous, sympathetic and loyal, but the children in the school were afraid of his tempers and his dominating behaviour. This type of drama work, in addition to counselling, relaxation techniques, behavioural programmes and strategies to boost self-esteem, formed a multifaceted approach to stabilizing George's behaviour.

A drama for older children

A mysterious lady (an auxiliary or even an older pupil from another class) is found by the wayside. She is dishevelled but uninjured. The teacher slowly leads the group towards her but, as they approach, she shrinks away because she is obviously very afraid.

The group have to discuss tactics to approach the lady without frightening her and also how to help her if they are able to approach. They need to find out what has happened for her to be so distressed.

Role of the teacher

1. To provide an air of mystery and suspense to hold the attention of the group.
2. To elicit feelings of concern and empathy for someone in trouble.
3. All problem solving needs to be carried out by the whole group, and all must listen to all ideas and evaluate them carefully.
4. Only a solution agreed upon by the whole group is acceptable, i.e. there must be a consensus of opinion.

The teacher needs to have some rapport and signal system (e.g. eye contact) with the 'lady' so that the approach and retreat develops at a speed that holds the suspense and gives the group time for discussion and to solve the mystery. It is not necessary to arrive at an explanation, e.g. the 'lady' may enter a hospital where the group takes on medical roles, etc. A great deal of creative art, writing, drama and oral work can come of such short sequences. Short video scenes can be attempted.

(Original ideas from Dorothy Heathcote, lecturer in drama (retired), University of Newcastle upon Tyne and Roger Hancock, Adviser for Drama, Newcastle upon Tyne.)

Mark

Mark was a 14-year-old who recently entered a new school out of his catchment area. His parents were aware that he had problems making friends and were wary of him being bullied. Mark was very small for his age and, in addition, he was a 'clumsy' child (see Chapter 3). Mark had coordination problems and walked in an ungainly manner, he was poor at games and sadly had mannerisms associated with his poor coordination. As with many clumsy children he was unable to enunciate his words clearly or quickly and became flustered and tongue-tied when provoked. Mark had witnessed a lot of marital disharmony and aggression when younger and from that time he had become fearful, anxious and lacking in confidence.

After a few months in his new school he became known as Mark the Martian because of his mannerisms. He was unable to shrug this off and ignore it. Because all his classmates, and others, kicked, punched and tripped him at every possible opportunity, he became so tense that he reacted in a volatile and dramatic way which earned him the reputation among staff of being aggressive. His reactions encouraged the bullies to continue.

No single incident was severe in itself but the accumulative effect was devastating. Mark did not have the confidence to approach a member of staff, and because the staff never saw any of the premeditated attacks, only his spontaneous response, they did not have a sympathetic attitude towards him.

The bullying came to a head when it was discovered that Mark was walking around the town all day in the winter weather rather than face school. At the same time the mother of one of his classmates 'phoned his parents and the school to say her son was becoming distressed at the extent of the bullying Mark was having to endure in school. Many of the children were disturbed by the events but no teacher had been aware of what had been taking place.

Role of the teacher

1. The parents and year tutor discussed the problem and strategies to help.

2. Mark was given an assurance that the bullying would end. He had been so afraid he had been unable to sleep. Constant vigilance was assured to enable him to return. Break times were spent inside school on a pretext provided by staff.
3. The bullies were taken to task by the school and it was made clear that bullying in any form was not permitted. Their parents were informed that it was considered to be a serious matter.
4. The staff were informed and asked for their support in supervising carefully during lesson time and to help Mark develop confidence and self-esteem. This was done particularly well in games. Mark was never chosen for a partner, so the teacher would often put the class in pairs or partner Mark himself.
5. Mark was too afraid to attend clubs but would have enjoyed chess had it been available. This would have given him a chance of success.

Within a few days all bullying stopped. Many children had been involved in a periphery fashion and so it took some time to end it completely. Within two weeks Mark was attending school without distress but the night fears and nervous flinching lasted many months. It was a year before he could approach a group of children with any confidence. The parents supported the work of the school by getting him to mix in groups of older people e.g. a sports club, where he gained experience and confidence in a non-threatening manner. He continued with chess activities after school and took up weighttraining which added to his confidence.

The following two cases are of two boys with very similar family backgrounds; however, one became a bully, the other a victim.

Simon

Simon was a boy in the first year of secondary school. He was reported as having frequent temper outbursts which would be followed by him running home, 3 miles away.

Role of the teacher

1. The teacher kept a desk diary of Simon's outbursts and found they occurred especially on a Monday morning. After an interview with Simon's mother who was separated from his father, it became clear that Simon expected his father to

call at the house for him each weekend, as promised. He waited each weekend but his father rarely came. Simon was intensely disappointed but refused to admit to his feelings.

2. An analysis of the antecedents to the flight home was made and it was found that Simon's classmates had discovered his emotional vulnerability and had spotted that, by provoking him, he would react in a dramatic and entertaining fashion. The bullying had spread from verbal to physical attack and from boys only to boys and girls joining in the attacks. Simon was well known in school and considered fair game.

3. An investigation of the records showed that Simon had experienced a number of changes of school and had never developed firm friendships.

4. The family situation could not be changed and so the teacher counselled Simon and helped him to realize that the way he was allowing his disappointment to affect him in school was exacerbating the situation.

5. A reward system helped Simon to stay nearer and nearer to school when distressed so that eventually he was able to sit quietly alone in class.

6. The teacher helped him to resist provocation by giving him practice in shrugging off abuse. Simon kept a diary to show the times he was able to resist.

7. The culprits were put on a reward system for not annoying others and for making positive statements and offering support to all classmates – not only Simon, as this would have spotlighted him even more.

8. The members of the group were warned that to support nasty remarks or attacks was as bad as being the culprits themselves and would be treated as such.

9. A group of children was quietly asked to support Simon, to keep an eye on him and to report any bullying.

10. Simon had been bullying younger children and that was discussed with him.

11. To elicit the goodwill of staff Simon had been hurrying his work which had resulted in it being done carelessly and untidily. This had brought him further trouble. He was helped to slow down his speed of working so that he gained better results.

12. Other ways of getting praise and success were discussed.

13. Simon had tried to break into inappropriate groups. It was pointed out to him that we can only choose friends from those willing to become friends. He played alone for a while and then became friendly with one or two willing boys. The costs and demands of friendships were discussed at length.

14. Simon had been thumb-sucking in class when distressed. He

was taught to twiddle his pencil in his fingers when anxious and to use other more age-appropriate tension habits until he became more relaxed.

Tom

Tom was a young boy of 10, but he was one of the largest and strongest boys in school. It was know that he was aggressive to others and disruptive in class, but only by observing him surreptitiously in the playground from a classroom window, was the extent of his bullying understood. It was noted that through-out the breaktimes Tom would take boys one by one behind the outbuildings and each would emerge looking tearful after a few minutes. This would happen many times over the hour-long lunchbreak.

Further observation and analysis showed that the victims were chosen, for example, if Tom wanted their football or other possessions or if they had annoyed him in class. There were supervisors in the playground but that small area was left unobserved.

Role of the teacher

1. Investigation unearthed the fact that Tom's father, separated from his mother, had rejected Tom from birth. Tom's brother and sister had outings with their father, presents and birthday cards, but Tom was conspicuously left out for no obvious reason. The father had a new family and Tom was devastated because he could not understand his father's negative and rejecting behaviour and, although never discussed, it is feasible that he may have suspected that he was the reason for his father leaving home. His mother felt no change would be possible and so the teacher decided to try to help Tom accept the situation.
2. Tom was challenged about his behaviour which he denied. Tom was confronted with a desk diary of the bullying incidents and, although angry, he did accept the evidence.
3. He agreed that he would stay in sight of the supervisors and that they would call to him every 5 minutes to report. If he complied he would be given a credit mark which was a system just started in the school.
4. After a week of success Tom was abusive to his teacher and had a fight in the yard. The teacher found out from his mother that Tom had been taken out by his father, for the first time,

and it was felt that he may have been under pressure when the incidents occurred. The teacher counselled him about this.

5. Tom managed well for 2 weeks but then was 'out' in a game of cricket and threw the bat at another boy in temper.

6. The headteacher decided to take severe measures but later looked at the credits Tom had gained in the previous 2 weeks and action was deferred.

7. Tom was asked to make a promise that he would not intimidate others but only to give the assurance if he intended to keep the promise. After some minutes he broke down and cried for the first time.

8. It was decided to give Tom the benefit of the doubt and he was allowed to resume, as normal, with the support of the credit system. The bullying and disruptive behaviour stopped and he managed to keep his promise. Tom is now a 'prefect' and a responsible class member.

Jennie

Jennie was a first-year pupil in a comprehensive school. There was a background of family problems but these were not affecting Jennie in any obvious way. The problems came to light in a Personal and Social Education lesson. A worksheet on bullying had been prepared as a stimulus to discussion. The discussion went well even though the class was known to be lively and could be difficult at times. In the discussion the tutor asked if anyone had ever experienced bullying. Jennie quietly explained that she felt that she was being bullied by the boys in the class. The boys vociferously denied that this was true.

Jennie explained that she had entered school out of her catchment area and so had no friends to offer her support. She had once lived in a disadvantaged area and was being teased about this by the boys in the class. Jennie felt that she was under a great deal of stress and she was unhappy.

The tutor asked the boys, there and then, for their reply. It was obvious that they had no idea that their teasing had distressed Jennie for they said it was only 'a bit of fun'. To the boys, verbal taunting did not seem like bullying.

It was discovered that, because of problems at home, Jennie reacted badly to the taunts, she hit out wildly and rose to provocation. This naturally made matters worse. Jennie had been taught to 'stick up for herself' and so she worked on the principle of hit out at what is hurting.

After the one discussion lesson, the problem was eradicated and the boys saw how hurtful such thoughtless behaviour can be and Jennie understood how her own reactions were maintaining the bullying. The lesson was guided by the teacher but he gave very little input. The problem was discussed and solved by the pupils themselves. It was especially gratifying that a sound solution was reached and carried out, because the group had the reputation of being aggressive and uncaring.

Wendy

Wendy was a 16-year-old girl who claimed that she was unable to go to school because she was bullied. No culprits were named, nor specific incidents given, but it was clear that she had great difficulty in attending school.

Role of the teacher

1. After contact with the home it became clear that Wendy and her mother were still grieving over the death of her father who had died suddenly 2 years previously.
2. Continued contact through other agencies involved indicated that it was Wendy's mother who was the more depressed and that she was still angry, without cause, about the medical attention her husband had received. This strong feeling had become diffused and confused with all those in authority so that the commitment to help Wendy back to school, which had seemed evident at first was, in fact, lacking.
3. A desensitization programme was initiated to ease Wendy back to school. She was gradually brought nearer and nearer school until, after a couple of weeks, she was able to enter and sit in a small room to do the work allocated by relevant teachers.
4. When the time came for Wendy to enter class she refused to cooperate and she stayed at home. Wendy was supported in this by her mother who said she would be under too much emotional stress if she returned.
5. Wendy had mixed feelings about returning to school. She enjoyed staying at home, sitting watching TV with her mother, and she was worried about leaving her mother alone. Wendy, however, was not unintelligent and realized that this was her mother's problem and at times she felt annoyed that her mother was stopping her from having a normal adolescent life.
6. Wendy's mother managed to prevaricate and delay matters to such an extent that after a few months Wendy reached school-leaving age before any solution was reached.

Tony

This last case study is included, even though I was not involved, because it illustrates a pattern of bullying which is not uncommon. These bullies became caught up in a situation which eventually led them to become afraid or ashamed of their own actions.

Tony entered the local secondary school where he made new friends but, by chance, still had to travel home alone each night across a small park. For several weeks a group of boys of his own age, from another school, waited for him in the park. These boys would taunt him, take or destroy his possessions, and eventually they started to hit Tony. As the boys were his own age Tony felt that he ought to be able to cope and so told no one about the attacks. Tony's parents began to realize something was wrong but could get no information from him. When he began to avoid going to school, and returned bruised when he did attend, his parents began to suspect bullying.

One day Tony arrived home with blood pouring from his nose and face. The boys had kicked and punched him but the damage was not severe and looked much worse than was actually the case. Tony told his parents about the bullying, but from that moment on it stopped, and he never saw the bullies again. Tony and his parents felt that the boys had been so afraid or ashamed of what they had done that they had decided to stop bullying.

Workshop and curriculum material

1. Curriculum topics

Friendships: making and keeping friends

1. The costs and benefits of friendships.
2. How to choose friends, and how to encourage friendships.
3. Coping with conflict.
4. Taking responsibility for oneself and others.
5. Interpreting moods of self and others.

Groups: entering groups

1. Signs of acceptance or rejection.
2. Feelings of rejection.
3. Choosing a group of friends.
4. Saying 'No' or refusing requests.

Conflict

1. How to cope, avoid or deflect.
2. Resisting provocation.
3. Having the last word.
4. Resolution – better for both so that neither loses face.
5. Confronting a problem.

Communities

1. Neighbourhood groups.
2. Religious groups.
3. Working in a community.

Witnessing bullying

1. How did it feel?
2. Why did it happen?
3. Did you discuss it?

Leadership and dominance

1. Do we need leaders?
2. Can we identify leaders?
3. Types of leaders.

4. Assertiveness, arrogance, aggression – the differences.
5. Leadership skills.

Cooperation and competition

1. What is the difference?
2. Are both necessary?

Being alone

1. Identifying those isolated.
2. What does it feel like?
3. Supporting those who are shy or friendless.

Bullying in the wider context

1. Historical.
2. Geographical and political.
3. Political leaders and propaganda.

Fear

1. Feeling afraid.
2. Keeping secrets.
3. Confronting fear.
4. Handling a crisis situation.

Influential individuals

1. Individual responses can be effective, e.g. Mother Teresa, Bob Geldof, Ghandi, etc.
2. Individuals who have influenced the pupils themselves.

Social situations

1. Confidence.
2. Meeting new people.
3. Entering a room.
4. Posture and non-verbal behaviour.
5. Initiating and maintaining a conversation.
6. Listening skills.
7. Making, meeting and refusing requests.

Methods

role play	discussion	poetry and literature
writing	art, collage	cartoons
video	TV, radio, media	drama

making books for others to read – for younger pupils, etc.

2. An example of a discussion in a personal, social and moral education lesson

A line drawing of a bullying situation was handed out and a class discussion was encouraged. The discussion was kept low-key, non-emotional and presented as a problem to be solved: 'Why are some pupils bullied and what is the best action to take if it happens to you?' The consensus of opinion was that pupils who remained uninvolved in the group were most disliked, especially if they rose to taunts or provocation.

The class was split into four groups to discuss the various actions which could be taken. Four choices of action to take against bullies were brought back to the full class group:

- *aggression:* 'beat them up!';
- *avoidance:* change school;
- *flight:* run away;
- *arbitration:* seek adult help.

The class group evaluated these responses and with no guidance from the teacher proposed that arbitration would be the most successful. The groups re-formed for a last time to discuss what could be done if arbitration failed.

The discussion was intellectually stimulating, each child having a chance to put forward an opinion. The lesson proved to be a sound reference point which later served to remind pupils how to cope.

3. Games

A wide range of social experiences can be gained from playing games:

- playground games;
- classroom games;
- party games;
- physical education and games lessons, i.e. small group or team games;
- board games, e.g. snakes and ladders, Monopoly, etc.;
- card games, e.g. happy families;
- skipping games and rhymes.

Parents can introduce games and rhymes used when they were young.

Reference and history books can offer games of long ago even from early civilizations.

Games can be collected from different countries or local areas, perhaps through pen pals, etc.

These can all be collated, organized into displays but, most importantly, learned and enjoyed. Markings for play areas – walls and ground – can be chosen by the children to extend the repertoire.

Games can facilitate social development by offering experiences in the following skills;

role taking	problem solving
reciprocity	logical thought
empathy	forward planning
motivation	supporting others
turn taking	physical awareness of others,
sharing	i.e. not being too
sustaining effort	boisterous, careless
handling competition	leadership

coping with winning and losing	compliance
patience	dominance
responsibility for equipment	teamwork
tidying away	verbal and non-verbal communication
ending appropriately to time	language development
sequencing	explaining rules, elaboration of sentences
evaluating options	decision making

4. Workshop exercise: approaching the school for help

In pairs – the possible negative responses of a school are discussed. One of the pair takes the role of a school refusing to become involved; the other takes the role of the concerned adult and tries to counter the responses given below:

1. If we don't know who the bullies are we can't do anything about it.
2. The victim provokes other children and is a nuisance in class, e.g. temper flashes, hits out, swears. Tries to bully as well.
3. Poor staffing ratio – no extra supervision available.
4. The victim irritates certain members of staff, but not others – never has the right books, equipment, always late.
5. Never complained to staff about being bullied.
6. Too dependent – can't get himself/herself around school.
7. Victim does not help matters – won't join in, tends to wander around alone. Not popular with other children.
8. We're here to teach not preach. No time for extras with a heavy exam curriculum to get through. What do you suggest we drop?
9. The victim is hopeless in games/art/woodwork/lessons. The others all laugh.
10. If it's happening outside the school, then it's out of our jurisdiction.
11. Over-sensitive parents, over-protected child.
12. It has always gone on/they'll learn to cope in time/boys will be boys.
13. There's nothing anyone can do about their size, colour, accent, etc.

5. Workshop on case studies

Ask pairs or small groups to:

1. Define bullying – giving consideration to gender differences, age differences, high risk pupils etc.
2. Discuss in depth any case of bullying they are involved in or have known about.
3. Take a case study and select areas for intervention from the spectrum of work given on the following pages.

4. Compile a detailed programme of work drawing from the areas they have chosen.

6. Suggested books and materials

All the following publications are reasonably priced and many are available from: Centre for Global Education, University of York, Heslington, York YO1 5DD and Changes Bookshop, 242 Belsize Road, London NW6 4BT. Tel: 01-328 5161.

General advice on parenting skills

All these titles are written in a light hearted manner but offer sound, practical advice..

Toddler Taming (1987) by C. Green. London: Century Hutchinson.

Seven Tactics for Superparents (1983) by K. Wheldall, D. D. Wheldall and S. Winter. Available from: Positive Products, 61 Selly Wick Drive, Selly Park, Birmingham B29 FJ0.

What Can Parents Do? A Handbook for Parents (1986) by Mickey and Terri Quinn. Veritas Family Resources, Dublin: Criterion Press.

Materials for schools

Kidscape Training Pack (1986) by Michelle Elliott. A Pack for use with primary age children. Available from: Kidscape, 82 Brook Street, London W1Y 1YG. Tel: 01-493 9845.

Keeping Safe: A Practical Guide to Talking with Children (1988) by Michelle Elliott. London: Hodder and Stoughton.

Teenscape (in preparation) by Michelle Elliott – for older pupils.

Steps to Success (1983) by J. Thacker. Windsor: NFER Nelson. An interpersonal problem solving approach for children.

Peace Education Project – a variety of materials available from: Peace Education Project, 6 Endsleigh Street, London WC1. Tel: 01-435 2182.

Let's Co-operate (1986) by Mildred Mascheder. London: Lithosphere Printing Co-operation.

Lets Play Together (in preparation) by Mildred Mascheder.

Booklets: *Violence and Non-violence; Co-operative Games; Coping with Conflict.*

Ways and Means: An approach to Problem Solving (1987) by Sue Bowers. The Handbook of Kingston Friends Workship in conjunction with the Learning Difficulties Project, Kingston Polytechnic. Available from: Quaker Meeting House, 76 Eden Street, Kingston upon Thames KT1 1DJ.

Using Student Team Learning (1986) by R. E. Slavin. Available from: The Centre for Social Organization of Schools, Johns Hopkins University, 3505, North Charles Street, Baltimore MQ21218, USA.

So Everybody Fights by Ita Sheehy. Irish Commission for Justice and Peace. 169 Booterstown Avenue, Blackrock, Co. Dublin, Republic of Ireland.

The Friendly Classroom for a Small Planet (1978) by P. Prutzman. Avery Publishing Group (A practical handbook).

Winners All-Co-operative Games For All Ages. Pax Christi, 9 Henry Road, London N4 21H.

Helping Kids Make Friends (1979) by H. Stocking, D. Arezzo and S. Leavitt and *Helping Friendless Children* (1983) by H. Stocking, D. Arezzo and S. Leavitt. (Boys Town Centre for The Study of Youth Development – Nebraska). Published by: Argus Communications. Allen, Texas 75002, USA.

First Year Tutorial Handbook (1986) by G. T. Davies. Oxford: Blackwell.

FIRM (Forum for Initiatives in Reparation and Mediation) Fact sheets and information available from Tony Marshall, 19 London End, Beaconsfield Road, Bucks. HP9 2HN.

Fiction about bullying to stimulate discussion

I'm The King of the Castle (1982) by Susan Hill (for older children). Oxford: Heinemann Education.

Willow Street Kids (1986) by Michelle Elliott (for younger children). London: Andre Deutsch.

Lord of the Flies (1954) by William Golding (for older children). London: Faber and Faber.

Looking Back (1973) by Camara Laye in *The African Child*. Short stories compiled by John L. Foster. London: Edward Arnold.

Bibliography

Abramson, L. Y., Seligman, M. E. P. and Teasdale, J. D. (1987). Learned helplessness in humans: Critique and reformulation. *Journal of Abnormal Psychology*, **87**, 49–74.

Ackers, R. L. (1968). Problems in the sociology of deviance. *Social Forces*, **46**, 463.

Adler, A. (1943). *Understanding Human Nature*. London: Allen and Unwin.

Adorno, T. W., Frenkel-Brunswick, E., Levinson, D. J. and Stanford, R. N. (1950). *The Authoritarian Personality*. New York: Harper.

Akhtar, S. and Stronach, I. (1986). They call me Blacky. *Times Educational Supplement*, 19 September, p. 23.

Allen, V. L. (1975). Self, social group and social structure. *In* D. Magnusson, A Dunér and G. Zetterholm (Eds), *Adjustment: A Longitudinal Study*. Stockholm: Almqvist and Wiksell.

Allport, G. W. (1954). *The Nature of Prejudice*. New York: Addison-Wesley.

Argyle, M. (1978). *The Psychology of Interpersonal Behaviour*. Harmondsworth: Penguin.

Ariès, P. (1960). *Centuries of Childhood*. Harmondsworth: Penguin.

Arora, C. M. T and Thompson, D. A. (1987). Defining bullying for a secondary school. *Education and Child Psychology*, **4**(3)(4), 110–20.

Asher, S. R. and Dodge, K. A. (1986). Identification of children who are rejected by their peers. *Developmental Psychology*, **22**, 444–9.

Asher, S. R. and Gottman, J. M. (Eds) (1981). *The Development of Children's Friendships*. Cambridge: Cambridge University Press.

Asher, S. R. and Renshaw, P. D. (1981). Children without friends: Social knowledge and social skill training. *In* S. R. Asher and J. M. Gottman (Eds), *The Development of Children's Friendships*. Cambridge: Cambridge University Press.

Askew, S. and Ross, C. (1988). *Boys Don't Cry*. Milton Keynes: Open University Press.

Bandura, A. (1969). *The Principles of Behaviour Modification*. New York: Holt, Rinehart and Winston.

Bandura, A. (1973a). Social learning theory of aggression. *In* J. F. Knutson (Ed.), *Control of Aggression: Implications for Basic Research*. Chicago: Aldine Atherton.

Bandura, A. (1973b). *Aggression: A Social Learning Analysis*. Englewood Cliffs, N.J.: Prentice-Hall.

Bandura, A. (1979). Psychological mechanisms of aggression. *In* M. von Cranach, K. Foppa, W. Lepenies and D. Ploog (Eds), *Human Ethology: Claims and Limits of a New Discipline*. Cambridge: Cambridge University Press.

Bandura, A., Ross, D. and Ross, S. A. (1963). Vicarious reinforcement and imitation learning. *Journal of Abnormal and Social Psychology*, **67**, 601–7.

Becker, H. S. (1963). *Outsiders*: Studies in the Sociology of Deviance, New York: Free Press.

Becker, W. C. (1964). Consequences of different kinds of parental discipline. *In* M. L. Hoffman and L. W. Hoffman (Eds), *Review of Child Development Research*, Vol. 1. New York: Russell Sage Foundation.

Becker, W. C., Masden, C. H., Arnold, C. R. and Thomas, B. A. (1967). The contingent use of teacher attention and praise in reducing classroom behaviour problems. *Journal of Special Education*, **I**(3), 287–307.

Bell, R. Q. and Harper, L. V. (1977). *Child Effects on Adults*. Hillsdale, N.J.: Lawrence Erlbaum Associates.

Berkowitz, L. (1962). *Aggression: A Social Psychological Analysis*. New York: McGraw Hill.

Berkowitz, M. W. (Ed.) (1985). *Peer Conflict and Psychological Growth: New Directions for Child Development*. San Francisco: Jossey Bass.

Berndt, T. J. (1983). Social cognition, social behaviour and children's friendships. *In* E. T. Higgins, D. N. Ruble and W. W. Hartup (Eds), *Social Cognition and Social Development: A Sociocultural Perspective*. Cambridge: Cambridge University Press.

Besag, V. E. (1986). Bullies, victims and the silent majority. *Times Educational Supplement*, 5 December, 22–3.

Besag, V. E. (1988). Report for Council for Cultural Co-operation. Report of the European Teachers Seminar on Bullying in Schools. Strasburg: CCC.

Bigelow, B. J. and La Gaipa, J. J. (1980). The development of friendship values and choice. *In* H. C. Foot, A. J. Chapman and J. R. Smith (Eds), *Friendship and Social Relations in Children*. Chichester: John Wiley.

Bird, C. (1980). Deviant labelling in schools – The pupils' perspective. *In* P. Woods (Ed.), *Pupil Strategies*. London: Croom Helm.

Bird, C., Chessum, R., Furlong, V. J. and Johnson, D. (1981). *Disaffected Pupils*. London: Brunel University.

Birleson, P. (1981). The validity of depressive disorder in childhood and the development of a self-rating scale: A research report. *Journal of Child Psychology and Psychiatry*, **22**, 73–88.

Bjorkquist, K., Ekman, K. and Lagerspetz, K. (1982). Bullies and victims: Their ego picture, ideal ego picture and normative ego picture. *Scandinavian Journal of Psychology*, **23**, 307–13.

Block, J. (1971). *Lives Through Time*. Berkeley, Calif.: Bancroft Books.

Borland, M. (Ed.) (1976). *Violence in the Family*. Manchester: Manchester University Press.

Bowers, K. S. (1973). Situationalism in psychology: An analysis and a critique. *Psychological Review*, **80**, 307–36.

Brandes, D. and Ginnis, P. (1986). *A Guide to Student Centred Learning*. Oxford: Blackwell.

Brophy, J. and Good, T. (1974). *Teacher–Student Relationships: Causes and Consequences*. New York: Holt, Rinehart and Winston.

Burden, R. (1981). Systems theory and its relevance to schools. *In* B. Gillham (Ed.), *Problem Behaviour in the Secondary School*. London: Croom Helm.

Burne, B. (1987). A study of the incidence and nature of bullies and whipping boys (victims) in a Dublin City post primary school for boys. Unpublished M.Ed. thesis, Trinity College, Dublin.

Cairns, R. B. (1979). Social Development. *The Origins and Plasticity of Interchanges*. San Francisco: W. H. Freeman & Co.

Cairns, R. B. (1986). A contemporary perspective on social development. *In* P. S. Strain, M. J. Guralnick and H. M. Walker (Eds), *Children's Social Behaviour, Development Assessment and Modification*. London and San Diego: Academic Press.

Caldwell, B. M. (1977). Aggression and hostility in young children, *Young Child*, **32**(2), 4–13.

Caplan, G. (1964). *Principles of Preventive Psychiatry*. London: Tavistock.

Cartwright, D. and Zander, A. (1960). *Group Dynamics, Research and Theory*. London: Tavistock.

Cashmore, E. (1979). *Rastaman: The Rastafarian Movement in England*. London: Allen and Unwin.

Chess, S. and Thomas, A. (1984). *Origins and Evolution of Behaviour Disorders*. New York: Raven Press.

Cicourel, A. V. and Kitsuse, J. I. (1963). *The Educational Decision-makers*. New York: Bobbs-Merrill.

Cicourel, A. V. and Kitsuse, J. I. (1968). The social organization of the high school and deviant adolescent careers. *In* E. Rubington and M. Weinberg (Eds), *Deviance: The Interactionist Perspective*. New York: Macmillan.

Clarke, A. B. D. and Clarke, A. M. (1984). Constancy and change in the growth of human characteristics. *Journal of Child Psychology and Psychiatry*, **25**(2), 191–210.

Clarke, R. V. G. (1985). Delinquency, environment and intervention. *Journal of Child Psychology and Psychiatry*, **26**(4), 505–23.

Coard, B. (1971). *How the West Indian Child is Made Educationally Subnormal in the British School System*. London: New Beacon Books.

Coffield, F., Robinson, P. and Sarsby, J. (1981). *A Cycle of Deprivation?* London: Heinemann.

Coffield, F., Borrill, C. and Marshall, S. (1986). *Growing up on the Margins*. Milton Keynes: Open University Press.

Cohen, S. (1971). *Images of Deviance*. Harmondsworth: Penguin.

Cohn, T. (1987). Sticks and stones may break my bones but names will never hurt me. *Multicultural Teaching*, **5**(3), 8–11.

Cole, R. J. (1977). The bullied child in school. Unpublished M.Sc. dissertation, University of Sheffield.

Coleman, J. S. (1966). The Coleman Report. *Equality of Educational Opportunity*. Washington: US Government Printing Office.

Condry, J. C. and Ross, D. F. (1985). Sex and aggression: The influence of gender label on the perception of aggression in children. *Child Development*, **56**, 223–5.

Corsaro, W. A. (1979). We're friends, right? Children's use of access rituals in a nursery school. *Language in Society*, **8**, 315–36.

Corsaro, W. A. (1981). Friendship in the nursery school: Social organisation in a peer environment. *In* S. R. Asher and J. M. Gottman (Eds), *The Development of Children's Friendships*. Cambridge: Cambridge University Press.

Cottle, T. J. (1981). *Like Fathers, Like Sons: Portrait of Intimacy and Strain*. Cambridge: Mass.: Harvard Medical School.

Coulton, G. G. (1967). *Life in the Middle Ages*. Cambridge: Cambridge University Press.

Council for Cultural Cooperation (1988). Report of the European Teachers' Seminar on *Bullying in Schools*. Strasbourg: CCC.

Cowen, E. L., Pederson, A., Babigian, H., Izzo, L. D. and Trost, M. A. (1973). Long-term follow-up of early detected vulnerable children. *Journal of Consulting and Clinical Psychology*, **41**, 438–46.

Daines, R. (1981). Withdrawal units and the psychology of problem behaviour. *In* B. Gillham (Ed.), *Problem Behaviour in the Secondary School*. London: Croom Helm.

Dancy, J. C. (1980). The notion of the ethos of a school. *Perspectives*, No. 1. Exeter: University School of Education.

Davey, A. G. (1983). *Learning to be Prejudiced: Growing up in a Multiethnic Britain*. London: Edward Arnold.

Davey, A. G. (1987). Giving parents a voice in multicultural education. *Multicultural Teaching*, **V**(3), 20–4.

Davie, R. (1980). Behaviour problems in schools and school-based in-service training. *In* G. Upton and A. Gobell (Eds), *Behaviour Problems in the Comprehensive School*. Cardiff: Faculty of Education, University College.

Davies, G. T. (1986). *A First Year Tutorial Handbook*. Oxford: Blackwell.

Deluty, R. H. (1981). Assertiveness in children: Some research considerations. *Journal of Clinical and Child Psychology*, **10**(3), 155–8.

Dewey, J. (1966). *Democracy and Education*. New York: Free Press.

Dodge, K. A., Coie, J. D. and Brakke, N. P. (1982). Behaviour patterns of socially rejected and neglected pre-adolescents – the roles of social approach and aggression. *Journal of Abnormal Child Psychology*, **10**(3), 389–410.

Dorking, L. (1987). How bullying scars the child. *The Teacher*, 5 October, p. 7.

Dorn, A. and Hibbert, P. (1987). A comedy of errors: Section 11 funding and education. *In* B. Troyna (Ed.), *Racial Inequality in Education*. London: Tavistock.

Douglas, J. (1967). *The Social Meaning of Suicide*. Princeton, N.J.: Princeton University Press.

Douvan, E. and Adelson, J. (1966). *The Adolescent Experience*. Chichester: John Wiley.

Drapkin, I. and Viano, E. (1975). *Victimology: A New Focus*. Lexington, Mass.: Lexington Books.

Duck, S. W. (1984). *Friends for Life: The Psychology of Close Relationships*. New York: St Martin's Press.

Duck, S. W., Miell, D. K. and Gaebler, H. C. (1980). Attraction and communication in children's interactions. *In* H. C. Foot, A. J. Chapman and J. R. Smith (Eds), *Friendship and Social Relations in Children*. Chichester: John Wiley.

Dubow, E. F. and Cappas, C. L. (1988). Peer social status and reports of children's adjustment by their teachers, by their peers and by their self ratings. *Journal of School Psychology*, **26**(1), 69–75.

Dunn, J. (1983). Sibling relationships in early childhood. *Child Development*, **54**, 787–811.

Dunn, J. and Kendrick, D. (1981). Depression in mothers – aggression in preschool boys. *Child Development*, **52**, 1265–73.

Dunn, J. and Kendrick, D. (1982). *Siblings: Love, Envy and Understanding*. London: Grant McIntyre.

Dunn, J. and Munn, P. (1986). Sibling quarrels and maternal intervention: Individual differences in understanding and aggression. *Journal of Child Psychology and Psychiatry*, **27**, 583–95.

Dunning, E., Murphy, P. and Williams, J. (1988). *The Roots of Football Hooliganism: An Historical and Sociological Study*. London: Routledge and Kegan Paul.

D'Zurilla, T. J. and Goldfried, M. R. (1971). Problem solving and behaviour modification. *Journal of Abnormal Psychology*, **78**, 107–26.

Edelman, M. S. and Omark, D. R. (1973). Dominance hierarchies in young children. *Social Sciences Information*, **12**(1), 103–10.

Eder, D. and Hallinan, M. T. (1978). Sex differences in children's friendships. *American Sociological Review*, **43**, 237–50.

Edwards, A. D. and Furlong, V. J. (1978). *The Language of Teaching*. London: Heinemann.

Edwards, A. D. and Hargreaves, D. (1976). Social scientific base of academic radicalism. *Education Review*, **28**, 83–93.

Egeland, B., Breitenbucher, M. and Rosenberg, D. (1980). Prospective study of the significance of life stress in the etiology of child abuse. *Journal of Consulting and Clinical Psychology*, **48**(2), 195–205.

Eisenberg, N. and Pasternack, J. F. (1983). Inequalities in children's prosocial behaviour: Whom do children assist? *In* R. L. Leahy (Ed.), *The Child's Construction of Social Inequality*. London and San Diego: Academic Press.

Elias, N. (1978). *The Civilizing Process*. Oxford: Blackwell.

Elizur, J. (1986). The stress of school entry: Parental coping behaviours and children's adjustment to school. *Journal of Child Psychology and Psychiatry*, **27**, 625–38.

Elliott, M. (1986). Kidscape Project. Unpublished research (personal communication). The Kidscape Primary Kit, Kidscape, 82 Brock Street, London W1Y 1YP.

Elliott, M. (1988). *Keeping Safe: A Practical Guide to Talking With Children*. London: Hodder and Stoughton.

Epps, S. (1985). Best practices in behavioural observation. *In* A. Thomas and J. Grimes (Eds), *Best Practices in School Psychology*. Kent, Ohio: National Association of School Psychologists.

Erikson, K. T. (1967). Notes on the sociology of deviance. *In* T. J. Scheff, *Mental Illness and Social Processes*, New York: Harper and Row.

Faull, C. and Nichol, A. R. (1986a). Abdominal pain in six year olds: An epidemiological study in a New Town. *Journal of Child Psychology and Psychiatry*, **27**(2), 251–60. Follow up study. (1986b). *Journal of Child Psychology and Psychiatry*, **27**(4), 539–44.

Feshbach, S. (1964). The function of aggression and the regulation of aggressive drive. *Psychology Revolution*, **71**, 257–72.

Feshbach, S. (1970). Aggression. *In* P. H. Mussen (Ed.), *Carmichael's Manual of Child Psychology*, Vol. 2, 3rd edition. Chichester: John Wiley.

Figg, J. and Ross, A. (1980). Analysing a school system: A practical exercise. *In* B. Gillham (Ed.), *Problem Behaviour in the Secondary School*. London: Croom Helm.

Fine, G. A. (1980). The natural history of preadolescent male friendship groups. *In* H. C. Foot, A. J. Chapman and J. R. Smith (Eds), *Friendship and Social Relations in Children*. Chichester: John Wiley.

Fine, G. A. (1981). Impression management and preadolescent behaviour: Friends as socializers. *In* S. R. Asher and J. M. Gottman (Eds), *The Development of Children's Friendships*. Cambridge: Cambridge University Press.

Firth, M. H. and Chaplin, L. (1987). Research note: The use of the Birleson Depression Scale with a non-clinical sample of boys. *Journal of Child Psychology and Psychiatry*, **28**(1), 79–85.

Fitzgerald, M. (1980). *Sociologies of Crime and Deviance*. D207 Block 1(9). Milton Keynes: Open University Press.

Foot, H. C., Chapman, A. J. and Smith, J. R. (Eds) (1980). *Friendships and Social Relations in Children*. Chichester: John Wiley.

Foy, B. (1977). Classroom aggression. *International Review of Education*, **23**, 97–117.

Frazer, J. G. (1923). *The Golden Bough*, 3rd edition. London: Macmillan.

Frude, N. and Gault, H. (Eds) (1984). *Disruptive Behaviour in Schools*, Chichester: John Wiley.

Furlong, V. J. (1985). *The Deviant Pupil: Sociological Perspectives*. Milton Keynes: Open University Press.

Furman, W., Rahe, D. F. and Hartup, W. W. (1979). Rehabilitation of socially withdrawn preschool children through mixed-age and same-age socialization. *Child Development*, **50**, 915–22.

Galloway, D. (1981). Institutional change or individual change? An overview. *In* B. Gillham (Ed.), *Problem Behaviour in the Secondary School*. London: Croom Helm.

Galloway, D., Martin, R. and Wilcox, B., (1986). Persistent absence from school and exclusion from school: The predictive power of school and community variables. *British Educational Research Journal*, **11**(1), 51–61.

Galloway, D., Ball, T., Blomfield, D. and Seyed, R. (1982). *Schools and Disruptive Pupils*. London: Longman.

Gallup, G. H. (1984). The 16th annual Gallup Poll of the public's attitude towards the Public Schools. *Phi Delta Kappa*, **66**, 23–38.

Galton, M. and Delafield, A. (1981). Expectancy effects in primary classrooms. *In* B. Simon and J. Willcocks (Eds), *Research and Practice in the Primary Classroom*. London: Routledge and Kegan Paul.

Galton, M. and Willcocks, J. (1983). *Moving from the Primary Class-room*. London: Routledge and Kegan Paul.

Garvey, C. (1984). *Children's Talk*. London: Fontana.

Garvey, C. and Berndt, R. (1975). The organisation of pretend play. Paper presented at the Annual Meeting of the American Psychological Association, Chicago, August.

George, C. and Main, M. (1979). Social interactions of young abused children: Approach, avoidance and aggression. *Child Development*, **50**, 306–18.

Gibbons, J. C. and Jones, J. F. (1975). *The Study of Deviance: Perspectives and Problems*. Englewood Cliffs, N.J.: Prentice-Hall.

Gibson, D. (1987). A case study of the 'consultation' process. *In* B. Troyna (Ed.), *Racial Inequality in Britain*. London: Tavistock.

Gillham, B. (1980). Psychological services and problems of adolescent behaviour. *In* G. Upton and A. Gobell (Eds), *Behaviour Problems in the Comprehensive School*. Cardiff: Faculty of Education, University College.

Gillham, B. (Ed.) (1981a). *Problem Behaviour in the Secondary School*. London: Croom Helm.

Gillham, B. (1981b). Rethinking the problem. *In* B. Gillham (Ed.), *Problem Behaviour in the Secondary School*. London: Croom Helm.

Ginsberg, D., Gottman, J. and Parker, J. (1986). The importance of friendship. *In* J. M. Gottman and J. G. Parker (Eds), *Conversations of Friends*. Cambridge: Cambridge University Press.

Glow, R. A. and Glow, P. H. (1980). Peer and self rating: Children's perception of behaviour relevant to hyperkinetic impulse disorder. *Journal of Abnormal Child Psychology*, **8**(4), 471–90.

Gobell, A. (1980). Three classroom procedures. *In* G. Upton and A. Gobell (Eds), *Behaviour Problems in the Comprehensive School*. Cardiff: Faculty of Education, University College.

Goffman, E. (1961). *Asylums*. New York: Doubleday Anchor.

Goffman, E. (1968). *Stigma: Notes on the Management of Spoiled Identity*. Harmondsworth: Pelican.

Goffman, E. (1974). *The Presentation of Self in Everyday Life*. Harmondsworth: Pelican.

Goldman, J. A., Corsini, D. A. and Urioste, R. (1980). Implications of positive and negative sociometric status for assessing the social competence of young children. *Journal of Applied Developmental Psychology*, **1**, 209–20.

Good, T. L. and Brophy, J. (1984). *Looking in Classrooms*. New York: Harper and Row.

Gottfredson, G. D. and Gottfredson, D. C. (1985). *Victimization in Schools*. New York: Plenum Press.

Gottman, J. M. (1986). The world of coordinated play: Same – and cross – sex friendship in children. *In* J. M. Gottman and J. G. Parker (Eds), *Conversations of Friends*. Cambridge: Cambridge University Press.

Gottman, J. M. and Mettetal, G. (1986). Friendship and acquaintance-ship through adolescence. *In* J. M. Gottman and J. G. Parker (Eds), *Conversations of Friends*. Cambridge: Cambridge University Press.

Gottman, J. M. and Parker, J. G. (Eds) (1986). *Conversations of Friends*. Cambridge: Cambridge University Press.

Gowar, M. (1986). *So Far, So Good*. London: Collins.

Gramsci, A. (1973). *Selections from Prison Notebooks*. London: Lawrence and Wishart.

Green, A. H. (1978). Self-destructive behaviour in battered children. *American Journal of Psychiatry*, **135**, 579–82.

Green, C. (1987). *Toddler Taming*. London: Century Hutchinson.

Green, E. H. (1933). Friendships and quarrels among pre-school children. *Child Development*, **3**, 237–52.

Grunsell, R. (1985). *Finding Answers to Disruption: Discussion Exercises for Secondary Teachers*. New York: Longman.

Hall, E. and Hall, C. (1988). *Human Relations in Education*. London: Routledge and Kegan Paul.

Hallinan, M. T. (1980). Patterns of cliquing among youth. *In* H. C. Foot, A. J. Chapman and J. R. Smith (Eds), *Friendship and Social Relations in Children*. Chichester: John Wiley.

Hallinan, M. T. (1981). Recent advances in sociometry. *In* S. R. Asher and J. M. Gottman (Eds), *The Development of Children's Friendships*. Cambridge: Cambridge University Press.

Halpern, H. A. (1973). Crisis theory: A definitional study. *Community Mental Health Journal*, **9**, 342–9.

Hamblin, D. H. (1974). *The Teacher and Counselling*. Oxford: Blackwell.

Hamblin, D. H. (1978a). *The Teacher and Pastoral Care*. Oxford: Blackwell.

Hamblin, D. H. (1978b). *Group Dynamics: Research and Theory*. Oxford: Blackwell.

Hargreaves, D. (1967). *Social Relations in a Secondary School*. London: Routledge and Kegan Paul.

Hargreaves, D. (1980). Teachers' knowledge of behaviour problems. *In* G. Upton and A. Gobell (Eds), *Behaviour Problems in the Comprehensive School*. Cardiff: Faculty of Education, University College.

Hargreaves, D. H. (1982). *Challenge for the Comprehensive School*. London: Routledge and Kegan Paul.

Hargreaves, D. H. (1984). *Improving Secondary Schools*. London: ILEA.

Hargreaves, D. H., Hester, S. K. and Mellor, F. J. (1975). *Deviance in Classrooms*. London: Routledge and Kegan Paul.

Hartup, W. W. (1974). *Determinants and Origins of Aggressive Behaviour*. The Hague: Mouton.

Hartup, W. W. (1978). Children and their friends. *In* H. McGurk (Ed.), *Issues in Childhood Social Development*. London: Methuen.

Hartup, W. W. (1983). Peer relations. *In* E. M. Hetherington (Ed.), *Handbook of Child Psychology: Vol. 4: Socialization, Personality and Social Development*. Chichester: John Wiley.

Hartup, W. W., Glazer, J. A. and Charlesworth, R. (1967). Peer reinforcement and sociometric status. *Child Development*, **38**, 1017–24.

Hastings, J. (1981). One school's experience. *In* B. Gillham (Ed.), *Problem Behaviour in the Secondary School*. London: Croom Helm.

Haward, L. R. C. (1981). Psychological consequences of being the victim of a crime. *In* S. Lloyd-Bostock (Ed.), *Law and Psychology*. Oxford: Centre for Socio-Legal Studies.

Hawton, K. (1982). Attempted suicide in children and adolescents. *Journal of Association of Child Psychology and Psychiatry*, **23**(4), 497–503.

Heinemann, P. P. (1973). *Mobbning. Gruppvåld blant barn og. vokane.* Stockholm: Natur och Kultur.

Hemming, J. (1983). The motivation for violence among adolescents. *Public Health*, **97**, 324–9.

Hentig, H. von (1948). *The Criminal and His Victim: Studies in the Sociobiology of Crime.* New Haven.

Herbert, M. (1987). *Behavioural Treatment of Children with Problems: A Manual,* 2nd edition. London and San Diego: Academic Press.

Hersov, L. A., Berger, M. and Shaffer, D. (Eds) (1978). *Aggressive and Anti-social Behaviour in Childhood and Adolescence.* Oxford: Pergamon Press.

Hertz-Lazarowitz, R. (1984). Internal dynamics of cooperative learning. *In* R. Slavin, S. Sharan, S. Kagan, R. Hertz-Lazarowitz, C. Webb and R. Smuck (Eds), *Learning to Cooperate, Cooperating to Learn.* New York: Plenum Press.

Hetherington, E. M., Cox, M. and Cox, R. (1977). The aftermath of divorce. *In* J. H. Stevens and M. Matthews (Eds), *Mother–Child, Father–Child Relations.* Washington, D.C.: National Association for the Education of Young Children.

Hinde, R. A. (1979). *Towards Understanding Relationships.* New York: Academic Press.

Hinde, R. A. (1988). Gender: A thorny issue. *The Psychologist*, **1**(1), 6.

Hinde, R. A., Titmus, G., Easton, D. and Tamplin, A. (1985). Incidence of friendship and behaviour toward strong associates versus nonassociates in preschoolers. *Child Development*, **56**, 234–45.

Hinde, R. A., Easton, D., Meller, R. E. and Tamplin A. (1983). The nature and determinants of preschoolers' differential behaviour to adults and peers. *British Journal of Developmental Psychology*, **1**(1), 3–19.

Hodson, P. (1988). *Letters to Growing Pains.* London: BBC Publications.

Hoffman, L. (1981). *Foundations of Family Therapy: A Conceptual Framework for Systems Change.* New York: Basic Books.

Holt, J. (1982). *How Children Fail,* revised edition. Harmondsworth: Penguin.

Hoppe, R. A., Simmel, E. C. and Milton, G. A. (Eds) (1970). *Early Experiences and the Processes of Socialization.* London and San Diego: Academic Press.

Hopper, B. (1987). *Co-operative Learning: An Overview.* Human Relations in Education 7. Nottingham: School of Education, University of Nottingham.

Hunter, J., Kysel, F. and Mortimore, P. (1985). *Children in Need: The Growing Needs of Inner London School Children.* Research and Statistics Branch, RS 994/85. London: ILEA.

Hyatt-Williams, A. (1983). Brutalization or Failure to Tame. *Public Health*, **97**, 320–3.

Hyde, J. S. (1984). How large are gender differences in aggression? A developmental meta-analysis. *Developmental Psychology*, **20**, 722–36.

Jahoda, G. and Lewis, I. M. (1987). *Acquiring Culture: Cross Cultural Studies.* New York: Croom Helm/Routledge.

Jamieson, J. H. (1984). Coping with physical violence: Some suggestions. *Maladjustment and Therapeutic Education*, **2**(2), 39–45.

Jamieson, J. H. (1988). Violence at home: life outside residential care. *Maladjusted and Therapeutic Education*, **6**(1), 3–13.

Janes, C. L. and Hesselbrock, V. M. (1978). Problem children's adult adjustment predicted from teachers' ratings. *American Journal of Orthopsychiatry*, **48**, 300–9.

Janes, C. L., Hesselbrock, V. M., Myers, D. G. and Penniman, J. H. (1979). Problem boys in young adulthood: Teachers' ratings and twelve-year follow-up. *Journal of Youth and Adolescence*, **8**, 453–72.

Jennings, H. H. (1950). *Popular Children*. New York: Longman Green.

Jersild, A. T., Markey, F. V. (1935). Conflicts between preschool children. *Child Development Monograph*, Vol. 21.

Jersild, A. T. (1966). *Child Psychology*, 5th edition. London: Staples Press.

Johnson, D. W. and Johnson, R. T. (1984). The internal dynamics of cooperative learning groups. *In* R. Slavin, S. Sharan, S. Kagan, R. Hertz-Lazarowitz, C. Webb and R. Smuck (Eds), *Learning to Cooperate, Cooperating to Learn*. New York: Plenum Press.

Jones, A. (1980). Adolescent behaviour and teacher stress. *In* G. Upton and A. Gobell (Eds), *Behaviour Problems in the Comprehensive School*. Cardiff: Faculty of Education, University College.

Jowett, S. and Sylva, K. (1986). Does kind of preschool matter? *Educational Research*, **28**(1), 21–31.

Kagan, J. (1981). *The Second Year: The Emergence of Self-awareness*. Cambridge, Mass.: Harvard University Press.

Kagan, J. (1982). The emergence of self. *Journal of Child Psychology and Psychiatry*, **23**, 363–81.

Kagan, J. (1984). Continuity and change in the opening years of life. *In* R. N. Emde and R. J. Harmon (Eds), *Continuities and Discontinuities in Development*. London: Plenum Press.

Kagan, J. and Moss, H. A. (1962). *Birth to Maturity: a study in psychological development*. Chichester: John Wiley.

Kaplan, H. (1980). *Deviant Behaviour in Defence of Self*. London and San Diego: Academic Press.

Kaplan, R. M., Konecni, V. J. and Novaco, R. W. (Eds) (1984). *Aggression in Childhood and Youth*. The Hague: Nijhoff.

Katz, P. A. (1983). Developmental foundations of gender and racial attitudes. *In* R. L. Leahy (Ed.), *The Child's Construction of Social Inequality*. London and San Diego: Academic Press.

Kazdin, A. E. and Petti, T. A. (1982). Self report and interview measures of childhood and adolescent depression, *Journal of Child Psychology and Psychiatry*, **23**, 437–57.

Kelly, E. and Cohn, T. (1988). *Racism in Schools: New Research Evidence*. Stoke-on-Trent: Trentham Books.

Kempe, C. H., Silverman, F. N. and Steele, B. F. (1962). The battered child syndrome. *Journal of the American Medical Association*, **181**, 17–240.

Kidder, L. H. and Stewart, M. V. (1975). *The Psychology of Intergroup Relations: Conflict and Consciousness*. New York: McGraw-Hill.

Klein, M. (1946). *Writings, Vol. 3: Notes on Some Schizoid Mechanisms*. London: Hogarth Press.

Klein, M. (1960). *Our Adult World and Its Roots in Infancy*. London: Tavistock Pamphlet no. 2.

Knoff, H. M. (1983). Personality assessment in the schools: Issues and procedures for school psychologists. *School Psychology Review*, **12**, 391–8.

Knowles, J. (1988). Teacher appraisal and peer group evaluation in the identification of early bullying/victim behaviour. Unpublished M.Sc. thesis, University of Newcastle upon Tyne.

Koch, H. (1960). The relation of certain formal attributes of siblings to attitudes held towards each other and towards their parents. *Monograph for the Society for Research into Child Development*, **25**, 4.

Kohlberg, L. (1981). *Essays in Moral Development: The Philosophy of Moral Development*, Vol. 1. New York: Harper and Row.

Kolvin, I., Garside, R. F., Nicol, A. R., McMillan, A., Wolstenholm, F. and Leitch, I. M. (1981). *Help Starts Here: The Maladjusted Child in the Ordinary School*. London: Tavistock.

Kosky, R. (1983). Childhood suicidal behaviour. *Journal of Association of Child Psychology and Psychiatry*, **24**(3), 457–68.

Kounin, J. S. (1970). *Discipline and Group Management in Classrooms*. New York: Holt, Rinehart and Winston.

Kramer, J. K. (1985). Best practices in parent training. *In* A. Thomas and J. Grimes (Eds), *Best Practices in School Psychology*. Kent, Ohio: National Association of School Psychologists.

Krebs, J. R. (1984). Natural selection and behaviour. *In* J. R. Krebs and N. B. Davies (Eds), *An Introduction to Behavioural Ecology*, 2nd edition. Oxford: Blackwell.

Kupersmidt, J. (1983). Predicting delinquency and academic problems from childhood peer status. *In* J. D. Coie (Chair), *Strategies for Identifying Children at Social Risk: Longitudinal Correlates and Consequences*. Biennial Meeting of the Society for Research in Child Development, Detroit.

Kureishi, H. (1986). *My Beautiful Launderette and the Rainbow Sign*. London: Faber.

Lacey, C. (1970). *Hightown Grammar*. Manchester: Manchester University Press.

La Gaipa, J. J. (1981). Children's friendships. *In* S. W. Duck and R. Gilmour (Eds), *Personal Relationships, Vol. 2: Developing Personal Relationships*. New York: Academic Press.

Lagerspetz, K. M. J., Bjorquist, K., Berts, M. and King, E. (1982). Group aggression among school children in three schools. *Scandinavian Journal of Psychology*, **23**, 45–52.

La Greca, A. M. and Stark, P. (1986). Naturalistic observations. *In* P. S. Strain, M. J. Guralnick and H. M. Walker (Eds), *Children's Social Behaviour, Development, Assessment and Modification*. London and San Diego: Academic Press.

Lambourne, D. M. (1979). *Labelling: A social theory of handicap* (a review of the literature). Unpublished dissertation B. Phil., Part 2, University of Newcastle upon Tyne.

Lancaster, J (1805). *Improvements in Education*. London: Darton and Harvey.

Larkin, P. (1974). *High Windows*. London: Faber and Faber.

Laslett, R. (1982). A children's court for bullies. *Special Education*, **9**(1), 9–11.

Laszlo, J. I. and Bairstow, P. J. (1985). *Perceptual-motor Behaviour: Developmental Assessment and Therapy*. London and San Diego: Holt Saunders.

Lawrence, J., Steed, D. and Young, P. (1984). *Disruptive Children, Disruptive Schools?* London: Croom Helm.

Lazanus, P. and Weinstock, S. (1984). Use of sociometric peer nominations in classifying socially ignored versus socially rejected children. *School Psychology International*, **5**(3), 139–46.

Leahy, R. L. (Ed.) (1983). *The Child's Construction of Social Inequality*. London and San Diego: Academic Press.

Lefkowitz, M. M., Eron, L. D., Walder, L. O. and Huesmann, L. R. (1977). *Growing up to be Violent*. New York: Pergamon Press.

Lemert, E. M. (1967). *Human Deviance, Social Problems and Social Control*, 2nd edition. Englewood Cliffs, N.J.: Prentice-Hall.

Lever, J. (1976). Sex differences in the games children play. *Social Problems*, **23**, 478–87.

Lewis, M. and Brooks-Gunn, J. (1979). *Social Cognition and the Acquisition of Self*. New York: Plenum Press.

Lewis, M., Gottesman, D. and Gurstein, S. (1979). The course and duration of crisis. *Journal of Consulting and Clinical Psychology*, **47**, 128–34.

Lewis, M., Young, G., Brooks, J. and Michalson, L. (1975). The beginning of friendship. *In* M. Lewis and L. A. Rosenbaum (Eds), *Friendship and Peer Relations*. Chichester: John Wiley.

Liazios, A. (1972). The poverty of the sociology of deviance. Nuts, sluts and perverts. *Social Problems*, **20**(1), 103–19.

Lippman, W. (1922). *Public Opinion*. London and San Diego: Harcourt Brace Jovanovich.

Lorenz, K. (1966). *On Aggression*. London: Methuen.

Lowenstein, L. F. (1976). Perception and accuracy of perception of the bullying child of potential victims. Unpublished research.

Lowenstein, L. F. (1978). Who is the bully? *Bulletin of the British Psychological Society*, **31**, 147–9.

Lowenstein, L. F. (1987). The Study, Diagnosis and Treatment of Socially Aggressive Behaviour (Bullying) of Two Adolescent Boys in a Therapeutic Community. Unpublished.

McAuley, R. (1982). Training parents to modify conduct problems in their children. *Journal of Child Psychology and Psychiatry and Allied Disciplines*, **23**(3), 335–42.

McClelland, D. (1975). *Power: The Inner Experience*. New York: John Wiley.

Maccoby, E. E. (1980). *Social Development: Psychological Growth and the Parent–Child Relationship*. New York: Harcourt Brace Jovanovich.

Maccoby, E. E. and Jacklin, C. N. (1975). *The Psychology of Sex Differences*. Stanford, Calif.: Stanford University Press.

Maccoby, E. E. and Jacklin, C. N. (1980a). Psychological sex differences. *In* M. Rutter (Ed.), *Scientific Foundations of Developmental Psychiatry*. London: Heinemann.

Maccoby, E. E. and Jacklin, C. N. (1980b). Sex differences in aggression: A rejoinder and a reprise. *Child Development*, **51**, 964–80.

McCord, W., McCord, J. and Howard, A. (1961). Familial correlates of aggression in non-delinquent male children. *Journal of Abnormal and Social Psychology*, **62**, 79–93.

MacFarlane, J. W. (1964). Perspectives on personality consistency and change from the Guidance Study. *Vita Humana*, **7**, 115–26.

McGuffin, P. (1984). Genetic influences on personality, neurosis and psychosis. *In* P. McGuffin, M. F. Shanks and P. Hodgson (Eds), *Scientific Principles of Psychopathology*. London: Grune and Stratton.

McGurk, H. (Ed.) (1978). *Issues in Childhood Social Development*. London: Methuen.

McKinley, I. and Gordon, N. (1980). *Helping Clumsy Children*. Edinburgh: Churchill Livingstone.

McNamara, D. E. J. and Karmen, A. (1983). *Deviants: Victims or Victimizers?* Beverly Hills, Calif.: Sage.

McRobbie, A. and Garber, J. (1976). Girls and subcultures. *In* S. Hall and T. Jefferson (Eds), *Resistance Through Rituals*. London: Hutchinson.

Magnusson, D., Endler, N. S. (Eds) (1977). *Personality at the Crossroads: Current Issues in Interactional Psychology*. Hillsdale, N.J.: Lawrence Erlbaum Associates. London: Wiley & Sons.

Malinowski, B. (1923). The meaning of meaning. *In* C. K. Ogden and I. A. Richards (Eds), *The Problem of Meaning in Primitive Languages*. London: Routledge and Kegan Paul.

Mannarino, A. P. (1980). The development of children's friendships. *In* H. C. Foot, A. J. Chapman and J. R. Smith (Eds), *Friendship and Social Relations in Children*. Chichester: John Wiley.

Manning, M. and Sluckin, A. M. (1984). The function of aggression in the pre-school and primary years. *In* N. Frude and H. Gault (Eds), *Disruptive Behaviour in Schools*. Chichester: John Wiley.

Markoff, M. (1971). Societal reaction and career deviance: A critical analysis. *Sociological Quarterly*, **12**, 204–18.

Marland, M. (1975). *The Craft of the Classroom: A Survival Guide*. London: Heinemann.

Marsh, P. and Campbell, A. (1982). *Aggression and Violence*. Oxford: Blackwell.

Marsh, P., Rosser, E. and Harré, R. (1978). *The Rules of Disorder*. London: Routledge and Kegan Paul.

Masters, J. (1952). *The Deceivers*. London: Sphere Books Ltd.

Matza, D. (1969). *Becoming Deviant*. Englewood Cliffs, N.J.: Prentice-Hall.

Maughan, B., Mortimore, P., Ouston, J. and Rutter, M. (1980). Fifteen thousand hours: A reply to Heath and Clifford. *Oxford Review of Education*, **6**(3), 289–303.

Mayhew, P. M., Clarke, R. V. G., Sturman, A. and Hough, J. M. (1976). *Crime as Opportunity*. Home Office Research Unit Publication. No. 34. London: HMSO.

Measor, L. and Woods, P. (1984). *Changing Schools: Pupil Perspectives on Transfer to a Secondary School*. Milton Keynes: Open University Press.

Meichenbaum, D. (1973). Cognitive factors in behaviour modification: Modifying what clients say to themselves. *In* C. M. Franks and G.

T. Wilson (Eds), *Annual Review of Behaviour Therapy, Theory and Practice*. New York: Brunner/Marzeld.

Meichenbaum, D. H. (1977). *Cognitive Behaviour Modification*. New York: Plenum Press.

Michelson, L. and Mannarino, A. P. (1986). Social skills training with children: Research and clinical application. *In* P. S. Strain, M. J. Guralnick and H. M. Walker (Eds), *Children's Social Behaviour*. London and San Diego: Academic Press.

Miller, A. (1987). *For Your Own Good: The Roots of Violence in Child Rearing*. London: Faber and Faber.

Milham, S., Bullock, R., Hosie, K. (1978). *Locking Up Children*. Aldershot: Saxon House.

Mills, W. C. P. (1976). Exhaustive study of seriously disruptive behaviour in secondary schools in one local authority. Unpublished M.Ed. thesis. University of Birmingham.

Mitchel, J. and O'Moore, M. (1988). *In* Report of the European Teachers' Seminar on *Bullying in Schools*. Strasbourg: Council for Cultural Cooperation.

Mitchell, A. (1984). *On the Beach at Cambridge*. London: Allison & Busby.

Mittler, P. (1971). *The Study of Twins*. Harmondsworth: Penguin.

Monane, M., Leichter, D. and Lewis, D. (1984). Physical abuse in psychiatrically hospitalized children and adolescents. *Journal of the American Academy of Child Psychiatry*, **23**(6), 653–8.

Monte, C. F. (1977). *Beneath the Mask: An Introduction to Theories of Personality*. New York: Praeger.

Moreno, J. L. (1953). *Who Shall Survive*. New York: Beacon House.

MORI Poll (1987). A poll conducted among parents of state secondary school pupils in May 1987 for Reader's Digest.

Mortimore, P. (1980). Misbehaviour in schools. *In* G. Upton and A. Gobell (Eds), *Behaviour Problems in the Comprehensive School*. Cardiff: Faculty of Education, University College.

Mortimore, P. (1984). *The ILEA Junior School Study*. Confidential Report. London: ILEA.

Mortimore, P. and Blackstone, T. (1982). *Disadvantage and Education*. London: Heinemann.

Mortimore, P., Sammons, P., Stoll, L., Lewis, D. and Ecob, R. (1988). *School Matters: The Junior Years*. London: Open Books.

Moszczynska, U. (1979). Family environment and emergence of aggression in children at age six and seven. *Psychologia Wychowaweza*, **22**(4), 531–9.

Mykletun, R. J. (1979). *Plaging i Skolen*. Stavenger: Rogalands Forskning.

National Crime Commission Report (1967). The Challenge of Crime in a Free Society. Report of the President's Commission on Law Enforcement and Administration of Justice. US Government Printing Office, Washington DC.

Nelson, S. and Menachem, A. (1973). Paper presented at the First International Symposium on Victimology, September, Jerusalem. Unpublished paper.

Newson, J. and Newson, E. (1976). Day to day aggression between parent and child. *In* N. Tutt (Ed.), *Violence*. London: HMSO.

Newson, J. and Newson, E. (1984). Parents' perspectives on children's behaviour in school. *In* N. Frude and G. Gault (Eds), *Disruptive Behaviour in Schools*. Chichester: John Wiley.

Nielsen, R. and Stigendal, L. (1973). *Varför mobbning? Gruppvald ur ett samhällsperspektiv*. Stockholm: M. and B. Fackboksforlaget.

Norwegian National Campaign (in prep.) Evaluation of the NNC – preliminary finding. Preliminary results in *Report of the European Teachers' Seminar on Bullying in Schools* (1988). Strasbourg: CCC and D. Tattum and D. Lane (1988) *Bullying in Schools*. Stoke-on-Trent: Trentham Press.

Oaklander, V. (1978). *Windows to our Children*. Moab, Utah: Real People Press.

Ogilvie, V. (1953). *The English Public School*. London: Batsford.

Olweus, D. (1973). *Hackkycklingar och översittare: Forskning om skolmobbring*. Stockholm: Almqvist and Wikzell.

Olweus, D. (1978). *Aggression in the Schools: Bullies and Whipping Boys*. Washington, D.C.: Hemisphere.

Olweus, D. (1979). Stability of aggressive reaction patterns in males: A review. *Psychological Bulletin*, **86**(4), 852–75.

Olweus, D. (1980). Familial and temperamental determinants of aggressive behaviour in adolescent boys: A causal analysis. *Developmental Psychology*, **16**, 644–60.

Olweus, D. (1981). Bullying among school boys. *In* N. Cantwell (Ed.), *Children and Violence*. Stockholm: Akademilitteratur.

Olweus, D. (1983). Low school achievement and aggressive behaviour in adolescent boys. *In* D. Magnusson and V. Allen (Eds), *Human Development: An Interactional Perspective*. London and San Diego: Academic Press.

Olweus, D. (1984). Aggressors and their victims: Bullying at school. *In* N. Frude and H. Gault (Eds), *Disruptive Behaviour in Schools*. Chichester: John Wiley.

Olweus, D. (1985a). 80,000 barn er innblandet i mobbing. *Norsk Skolebad* (Oslo), **2**, 18–23.

Olweus, D. (1985b). Undersökning om mobbning bland 17,000 svenska elever. Mimeo.

Olweus, D. (1987). Bully/victim problems among school-children in Scandinavia. *In* J. P. Myklebust, and R. Ommundsen (Eds), *Psykologprofesjonen mot ar 2000*. Oslo: Universitetsforlaget.

Olweus, D. and Roland, E. (1983). *Hobbing-bakgrunn og tiltak*. Oslo, Norway: Kirke-og undervisnings departementet.

Omark, D. R., Omark, M. and Edelman, M. S. (1975). Formation of dominance hierarchies in young children. *In* T. R. Williams (Ed.), *Action and Perception in Psychological Anthropology*. The Hague: Mouton.

Omark, D. R. *et al.* (1980). *Dominance Relations: An Ethological Review of Human Conflict and Social Interactions*. Garland.

O'Moore, M. (1988). *In* Report of the European Teachers' Seminar on *Bullying in Schools*. Strasbourg: Council for Cultural Cooperation.

Orton, W. T. (1982). Mobbing. *Public Health*, **96**, 172–4.

Osgood, C. (1964). Semantic differential technique in the comparative study of cultures. *American Anthropologist*, **66**(3), Part 2, 171–200.

Ouston, J. (1981). Differences between schools: The implications for school practice. *In* B. Gillham (Ed.), *Problem Behaviour in the Secondary School*. London: Croom Helm.

Page, R. (1984). *Stigma: Concepts in Social Policy 2*. London: Routledge and Kegan Paul.

Patterson, G. R. (1982). *Coercive Family Practices*. Eugene, Oregon: Castalia.

Patterson, G. R. (1984). A microsocial process: A view from the boundary. *In* J. C. Masters and K. L. Yarkin (Eds), *Boundary Areas in Psychology: Social and Developmental Psychology*. London and San Diego: Academic Press.

Patterson, G. R. and Guillon, M. (1976). *Living with children: New Methods for Parents and Teachers*. Champaign, Ill.: Research Press.

Patterson, G. R. and Stouthamer-Loeber, M. (1984). The correlation of family management practices and delinquency. *Child Development*, **55**, 1299–307.

Patterson, G. R., Littman, R. A. and Bricker, W. (1967). Assertive behaviour in children: A step towards a theory of aggression. *Monographs of the Society for Research Child Development*, **32**, 5.

Patterson, G. R., Cobb, J. A. and Ray, R. S. (1973). A social engineering technology for retraining families of aggressive boys. *In* H. E. Adams, I. P. Unikel (Eds), *Issues and Trends in Behaviour Therapy*. Springfield, Illinois: C.C. Thomas.

Patterson, G. R., Reid, J. G., Jones, R. R. and Conger, R. E. (1975). *Social Learning Project: A Social Learning Approach to Family Intervention, Vol. I*. Eugene, Oreg.: Castalia.

Pearce, J. B. (1978). The recognition of depressive disorders in children. *Journal of the Royal Society of Medicine*, **71**, 494–500.

Pik, R. (1981). Confrontation systems and teacher support systems. *In* B. Gillham (Ed.), *Problem Behaviour in the Secondary School*. London: Croom Helm.

Pikas, A. (1975a). *Så Stoppar vi Mobbning!* Lund: Berlingska-boktryckeriet.

Pikas, A. (1975b). Treatment of mobbing in school: principles for and the results of the work of an anti mobbing group. *Scandinavian Journal of Education Research*, **19**, 1–12.

Pikas, A. (1976). *Slik Stopper in Mobbning*. Oslo: Gyldendal.

Pikas, A. (1987a). Unpublished paper presented in absence at Council of Europe Conference on Bullying in Schools, Stavanger 1987.

Pikas, A. (1987b). *Sa Bekamper vi Mobbning Iskolan*. Uppsala A.M.A. Dataservice.

Pizzey, E. (1974). *Scream Quietly or The Neighbours Will Hear*. Harmondsworth: Penguin.

Plummer, K. (1979). Misunderstanding labelling perspectives. *In* D. Downes and P. Rock (Eds), *Deviant Interpretations*. Oxford: Martin Robertson.

Preece, A. (1987). The range of narrative forms conversationally produced by young children. *Child Language*, **14**, 353–73.

Presland, J. L. (1980). Behaviour modification and secondary schools. *In* G. Upton and A. Gobell (Eds), *Behaviour Problems in the Comprehensive School*. Cardiff: Faculty of Education, University College.

Pring, R. (1978). Teacher as researcher. *In* D. Lawton, P. Gordon,

M. Ing, B. Gibby, R. Pring and T. Moore (Eds), *Theory and Practice of Curriculum Studies*. London: Routledge and Kegan Paul.

Pring, R. (1984). *Personal and Social Education in the Curriculum*. London: Hodder and Stoughton.

Pringle, M. L. K. (Ed.) (1971). *Deprivation and Education*. London: Longmans.

Pringle, M. L. K. (1986). *The Needs of Children*. London: Hutchinson.

Pringle, M. L. K. and Clifford, L. (1965). Conditions associated with emotional maladjustment among children in care. *In* M. L. K. Pringle (Ed.), *Deprivation and Education*. London: Longmans.

Putallaz, M. and Gottman, J. (1981). Social skills and group acceptance. *In* S. R. Asher and J. M. Gottman (Eds), *The Development of Children's Friendships*. Cambridge: Cambridge University Press.

Quinn, D. (1985). An interpersonal problem-solving programme in a primary school. Unpublished M.Sc. dissertation. University of Newcastle upon Tyne.

Quinton, D. and Rutter, M. (1985a). Family pathology and child psychiatric disorder: A four-year prospective study. *In* A. R. Nicol (Ed.), *Longitudinal Studies in Child Care and Child Psychiatry*. Chichester: John Wiley.

quinton, D. and Rutter, M. (1985b). Parenting behaviour of mothers raised in care. *In* A. R. Nicol (Ed.), *Longitudinal Studies in Child Psychology and Psychiatry*. Chichester: John Wiley.

Rabinowitz, A. (1981). The range of solutions: A critical analysis. *In* B. Gillham (Ed.), *Problem Behaviour in the Secondary School*. London: Croom Helm.

Raven, J. (1979). School rejection and its amelioration. *Educational Research*, **20**, 3–9.

Redl, F. and Wineman, D. (1957). *The Aggressive Child*. New York: Free Press.

Reid, D. W. (1977). Locus of control as an important concept for an interactionist approach to behaviour. *In* D. Magnusson, N. S. Endler (Eds), *Personality at the Crossroads: Current Issues in Interactional Psychology*. New Jersey: Lawrence Erlbaum Associates.

Reid, K. (1983). Retrospection and persistent school absenteeism. *Educational Research*, **2**(25), 110–15.

Reid, K. (1984). Disruptive behaviour and persistent school absenteeism. *In* N. Frude and H. Gault (Eds), *Disruptive Behaviour in Schools*. Chichester: John Wiley.

Reid, K. (1985). *Truancy and School Absenteeism*. London: Hodder and Stoughton.

Renvoize, J. (1978). *Web of Violence: A Study of Family Violence*. London: Routledge and Kegan Paul.

Reynolds, D. (Ed.) (1985). *Studying School Effectiveness*. Lewes: Falmer Press.

Reynolds, D. and Murgatroyd, S. (1977). The sociology of schooling and the absent pupil: The school as a factor in the generation of truancy. *In* H. C. M. Carroll (Ed.), *Absenteeism in South Wales: Studies of Pupils, Their Homes and Their Secondary Schools*. Swansea: Faculty of Education, University College.

Reynolds, D. and Sullivan, M. (1981). The effects of school: A radical faith re-stated. *In* B. Gillham (Ed.), *Problem Behaviour in the Secondary School.* London: Croom Helm.

Rhoades, S. L. and Strickland, B. (1980). A flip side look at self concept. *Clearing House,* **54**(4), 158–9.

Richman, N., Stevenson, J. and Graham, P. J. (1982). *Preschool to School: A Behavioural Study.* London: Academic Press.

Riley, D. (1988). Bullying: A study of victim and victimisers within one inner city secondary school. In-service B.Ed. Inquiry Report, Crewe and Alsager College of Higher Education.

Robins, L. N. (1966a). *Deviant Children Grown up: A Sociological and Psychiatric Study of Sociopathic Personality.* Baltimore, Ohio: Williams and Wilkins.

Robins, L. N. (1966b). Sturdy childhood predictors of adult anti-social behaviour: Replications from longitudinal studies. *Psychological Medicine,* **8**, 611–22.

Roff, M., Sells, S. B. and Golden, M. M. (1972). *Social Adjustment and Personality Development in Children.* Minneapolis, Minn.: University of Minnesota Press.

Roland, E. (1983). *Strategi mot mobbing.* Stavanger: Universitetsforlag.

Roland, E. (1988). Reported in Council for Cultural Cooperation Report of the European Teachers Seminar on Bullying in Schools. Strasbourg: CCC.

Roland, E. (in prep.). Familial and school determinants on bullying in school. Contact: Stavanger College of Education.

Rosenthal, R. and Jacobson, L. (1968). *Pygmalion in the Classroom: Teacher Expectation and Pupils' Intellectual Development.* New York: Holt, Rinehart and Winston.

Rotter, J. B. (1966). Generalized expectancies for internal versus external locus of control of reinforcement. *Psychological Monographs,* **80**(1, Whole No. 609).

Rowe, D. C. and Plomin, R. (1981). The importance of shared environmental influences in behavioural development. *Developmental Psychology,* **17**, 517–31.

Rubin, K. H. (1982). Social and social-cognitive developmental characteristics of young isolated, normal and sociable children. *In* K. H. Rubin (Ed.), *Peer Relationships and Social Skills in Childhood.* New York: Springer-Verlag.

Rubin, K. H. and Pepler, D. J. (1980). The relationship of child's play to social-cognitive growth and development. *In* H. C. Foot, A. J. Chapman and J. R. Smith (Eds), *Friendship and Social Relations in Children.* Chichester: John Wiley.

Rubin, Z. (1980). *Children's Friendships.* London: Fontana.

Rubin, Z., Provenzano, F. J. and Luria, Z. (1974). The eye of the beholder: parents' views on the sex of newborns. *American Journal of Orthopsychiatry,* **44**, 512–19.

Rutherford, R. B. Nelson, C. M. and Forness, S. R. (1987). *Severe Behaviour Disorders of Children and Youth.* Boston: Little, Brown & Co.

Rutter, M. (1971). Parent–child separation: Psychological effects on the children. *Journal of Child Psychology and Psychiatry,* **12**(4), 233–60.

Rutter, M. (1972). Relationships between child and adult psychiatric disorders: Some research considerations. *Acta Psychiatrica Scandinavia*, **48**, 3–21.

Rutter, M., Maughan, B., Mortimore, P. and Ouston, J. (1979). *Fifteen Thousand Hours: Secondary Schools and Their Effects on Children*. London: Open Books.

Ryan, W. (1971). *Blaming the Victim*. London: Orbach and Chambers.

St John Brooks, C. (1985). The school bullies. *New Society*, 6 December, 262–5.

Sarason, I. G. and Ganzer, V. J. (1973). Modelling and group discussions in the rehabilitation of juvenile delinquents. *Journal of Counselling Psychology*, **20**(5), 442–50.

Savin-Williams, R. C. (1979). Dominance hierarchies in groups of early adolescents. *Child Development*, **50**, 923–35.

Savin-Williams, R. C. (1980). Social interactions of adolescent females in natural groups. *In* H. C. Foot, A. J. Chapman and J. R. Smith (Eds), *Friendship and Social Relations in Children*. Chichester: John Wiley.

Schacter, S. (1960). Deviation, rejection and communication. *In* D. Cartwright and A. Zander (Eds), *Group Dynamics, Research and Theory*. London: Tavistock.

Schafer, S. (1977). *Victimology: The Victim and His Criminal*. Reston, Virginia: Reston Publishing Co. (Prentice-Hall).

Schmuck, R. A. and Schmuck, P. A. (1971). *Group Processes in the Classroom*. Dubuque, Iowa: Wm. C. Brown Company.

Schools' Council (1968). *Young Leavers Enquiry*. London: HMSO.

Schultz, M. R. (1975). The semantic derogation of women, language and sex. *In* B. Thorne and N. Henley (Eds), *Language and Sex: Difference and Dominance*. Rowley, Mass.: Newbury House Publishers.

Schweinhart, L. J. and Weikart, D. P. (1980). *Young Children Grow up: The Effects of the Perry Preschool Program on Youths through Age 15*. Monographs of the High/Scope Educational Research Foundation Monographs No. 7, Ypsilanti, MIs.: High/Scope.

Sears, R. R., Maccoby, E. E. and Levin, H. (1957). *Patterns of Child Rearing*. Evanston, Ill.: Row, Peterson.

Sears, R. R., Rau, L. and Alpert, R. (1965). *Identification and Child Rearing*. Stanford, Calif.: Stanford University Press.

Seligman, M. E. P. and Peterson, C. (1986). A learned helplessness perspective on childhood depression: theory and research. *In* M. Rutter, C. E. Izard and P. B. Read (Eds), *Depression in Young People*. New York: Guilford.

Shaffer, D. (1974). Suicide in childhood and early adolescence. *Journal of Child Psychology and Psychiatry*, **15**, 275–91.

Shaffer, L. S. (1984). Fatalism as an animistic attribution process. *Journal of Mind and Behaviour*, **5**(3), 351–61.

Shaffer, L. S. *et al.* (1985). Why me? An attributional theory: Adjustment to victimization. Paper presented to the Annual Meeting of the Eastern Psychological Association, March.

Shaffer, M. B. (1985). Best practices in counselling senior high school students. *In* A. Thomas and J. Grimes (Eds), *Best Practices in School Psychology*. Kent, Ohio: National Association of School Psychologists.

Shantz, C. U. (1987). Conflicts between children. *Child Development*, **58**, 283–305.

Shapiro, B. Z. (1967). Dissolution of friendship ties in groups of children. *Dissertation Abstracts*, **27**(10–A) 3517–18.

Sherif, M. and Sherif, C. (1953). *Groups in Harmony and Tension*. New York: Harper and Brothers.

Simmel, G. (1964). *Conflict and the Web of Group Affiliation*. London: Collier-Macmillan.

Slavin, R. E. (1984). An introdction to cooperative learning and research. *In* R. E. Slavin, S. Sharan, S. Kagan, R. Hertz-Lazarowitz, C. Webb and R. Schmuck (Eds), *Learning to Cooperate, Cooperating to Learn*. New York: Plenum Press.

Sluckin, A. (1981). *Growing up in the Playground: The Social Development of Children*. London: Routledge and Kegan Paul.

Smead, V. S. (1985). Best practices in crisis intervention. *In* A. Thomas and J. Grimes (Eds), *Best Practices in School Psychology*. Kent, Ohio: National Association of School Psychologists.

Sparks, J. P. (1983). Mobbing in an independent secondary boarding school and the reaction of staff to it. *Public Health*, **97**, 316–19.

Spence, S. (1983). Teaching social skills to children. *Journal of Association of Child Psychology and Psychiatry*. **24**(4), 621–7.

Spivack, G. and Shure, M. B. (1974). *Social Adjustment of Young Children. A Cognitive Approach to Solving Real Life Problems*. San Francisco: Jossey Bass.

Staub, E. (1971). The learning and unlearning of aggression. *In* J. L. Singer (Ed.), *The Control of Aggression and Violence*. London and San Diego: Academic Press.

Stephenson, P. and Smith, D. (1987a). The playground bully. *The Teacher*, 28 September.

Stephenson, P. and Smith, D. (1987b). Anatomy of a playground bully. *Education*, 18 September, 236–7.

Stephenson, P. and Smith, D. (1988). Bullying in the junior school. *In* D. Tattum and D. Lane (Eds), *Bullying in Schools*. Stoke-on-Trent: Trentham Books.

Stilwell, R. and Dunn, J. (1985). Continuities in sibling relationships: Patterns of aggression and friendliness. *Journal of Child Psychology and Psychiatry*, **26**(4), 627–37.

Stocking, S. H., Arezzo, D. and Leavitt, S. (1979). *Helping Kids Make Friends: A Guide for Teachers and Parents*. Boys Town, Nebraska: Boys Town Centre for the Study of Youth Development.

Stocking, S. H., Arezzo, D. and Leavitt, S. (1980). *Helping Friendless Children: A Guide for Teachers and Parents*. Boys Town, Nebraska: Boys Town Centre for the Study of Youth Development.

Storr, A. (1975). *Human Aggression*. Harmondsworth: Penguin.

Strain, P. S., Guralnick, M. J. and Walker, H. M. (Eds) (1986). *Children's Social Behaviour, Development, Assessment and Modification*. London and San Diego: Academic Press.

Straus, M. A., Gelles, R. J. and Steinmetz, S. K. (1980). *Behind Closed Doors: Violence in the American Family*. Garden City, New York: Anchor-Doubleday.

Strayer, F. F. (1980). Child ethology and the study of preschool social relations. *In* H. C. Foot, A. J. Chapman and J. R. Smith (Eds), *Friendship and Social Relations in Children*. Chichester: John Wiley.

Strayhorn, J. M. and Strain, P. S. (1986). Social and language skills for preventive mental health: What, how, who and when. *In* R. B. Cairns (Ed.), *Children's Social Behaviour*. London: Academic Press.

Sullivan, H. S. (1953). *The Interpersonal Theory of Psychiatry*. New York: Norton.

Swann Report (1985). *Education for All*. The Report of the Committee of Inquiry into the Education of Children from Ethnic Minority Groups. London: HMSO.

Szasz, T. S. (1961). *The Myth of Mental Illness: Foundations of a Theory of Personal Conduct*. New York: Hoeber-Harper.

Tattum, D. and Lane, D. (1988). *Bullying in Schools*. Stoke-on-Trent: Trentham Books.

Taylor, I. (1979). Soccer consciousness and soccer hooliganism. *In* S. Cohen (Ed.), *Images of Deviance*. Harmondsworth: Penguin, pp. 134–64.

Thio, A. (1978). *Deviant Behaviour*. Boston: Houghton Mifflin.

Thomas, A. and Chess, S. (1976). Evolution of behaviour disorders into adolescence. *American Journal of Psychiatry*, **133**, 5–13.

Thomas, A. and Chess, S. (1977). *Temperament and Development*. New York: Brunner/Mazel.

Thomas, A. and Grimes, J. (Eds) (1985). *Best Practices in School Psychology*. Kent, Ohio: National Association of School Psychologists.

Thomas, A., Chess, S., Birch, H. G., Hertzig, M. E. and Korn, S. (1963). *Behavioural Individuality in Early Childhood*. New York: New York University Press.

Tieger, T. (1980). On the biological basis of sex differences in aggression. *Child Development*, **51**, 943–63.

Tiffen, K. and Spence, S. H. (1986). Responsiveness of isolated versus rejected children to social skills training. *Journal of Child Psychology and Psychiatry*, **27**(3), 343–55.

Tomlinson, S. (1987). Curriculum option choices in multi-ethnic schools. *In* B. Troyna (Ed.), *Racial Inequality in Education*. London: Routledge.

Topping, K. (1983). *Educational Systems for Disruptive Adolescents*. London: Croom Helm.

Trad, P. V. (1987). *Infant and Childhood Depression: Developmental Factors*. New York: John Wiley.

Troyna, B. (1987). *Racial Inequality in Britain*. London: Tavistock.

Troyna, B. and Ball, W. (1985). Styles of LEA policy intervention in multicultural/antiracist education. *Educational Review*, **37**(2), 165–73.

Tuetsch, H. M. and Tuetsch, C. K. (1975). Victimology: An effect of consciousness, interpersonal dynamics and human physics. *International Journal of Criminology and Penology*, **3**, 249.

Turk, A. T. (1969). *Criminality and Legal Order*. Chicago: Rand McNally.

Tutt, N. (1981). Treatment under attack. *In* B. Gillham (Ed.), *Problem Behaviour in the Secondary School*. London: Croom Helm.

Tversky, A. and Kahnmann, D. (1974). Judgement under uncertainty: heuristics and biases. *Science*, **185**, 1124–31.

Upton, G. (1980). The nature and development of behaviour problems.

In G. Upton and A. Gobell (Eds), *Behaviour Problems in the Comprehensive School.* Cardiff: Faculty of Education, University College.

Upton, G. and Gobell, A. (Eds) (1980). *Behaviour Problems in the Comprehensive School.* Cardiff: Faculty of Education, University College.

Vygotsky, L. (1962). *Thought and Language.* New York: John Wiley.

Wachtel, P. L. (1973). Psychodynamics, behaviour therapy and the implacable experimenter: An inquiry into the consistency of personality. *Journal of Abnormal Psychology,* **83**, 324–34.

Wagner, B. J. and Heathcote, D. (1979). *Drama as a Learning Medium.* London: Hutchinson.

Wahler, R. G. and Dumas, J. E. (1986). A chip off the old block. *In* P. S. Strain, M. J. Guralnick and H. M. Walker (Eds), *Children's Social Behaviour, Development, Assessment and Modification.* London and San Diego: Academic Press.

Waldrop, M. F. and Halverson, C. F. (1975). Intensive and extensive peer behaviour: Longitudinal and cross-sectional analysis. *Child Development,* **46**, 19–26.

Wall Street Journal (1985). 12 November.

Wedge, P. and Essen, J. (1983). *Children in Adversity.* London: Pan.

Wedge, P. and Prosser, H. (1973). *Born to Fail.* London: Arrow Books.

West, D. J. (1982). *Delinquency: Its Roots, Careers and Prospects.* London: Heinemann.

West, D. J. and Farrington, D. P. (1973). *Who Becomes Delinquent?* London: Heinemann.

Wheldall, K., Merret, F. and Russel, A. (1983). *BATPAC: The Behavioural Approach to Teaching Project.* Birmingham: Centre for Child Studies, Department of Educational Psychology, University of Birmingham.

White, M. (1987). *The Japanese Educational Challenge.* London: Free Press/Macmillan.

White, R. and Lippitt, R. (1960). Leader behaviour and member reaction in three 'social climates'. *In* D. Cartwright and A. Zander (Eds), *Group Dynamics, Research and Theory.* London: Tavistock.

Whiting, B. and Whiting, J. W. M. (1975). *Children of Six Cultures.* Cambridge, Mass.: Harvard University Press.

Willis, P. (1977). *Learning to Labour.* Farnborough: Saxon House.

Wilson, J. R. and Irvine, S. R. (1978). Education and behaviour problems in Northern Ireland. *Behavioural Disorders,* **3**, 276–87.

Wilson, P. and Bottomley, V. (1980). The emotional climate in the classroom: The interaction between adult teacher and early adolescent students. *In* G. Upton and A. Gobell (Eds), *Behaviour Problems in the Comprehensive School.* Cardiff: Faculty of Education, University College.

Wolff, S. (1986). *Knowledge and Treatment in the Practical Treatment and Understanding of Disturbed Children.* Workshop Perspectives I. Association of Workers for Maladjusted Children.

Wooster, A. and Hall, E. (Eds) (1985). *Human Relations Training in Schools.* Human Relations in Education 1. Nottingham: School of Education, University of Nottingham.

Wooster, A. and Hall, E. (1985). *Communication and Social Skills: A Course*

Guide. Human Relations in Education 2. Nottingham: School of Education, University of Nottingham.

Wragg, E. C. (1980). Training teachers in class management. *In* G. Upton and A. Gobell (Eds), *Behaviour Problems in the Comprehensive School*. Cardiff: Faculty of Education, University College.

Wragg, E. C. (1981). *Class Management and Control*. DES Teacher Education Project Focus Workbook. London: Macmillan.

Wragg, E. C. (1982). *A Review of Research in Teacher Education*. Windsor: NFER/Nelson.

Wright, C. (1985). Black students: white teachers. *In* B. Troyna (Ed.), *Racial Inequality in Britain*. London: Tavistock.

Yamazaki, K., Inomata, J., Makita, K. and MacKenzie, J. A. (1986). Japanese culture and the feature of neurotic manifestation in childhood and adolescence. Paper presented at 11th International Congress, Paris. International Association for Child and Adolescent Psychiatry and Allied Professions.

Youngman, M. B. and Lunzer, E. (1977). *Adjustment to Secondary Schools*. University of Nottingham, School of Education.

Youniss, J. (1980). *Parents and Peers in Social Development: A Sullivan–Piaget Perspective*. Chicago: University of Chicago Press.

Youniss, J. (1983). Understanding differences within friendships. *In* R. L. Leahy (Ed.), *The Child's Construction of Social Inequality*. London and San Diego: Academic Press.

Youniss, J. and Volpe, J. (1978). A relational analysis of friendship. *In* W. Damon (Ed.), *Social Cognition*. San Francisco: Jossey Bass.

Zeiller, B. (1982). Physical and Psychological Abuse: A follow-up of abused delinquent adolescents. *Child Abuse and Neglect*, **6**(2), 207–10.

Zillman, D. (1984). *Connections Between Sex and Aggression*. Hillside, N.J.: Lawrence Erlbaum Associates.

Index